Yours to Keep AUG 07 2015
Withdrawn/ABCL

THE TIME THAT REMAINS

D0744885

Yours to Keep
Withdrawn/ABCL

AUG 07 2013

MERIDIAN

Crossing Aesthetics

Werner Hamacher

Editor

Translated by Patricia Dailey

Stanford
University
Press

———

Stanford
California

Yours to Keep
Withdrawn/ABCL

3 9075 04987028 7

THE TIME THAT REMAINS

A Commentary on the Letter to the Romans

Giorgio Agamben

You're to Keep
Withdrawn/ABCL

Stanford University Press
Stanford, California

English translation © 2005 by the Board of Trustees of the
Leland Stanford Junior University. All rights reserved.

No part of this book may be reproduced or transmitted in
any form or by any means, electronic or mechanical, including photocopying and recording, or in any information stor-
age or retrieval system without the prior written permission
of Stanford University Press.

The Time That Remains was originally published in Italian
under the title *Il tempo che resta. Un commento alla Lettera ai
Romani* © 2000 Bollati Boringhieri.

Permission granted by James J. Wilhelm to reprint his translation of Arnaud Daniel's *"Lo ferm voler qu'el cor m'intra"*
from *Il Miglior Fabbro. The Cult of the Difficult in Daniel,
Dante, and Pound* (Orono: National Poetry Foundation,
University of Maine at Orono, 1982).

Printed in the United States of America
on acid-free, archival-quality paper

Library of Congress Cataloging-in-Publication Data

Agamben, Giorgio, 1942–
    [Tempo che resta. English]
    The time that remains : a commentary on the letter to the
Romans / Giorgio Agamben ; translated by Patricia Dailey.
        p.   cm. — (Meridian, crossing aesthetics)
    Includes index.
    ISBN 0-8047-4382-7 (alk. paper)
    ISBN 0-8047-4383-5 (pbk. : alk. paper)
    1. Bible. N.T. Paul—Commentaries.   I. Title. II. Series:
Meridian (Stanford, Calif.)

BS2665.53.A33 2005
227'.107—DC22

                                                      2004016692

Original Printing 2005

Last figure below indicates year of this printing:
14   13   12

Contents

Acknowledgments and
Translator's Note

The ideas in this book developed over a series of seminars: initially, in a shorter format, at the Collège International de Philosophie in Paris, in October, 1998; then at the University of Verona, in Winter 1998–99; finally, at Northwestern University, in April, 1999, and the University of California, Berkeley, in October, 1999. The book represents the fruit of these seminars and is indebted to discussions with participating students and professors. The form of the leading idea remained constant throughout each seminar: it always consisted in a commentary *ad litteram*, in every sense of the word, on the first ten words of the first verse of the Letter to the Romans.

In the transliteration of Greek terms, I have simplified diacritical marks and only indicate long syllables in the Greek by the use of a macron over the corresponding vowel. The reader may, however, find those passages of selected original Greek texts that were closely analyzed and immediately linked to this seminar in the Appendix. The Greek text used is that of Eberhard Nestle (*Novum Testamentum graece et latine*, edited by Erwin Nestle and Kurt Aland, United Bible Societies, London, 1963). The interlinear translation is that of Morgan Meis.

[*Translator's note.* In accordance with the desire of the author, all citations of Paul's Letters were translated into English as closely as possible with regard to the author's personal translation. Various translations were consulted, used, and modified, including the King James Version, the New International Version, the American Standard Version, the Interlinear Greek New Testament, and the International Standard Version. A special thanks to Morgan Meis for his time and meticulous interlinear translation of the Greek in the Appendix, and to Arne de Boever, Alessia Ricciardi, Dana Hollander, Gil Anidjar, Stathis Gourgouris, and Neslihan Senocak.]

THE TIME THAT REMAINS

מַשָּׂא דּוּמָה אֵלַי קֹרֵא מִשֵּׂעִיר
שֹׁמֵר מַה־מִּלַּיְלָה שֹׁמֵר מַה־מִּלֵּיל

An oracle of silence
Someone calls to me from Seir,
Watchman, what is left of the night?
Watchman, what is left of the night?
—Isaiah 21:11

§ The First Day

Paulos doulos christou Iēsou

First and foremost, this seminar proposes to restore Paul's Letters to the status of the fundamental messianic text for the Western tradition. This would seem a banal task, for no one would seriously deny the messianic character of the Letters. And yet, this is not self-evident, since two thousand years of translation and commentary coinciding with the history of the Christian church have literally cancelled out the messianic, and the word *Messiah* itself, from Paul's text. Not that one should conclude that there was something like a premeditated strategy of neutralizing messianism, but anti-messianic tendencies were doubtlessly operating within the Church as well as the Synagogue, at various times and in diverse ways; nevertheless, the problem raised here touches on more essential matters. For reasons that will become clear over the course of the seminar, a messianic institution—or rather, a messianic community that wants to present itself as an institution—faces a paradoxical task. As Jacob Bernays once observed with irony, "to have the Messiah behind you does not make for a very comfortable position" (Bernays, 257). But to have him perennially ahead of you can also, in the end, be discomforting.

In both cases, we are confronted with an aporia that concerns the very structure of messianic time and the particular conjunction of memory and hope, past and present, plenitude and lack, origin and end that this implies. The possibility of understanding the Pauline message coincides fully with the experience of such a time; without this, it runs the risk of remaining a dead letter. The restoration of Paul to his messianic context therefore suggests, above all, that we attempt to understand the meaning and internal form of the time he defines as *ho nyn kairos*, the "time of the now." Only after this can we raise the question of how something like a messianic community is in fact possible.

In this vein, one could say that a kind of subterranean solidarity had existed between the Church and the Synagogue in presenting Paul as the founder of a new religion. All evidence indicates that Paul would have never dreamed of claiming this status, given that he expected the imminent expiration of time. The reasons for this complicity between Church and Synagogue are clear: for the one as for the other, the aim is to cancel out or at least mute Paul's Judaism, that is to say, to expunge it from its originary messianic context.

For this reason, a long-standing Hebrew literature on Jesus presents him in benevolent terms—as "a nice guy,"[1] as Jacob Taubes jokingly notes, or as *Bruder Jesus*, to quote the title of Ben Chorin's book, published in 1967. Only recently have several Jewish scholars undertaken serious reexamination of Paul's Jewish context. In the 1950s, when W. D. Davies's book *Paul and Rabbinic Judaism* emphatically called attention to the substantially Judeo-messianic character of Pauline faith, Jewish studies were still dominated by Buber's book *Two Types of Faith*. The thesis of this book, to which we will later return, and which Taubes notes as being "highly dubious but from which I learned a great deal" (Taubes, 6), opposes the Jewish *emunah*, an immediate and objective trust in the community to which one belongs, to the Greek *pistis*, the subjective recognition of a faith one judges to be true and to which one converts. For Buber, the first is the faith *of* Jesus (*Glauben Jesu*), while the second, the faith *in* Jesus (*Glauben an Jesus*), is, naturally, Paul's. But since then, things have clearly changed, and in Jerusalem as in Berlin and the United States, Jewish scholars have started to read Paul's letters with regard to their own context, even if they have not yet considered them for what they really are, that

1. This expression appears in English in Taubes.

is, as the oldest and the most demanding messianic texts of the Jewish tradition.

From this perspective, Taubes's posthumous work *The Political Theology of Paul* (2004) marks an important turning point, despite its being the record of a seminar that lasted only a week. Taubes, who belonged to an old family of Ashkenazi rabbis and had worked in Jerusalem with Scholem (whose relation to Paul is, as we shall see, as complicated as his relation to Benjamin), finds Paul to be the perfect representative of messianism. Since our seminar proposes to interpret messianic time as a paradigm of historical time, now, eleven years after his Heidelberg seminar, we cannot begin without a dedication *in memoriam*.

In Memoriam: Jacob Taubes

Paul's Letters are written in Greek, but what kind of Greek are we talking about? Are we referring to New Testament Greek, about which Nietzsche said that God gave proof of his tactfulness in choosing such an impoverished language? Philosophical lexicons as well as dictionaries and grammars of New Testament Greek consider the texts that comprise the canon of the New Testament as though they were perfectly homogeneous. From the perspective of thought and of language, this is, of course, untrue. Paul's Greek, unlike that of Matthew or Mark, does not consist of a translation behind which an attentive ear, like Marcel Jousse's, could perceive the rhythm and idiom of Aramaic. Wilamowitz-Möllendorf's anti-Nietzscheanism is finally right in characterizing Pauline Greek as a writer's language. "The fact that his Greek has nothing to do with a school or a model, but rather flows directly out of his heart in a clumsy fashion and in an uncontrollable outburst, and the fact that his Greek is not translated Aramaic (as are the sayings of Jesus), makes him a classic of Hellenism" (Wilamowitz-Möllendorf, 159).

Paul's Language

Describing him as a "classic of Hellenism" is nevertheless particularly infelicitous. Taubes's anecdote on this subject proves enlightening. One day in Zurich during the war, Taubes was taking a stroll with Emil Staiger, the renowned Germanist, who was also an excellent Hellenist (and who had engaged in an interesting epistolary exchange with Heidegger on the interpretation of a line of Mörike's poetry). "One day we were walking along the Rämistrasse from the university to the lake, to Bellevue, and he turned a corner, and I was continuing on to the Jewish quarter in Enge, and he said to me: You know, Taubes, yesterday I was read-ing the Letters of the Apostle Paul. To which he added, with great bitterness: But that isn't Greek, it's Yiddish! Upon which I said: Yes, Professor, and that's why I understand it!'" (Taubes, 4). Paul belongs to a Jewish Diaspora community that thinks and speaks in Greek (Judeo-Greek) in precisely the same manner that Sephardim would speak Ladino (or Judeo-Spanish) and the Ashkenazi Yiddish. It is a community that reads and cites the Bible in the Septuagint, which Paul does whenever necessary (even if he occasionally appears to use a corrected version that is based on the original, using what we would nowadays call a "personal-ized" version). Unfortunately, this is not the occasion for us to elaborate on this Judeo-Greek community and its having remained in the shadow of the history of Judaism—the reasons for which undoubtedly concern Paul at the core. The opposition between Athens and Jerusalem, between Greek culture and Judaism has become commonplace, starting at least with Shestov's book (1938), which Benjamin characterizes as "admirable, but absolutely useless" (Benjamin 1966, 803), and is particularly pop-ular with those who are not experts in either field. According to this commonplace assumption, the community to which Paul belonged (which also produced Philo and Flavius Josephus, as well as numerous other works requiring further study) was subject to distrust because it was imbued with Greek culture and because it read the Bible in the language of Aristotle and Plato. This is the equivalent of saying, "Trust not the Spanish Jews, because they read Góngora and translated the Bible into Ladino," and "Trust not the Eastern Jews, because they speak a kind of German." Yet there is nothing more genuinely Jewish than to inhabit a language of exile and to labor it from within, up to the point of confound-ing its very identity and turning it into more than just a grammatical language: making it a minor language, a jargon (as Kafka called Yiddish), or a poetic language (like Yehuda Halevi's and Moshe ibn Ezra's Judeo-Andalusian *kharjas*, discovered in the Cairo *genizah*). And yet, in each case it is also a mother tongue, even though, as Rosenzweig says, it bears witness to the fact that "so far as his language is concerned, the Jew feels always he is in a foreign land, and knows that the home of his language is in the region of the holy language, a region everyday speech can never invade" (Rosenzweig, 302). (In Scholem's letter to Rosenzweig, dated December 1926—one of the few texts in which Scholem adopts a prophetic tone in describing the religious force of a language that revolts against the very people who speak it—we witness one of the most intense rejections of the Hebrew language as a language of everyday use.)

This is the perspective from which we should account for Paul's language and this Judeo-Greek community that constitutes just as important a chapter in the Jewish Diaspora as does Sephardic culture up to the eighteenth century and Ashkenazi culture in the nineteenth and twentieth centuries. Hence the meaning of both Staiger's observation ("It's not Greek, it's Yiddish!") and Norden's reserve, which he expresses in his excellent book *Die antike Kunstprosa*: "Paul's style, globally speaking, is not Hellenistic" (Norden, 509). Nevertheless, Paul's style does not have a peculiarly Semitic coloring either. Being neither Greek, nor Hebrew, nor *lashon ha-qodesh*, nor secular idiom, is what makes his language so interesting (even if we are not yet at the point of confronting the problem of its messianic status).

I would like to have read and gone through all of this non-Greek in the Letter to the Romans with you today word by word, given that it is the testamentary   *Methodos* compendium of Paul's thought, of his gospel, par excellence. But since we do not have time for such an endeavor, in addition to reasons I will not pursue at this moment, we will have to place our stakes in this brief time, on this radical abbreviation of time that is the time *that remains*. For Paul, the contraction of time, the "remaining" time (1 Cor. 7:29: "time contracted itself, the rest is") represents the messianic situation par excellence, the only real time. I have subsequently decided on our reading only the first verse of the letter, and translating and commenting on it, word for word. I will be satisfied if, at the end of this seminar, we are able to understand the meaning of this first verse, in its literal sense and in every other aspect. This is a modest endeavor, but it depends on a preliminary wager: we will be treating this first verse as though its first ten words recapitulate the meaning of the text in its entirety.

Following epistolary practices of the period, Paul generally begins his letters with a preamble in which he presents himself and names his addressees. The fact that the greeting of the Letter to the Romans differs from others in its length and doctrinal content has not gone unnoticed. Our hypothesis pushes further, for it supposes that each word of the incipit contracts within itself the complete text of the Letter, in a vertiginous recapitulation. (*Recapitulation* is an essential term for the vocabulary of messianism, as we shall see later.) Understanding the incipit therefore entails an eventual understanding of the text as a whole.

PAULOS DOULOS CHRISTOU IESOU, KLETOS APOSTOLOS APHORIS-
MENOS EIS EUAGGELION THEOU. The Latin

The Ten Words   translation by Jerome used for centuries by the Catholic Church reads: *Paulus servus Jesu Christi, vocatus apostolus, segregatus in evangelium Dei.* A current literal English translates, "Paul, a servant of Jesus Christ, called to be an apostle, separated to the gospel of God."

One preliminary philological observation. We read the Pauline text in modern versions. (In our case Nestle-Aland's critical edition, which is a revised edition, published in 1962, of Eberhard Nestle's 1898 edition that abandoned the Erasmian *Textus receptus* and instead based itself on a comparison between the 1869 Tischendorf text and the 1881 Westcott-Hort text.) In contrast to the manuscript tradition, these editions necessarily introduce modern conventions of writing, like punctuation, into the text, and in doing so they occasionally presuppose semantic choices. This is why, in our verse, the comma after *Iēsou* makes for a syntactic break, separating *doulos* from *klētos*, that refers the latter to *apostolos* ("servant of Jesus Christ, called to be an apostle"). Yet nothing prevents us from opting for a different scansion, reading *Paulos doulos christou Iēsou klētos, apostolos aphōrismenos eis euaggelion theou* as "Paul, called as slave of Jesus the Messiah, separated as apostle for the announcement of God." This second reading would, among other things, better correspond with Paul's explicit affirmation (1 Cor. 15:9): *ouk eimi hikanos kaleisthai apostolos* ("I am not worthy to be called apostle"). Without yet choosing one over the other, at this point we should remember that, from the syntactic point of view, the verse presets itself like a single nominal syntagma that is absolutely paratactic, uttered in one single breath, moving according to the crescendo: *servitude, calling, envoi, separation.*

I will spare you the endless discussions on the subject of the name Paulos, concerning whether, as a Roman name, it is actually a *praenomen* or a *cognomen*, or perhaps even   *Paulos* a *signum* or a *supernomen* (that is to say, a surname), and the reasons for which "the young Jew with the proud biblical-Palestinian name of Sha'ul, which at the same time emphasized the descent of his family from the tribe of Benjamin, was given this Latin *cognomen*" (Hengel, 9). Why doesn't Paul ever give his full name, if, according to a completely unfounded conjecture, his name was Caius Julius Paulus? What relation exists between his Roman name and Sha'ul, his Hebrew name (which, in the Septuagint, is written as *Saoul* or *Saoulos*, and not *Saulos*)? These problems as well as others stem from a passage in Acts 13:9, which reads, *Saulos ho kai Paulos* (*ho kai* is the Greek equivalent of the Latin *qui et*, which usually introduces a surname and can mean "who is also called").

My methodological choice (which also entails basic philological precaution) consists here—and in general for the interpretation of Pauline texts—in not taking into account later sources, even if they are other New Testament texts. In his letters, Paul always and only calls himself *Paulos*. And this is all there is, nothing more to add. For those who would like to know more on this subject, permit me to refer you to the early study by Hermann Dessau (1910) or to the more recent work—though by no means more astute— by Gustave Adolphus Harrer (1940). Most of what you find there, however, is simply gossip, which is also the case for all the speculations on Paul's trade, on his studies with Gamaliel, and so on. This does not mean that gossip cannot be interesting; on the contrary, to the extent that it entertains a nontrivial relation to truth that eludes the problem of verification and falsification and claims to be closer to truth than factual adequation, gossip is certainly a form of art. The peculiarity of its epistemological status lies in the fact that in itself it accounts for the possibility of an error that does not entirely undermine the definition of truth. Intelligent gossip therefore interests us independently of its verifiable character. That said, to treat gossip as though it were information is truly an unforgivable *apaideusia* [lack of refinement].

While it may not be legitimate to unhesitatingly deduce from a text information that supposedly refers to the biographic reality of its author or characters, such information may still be used as a starting point for a better understanding of the text itself, or for the internal function that the author, the characters, or their respective names assume within the text. In other words, the good use of gossip is not excluded. In this vein, when the author of the Acts changes to *Paulos* the name of the character who up to that point had been called *Saulos*, we can read a significance in the sudden shift. In literary texts, we occasionally find that an author changes identity over the course of the narration—for example, when Guillaume de Lorris, the supposed author of *The Romance of the Rose*, gives way to an equally unknown Jean de Meun, or when Miguel de Cervantes declares at a certain point that the real author of the novel he is writing is not himself, but a so-called Cid Hamete Benengeli. (In this case, Benengeli is actually the transcription of an Arabic word that means "son of a stag," which is probably an ironic allusion to the hazy circumstances surrounding the author's birth, taking into account those laws concerning the *limpieza del*

On the Good Use of Gossip

sangre, purity of blood, that discriminate against those with Hebrew or Moorish ancestry.)

In the Hebrew context, the archetype for metanomasia, that is, for the changing of a name of a character, is found in Genesis 17:5, when God himself intervenes and changes the names of Abraham and Sarah, adding a letter to each name. Philo dedicates an entire treatise, *De mutatione nominum*, to this problem and comments at length on the Abraham and Sarah episode (as do two of his *Quaestiones et solutiones in Genesin*). Contra those who ridicule God's going out of his way to give Abraham the gift of one mere letter, Philo brings attention to the fact that this slight addition actually changes the meaning of the whole name—and, as a result, the entire person of Abraham himself. On the addition of *rho* to the name Sarah, Philo writes, "What seems to merely be the simple addition of a letter, in reality produces a new harmony. Instead of producing the small, it produces the great; instead of the particular, the universal; instead of the mortal, the immortal" (Philo, 124–25).

The fact that this treatise is not even mentioned in the recent literature on the name of the apostle (but is cited many times in Origen's and Erasmus's commentaries) is a prime example of what Giorgio Pasquali used to call *coniunctivitis professoria* (or in this instance, *theologico-professoria*).[2] In changing only one letter of his name, in replacing *pi* by *sigma*, Saulos could have possibly had—according to the author of the Acts, who was well versed in Hellenized Judaism—an analogous "new harmony" in mind. Saulos is in fact a regal name, and the man who bore this name surpassed all Israelites, not only in beauty, but also in stature (1 Sam. 9:2; this is why, in the Koran, Saul is called *Talut*, the highest). The substitution of *sigma* by *pi* therefore signifies no less than the passage from the regal to the insignificant, from grandeur to smallness—*paulus* in Latin means "small, of little significance," and in 1 Corinthians 15:9 Paul defines himself as "the least [*elachistos*] of the apostles."

Paul is therefore a surname, the messianic *signum* (which is the same as a *supernomen*) that the apostle bestows on himself at the moment he fully assumes the messianic vocation. The formula *ho*

2. *Translator's note*: See Giorgio Pasquali's *Pagine stravaganti di un philologo* (Florence: Editrice Le Lettere, 1994).

kai leaves no room for speculation around its referring to a surname and not a cognomen, and it is hard to believe that, after
Lambertz's studies on surnames in the Roman Empire, anyone
could ever support arguments to the contrary. According to a
practice that spread from Egypt to all of Asia Minor, *ho kai* is the
formula that normally introduces a surname. Among the examples
catalogued by Lambertz we find a *ho kai Paulos* that the scholar
thought was taken from the name of the apostle but which most
likely only repeats within itself the implicit gesture of humility
(Lambertz 1914, 152). Scholars of onomastics have long since noted
that as the Roman trinomial system began to wane and give way
to the modern uninomial system, many of the new names were
actually only surnames, often diminutives or perjoratives, which
were taken for proper names in keeping with the Christian claim
for creaturely humility. We possess lists of these surnames, lists
that document *in flagranti* the transition from noble Latin onomastics to the new Christian quasi name:

> *Januarius qui et Asellus*
> *Lucius qui et Porcellus*
> *Ildebrandus qui et Pecora*
> *Manlius qui et Longus*
> *Amelia Maura qui et Minima . . .*

Saulos qui et Paulos therefore carries within itself an onomastic
prophecy that would sustain a long legacy. Metanomasia realizes
the intransigent messianic principle articulated firmly by the apostle, in which those things that are weak and insignificant will, in
the days of the Messiah, prevail over those things the world con-
siders to be strong and important (1 Cor. 1:27–28: "But God hath
chosen . . . the weak things of the world to confound the things
which are mighty, . . . and things which are not, to bring to
nought the things that are"). The messianic separates the proper
name from its bearer, who from this point on may bear only an
improper name, a nickname. After Paul, all of our names are only
signa, surnames.

Confirmation of the messianic significance of metanomasia can
even be found in the verse on which we are commenting. In this

instance, the name Paul is immediately linked to the word *doulos,* "slave." Since slaves did not have any juridical status in classical antiquity, they did not have veritable names and could be given names only by their owners, according to the owners' whim. Slaves frequently received a new name upon acquisition (Lambertz 1906–8, 19). Plato (*Cratylus* 384d) alludes to this custom, writing, "We frequently change the names of our slaves, and the newly imposed name is as good as the old." Philostratus recalls that Herod Atticus bestowed the twenty-four letters of the alphabet as names to his slaves, so that his son could train himself in calling them. Among these non-names, these mere *signa* of slaves, aside from names that indicate geographical provenance, we often find nicknames that describe a physical quality, such as *micos, micros, micrine* (little, tiny) or *longus, longinus, megellos* (tall, large). At the very moment when the call transforms him who is a free man into "the slave of the Messiah," the apostle must, like a slave, lose his name, whether it be Roman or Jewish. From this point on he must call himself by a simple surname. This did not escape the sensibility of Augustine, who—in countering a misleading suggestion made by Jerome, repeated again by the moderns, that the name Paul supposedly came from the name of the proconsul whom he converted—knew perfectly well that Paul simply means "little" ("Paulum . . . minimum est"; *Enarrationes in Psalmos* 72:4). This should do for gossip.

(•) The methodological precaution of excluding everything that comes after a specific text is impossible here. The memory of a cultivated reader is comparable to a historical dictionary containing all of the uses of a term, from a term's first appearance up to the present day. A historical being (as is, by definition, language) monadically carries within himself the entirety of his history (or as Benjamin would say, all of his pre- and posthistory). One may consequently attempt to disregard the given meanings of a term after a certain date—which is what we shall be attempting here, with the highest possible degree of meticulousness. Keeping distinct the successive moments of a word's semantic history is not always easy, especially when, as with the Pauline text, this history coincides with the history of Western culture as a whole, with its decisive caesuras and continuities. If the interpretation of the New

Testament is inextricable from the history of its tradition and translations, then, for this very reason, precaution becomes all the more necessary. It is often the case that a later meaning, the product of ages of theological discussions, is integrated into lexicons and is uncritically pro-
jected back onto the text. The task thus remains of creating a Pauline
lexicon of technical terms (not to be confused with a lexicon of the New
Testament as a whole). Our seminar would like to consider itself as an
initial contribution, however partial, to this task.

This precaution does not imply any judgment on the historical value of
a text like the Acts, itself the subject of much debate. As we have seen,
this precaution is only valid when taken in a general philological and
conceptual way. To be able to distinguish what is of true historical value
and what is part of a hagiographic construction in Luke's text (to dis-
cern, for example, if the "cloven tongues like as of fire" mentioned in
Acts 2:3 pertain to any historical event) is, without a doubt, a task
beyond our present means.

The importance of the term *doulos* (servant, slave) in Paul is
witnessed in the term's frequent use. It appears 47 times
Doulos   in the Pauline text, more than a third of the 127 occurrences in the New Testament. Even before he presents
himself as an apostle, Paul chooses to present himself to the
Romans as a slave (as he does in Phil. 1:1 and in Titus 1:1). But
what does it mean to be "a slave of the Messiah"? In tracing out
the semantic history of the term *doulos*, the New Testament lexicons habitually contrast the predominantly juridical meaning that
the term acquired in the classical world—which technically refers
to the slave inasmuch as he is subjected to the power of the *domi-
nus-despotēs* (if the Greeks wanted to stress the generic relation of
a slave's belonging to the *oikos* of his owner they would use the
term *oiketēs*)—to the markedly religious connotation that the corresponding Hebrew word *'ebed* (like the Arabic *'abd*) acquires in
the Semitic world. The opposition does not aid our understanding of how *doulos* is used technically in the Pauline text, for, in
Paul, *doulos* refers to a profane juridical condition and at the same
time refers to the transformation that this condition undergoes in
its relation to the messianic event.

The juridical usage of the term becomes evident in passages that oppose *doulos* to *eleutheros* (free) and follow the antithesis Jew/Greek (such as 1 Cor. 12:13: "For by one Spirit we were all baptized into one body—Jews or Greeks, slaves or free"; in addition, see Gal. 3:28 and Col. 3:11). Here Paul is concurrently evoking the two fundamental divisions of people: one according to Hebrew law (Hebrew *goyim* reaffirmed in Gal. 2:7 in the form "circumcision-foreskin"), and the other according to Roman law.[3] In the first book of *The Digest of Justinian*, under the rubric of *de statu hominum*, we read "summa . . . de iure personarum divisio haec est, quod omnes aut liberi sunt aut servi [certainly, the great divide in the law of persons is this: all men are either free or slaves]" (Justinian, 15).

Doulos acquires a technical meaning in Paul (as in "slave of the Messiah," or the quasi-slang *hyper doulon*, "super-slave, beyond-slave," in Philem. 1:16). It is used to express the neutralization that the divisions of the law and all juridical and social conditions in general undergo as a consequence of the messianic event. The definitive passage for understanding the usage of the term is 1 Corinthians 7:20–23: "Let every man abide in the same calling wherein he was called. Art thou called being a slave? Care not for it: but if thou mayest be made free, use it rather. For he that is called in the Lord, being a slave, is the Lord's freeman: likewise also he that is called being free, is slave of the Messiah." Because this passage necessitates lengthy commentary in order to interpret the terms *klētos* and *klēsis*, I will postpone this analysis until later. We may nevertheless anticipate one thing: that the syntagma "slave of the Messiah" defines the new messianic condition for Paul, the principle of a particular transformation of all juridical conditions (which, for this reason, are not simply abolished). Moreover, we may note that the comparison with 1 Corinthians 7:22—in terms of the strong tie this passage sets up between the verb group *kaleō* ("I call") and the term *doulos*—permits for reading a different scansion in our incipit: "Paul, called (as) a servant of Jesus Christ, an apostle separated unto the announcement of God." In its being situated precisely at the center of the ten words

3. *Translator's note.* Agamben uses *prepuzio*, the Italian word for foreskin rather than uncircumscribed or uncircumcision, so I have done the same in order to render audible the bodily quality of Paul's language.

that comprise this verse, *klētos*, "calling," constitutes a kind of conceptual pivot, which can be turned just as much toward the first half (toward him who was free but now becomes a slave of the Messiah) as toward the second half (toward him who was not worthy of being called apostle and becomes separated as such). In either case, the messianic calling is a central event in Paul's individual history, as it is for the history of humanity.

ℸ Although studies on the relation between Roman law and Hebrew law, and on Paul's position with regard to both, remain largely insufficient, they are nevertheless promising. (Alan Watson's books provide interesting starting points concerning the relation of Jesus to Hebrew and Roman law, especially *Jesus and the Law* and *Ancient Law and Modern Understanding*; Boaz Cohen's book *Jewish and Roman Law* is, however, not as helpful. On the relation between Paul and Hebrew law, see Peter Tomson's *Paul and the Jewish Law*, which provides a good demonstration of the current reversal among scholars, who are now hurrying, undoubtedly for good reasons, to find the *Halacha* in the Pauline text regardless of consequence.) Nevertheless, the feeble opposition that sets the classical world against Judaism reveals its shortcomings precisely at this point. At first sight, Mishnah and Talmud, in their formal structure, seem to find no corresponding resemblance in all of Western culture. However, even the reader without any knowledge of the history of the law quickly notices that a fundamental work in Western culture resembles the Jewish compilations to the extent of being quasi-identical to them. We are referring to *The Digest*, that is, the book of the *Corpus iuris civilis*, in which Justinian brings together the opinions of great Roman jurisconsults. One after the other, opinions of jurists of different ages are listed in response to various questions, sometimes in sharp contrast to one another, in exactly same way that the Mishnah and Talmud draw up a list of the opinions of rabbis from the houses of Shammai and Hillel. In the following passage taken from *The Digest*, one only need replace Roman names with Hebrew names to confirm the formal analogy beyond doubt:

Ulpian, *Sabinus, book 22*: When someone legates stores, let us see what is embraced by the legacy. Quintus Mucius writes in the second book of his *Civil Law* that things intended to be eaten and drunk are includ-

Talmud and Corpus iuris

ed in a legacy of stores. Sabinus writes to the same effect in his books on Vitellius. Whatever of these, he says, [are kept for the use of] the head of the household, or his wife, or children, or the household which habitually surrounds them; likewise, of pack animals which are kept for the owner's use. But Aristo notes that things which are not for eating and not for drinking are also included in the legacy, as, for instance, those things in which we are accustomed to eat things, such as oil, fish sauce, brine, honey, and other similar items. Admittedly, he says, if edible stores are legated, Labeo writes in the ninth book of his *Posthumous Works* that none of these things goes with the legacy, because we are accustomed not to eat these things but to eat other things by means of them. In the case of honey, Trebatius states the opposite, rightly, because we are accustomed to eat honey. But Proculus correctly writes that all these things are included, unless the testator's intention should appear otherwise. Did he legate as eatables those things which we are accustomed to eat or also those things by means of which we eat other things? The latter should also be considered to be included in the legacy, unless the intention of the head of the household is shown to be otherwise. Certainly, honey always goes with edible stores, and not even Labeo denied that fish too, along with their brine, are included (Justinian, 33, 9). The analogy is all the more noteworthy in that the *Corpus iuris civilis* and the Talmud are contemporary with each other (both dating back to the mid-sixth century C.E.).

If you look at a current rendering of our verse, it is impossible not to notice that from the Vulgate on, several terms in the Greek are not translated but are instead substituted with a calque: apostle *Christou Iēsou* for *apostolos,* evangel for *euaggelion* and, above all, Christ for *Christos.* Each reading and each new translation of the Pauline text must begin by keeping in mind the fact that *christos* is not a proper name, but is, already in the Septuagint, the Greek translation of the Hebrew term *mashiah,* "the anointed," that is, the Messiah. Paul has no familiarity with Jesus Christ, only with Jesus Messiah or the Messiah Jesus, as he writes interchangeably. In the same fashion, he never uses the term *christianos* and even if he knew of this term (which seems to be implied in Acts 11:26), this would only have meant "messianic," especially in the sense of disciple of the Messiah. This presupposition is obvious in the sense that no one could seriously claim the contrary; nevertheless, it is anything but trivial. A millenary tradition that left the word *christos* untranslated ends by making the term *Messiah* disappear from Paul's text. The *euaggelion tou christou* of Romans 15:19 is the announcement of the coming of the Messiah. The formula *Iēsous estin ho christos* (Jesus is the Christ)—which in John 20:31 and Acts 9:22 signifies the messianic faith of the community Paul address-es—would not make any sense if *christos* were a proper name. It is absurd to refer to a "messianic conscience" of Jesus or his apostles (as do some modern theologians), if one has to first hypothesize that the apostles took *christos* for a proper name. Admitting that one can talk of a Christology in Paul, it coincides fully with the doctrine of the Messiah.

We will therefore always translate *christos* as "Messiah." That the term *Christ* consequently never appears in our text is not meant to signal any polemic intention nor a Judaizing reading of the Pauline text; rather, it entails an elementary philological scruple that all translators should follow, whether or not they be equipped with an *imprimatur*.

The assertion, often found in modern commentaries, that the syntagma *Christos Iēsous* (or *Iēsous Christos*) is

Proper Names   supposed to construct only one proper name obviously lacks any philological basis. The dis-tinction between *Christos* (capitalized) and *christos* as an appella-tion was introduced by modern editors. Not only do the most ancient manuscripts fail to distinguish between capitalized and noncapitalized words, they also write *christos*—as with other *nomina sacra* such as *theos, kyrios, pneuma, Iēsous,* and so on—in an abbreviated form (which, according to Ludwig Traube, stems from the Hebrew interdiction of pronouncing the tetragrammaton). But, in the preface to the Nestle-Aland edition, we find "*christos* will be written in lower case when it signals 'the official designa-tion' (*Amstbezeichnung*) of the Messiah (for example Matt. 16:16), and in upper case when it has clearly become a proper name (for example, in Gal. 3:24–29)." The real difficulty with this more or less conscious transgression of the most basic philological principles, lies in determining this self-evident "when." This was certainly not a problem for the evangelists, who knew perfectly well what the term *christos* signified ("We have found the Messiah, which is, being interpreted, *christos*"; John 1:41). Nor was it a problem for the Church Fathers, from Origen (*tēn christos prosegorian* ["the title christ"]; *Commentary on the Gospel According to John*, 72),[4] to Justin (who otherwise would not have said to the Jew Trypho, "We are all awaiting the christ").

The distinction between *ho christos* with the article and *christos* without the article is just as devoid of value in the Pauline text, given that, in a completely analogous fashion, Paul writes the word *nomos* sometimes with an article and sometimes without, never meaning for him that *nomos* has become a proper name. To the contrary, a formal analysis of the Pauline text shows that *christos* could only be an appellative, from the instant that the apostle refrains from writing *kyrios christos* (uniting two appellatives with differing connotations), and only writes *kyrios Iēsous christos, kyrios Iēsous, christos Iēsous kyrios emōn* (Coppens, 133). In general, one should never forget that it is beyond an author's power to take a term that is in current use in the linguistic context of his life and make it into a proper name, especially with regard to a fundamental concept, such as that of the Messiah for a Jew. The problem of distinguishing those passages in which the term maintains its "Old Testament" meaning is a pseudoproblem from the very start, for not only is it impossible for Paul to distinguish between an Old and New Testament in the way we do now, that is, as two textual wholes, but his reference to the *kainē diathēkē* is an "Old Testament" citation (Jer. 31:31) that specifically refers to the messianic accomplishment of the Torah. (The *palaia diathēkē* "is made inoperative in the Messiah"; 2 Cor. 3:14.)

When, in a modern commentary on the Letter to the Romans, we find, "Here we first read Christ Jesus, then Jesus Christ. The two formulas constitute one sole proper name, in which the appellative meaning of the Messiah tends to fade away" (Huby,

---

4. *Translator's note.* For the Greek see the bilingual Greek/French edition used by Agamben: *Commentaire sur saint Jean, 1: Books 1–5*, ed. Cécile Blanc (Paris: Editions du Cerf, 1996). This passage is found in book 1, paragraph 191, pp. 154–55.

38–39), we may completely disregard its claim, for it projects our forgetting of the original meaning of the term *christos* back onto the Pauline text. This is clearly no accident but one of the secondary effects of the admirable works of constructing the section of Christian theology the moderns called Christology. Our seminar does not set out to measure itself against the Christological problem; rather, more modestly and more philosophically, it seeks to understand the meaning of the word *christos*, that is, "Messiah." What does it mean to live in the Messiah, and what is the messianic life? What is the structure of messianic time? These questions, meaning Paul's questions, must also be ours.

§ The Second Day

Klētos

The term *klētos*, which comes from the verb *kaleō*, to call, means "calling" (Jerome translates it as *vocatus*). This term appears in the greeting of the first Letter to the Corinthians; in the other letters, we often find the following formula: "apostle by the will of God." We should pause to reflect on this term, for in Paul the linguistic family of the word *kaleō* acquires a technical meaning that is essential to Paul's definition of messianic life, especially when found in the deverbative form *klēsis*, meaning "vocation, calling." The definitive passage is 1 Corinthians 7:17–22:

> But as God hath distributed to every man, as the Lord hath called every one, so let him walk. And so ordain I in all communities [*ekklēsías*, another word from the same family as *kaleō*]. Is any man called being circumcised? let him not remove the mark of circumcision. Is any called with a foreskin? let him not be circumcised! Circumcision is nothing, and the foreskin is nothing. . . . Let every man abide in the same calling wherein he was called. Art thou called being a slave? care not for it: but if thou mayest be made free, use it rather. For he that is called in the Lord, being a slave, is the Lord's freeman: likewise also he that is called, being free, is slave of the Messiah.

What does *klēsis* mean here? What does the following phrase mean: "Let every man abide in the same calling wherein he was called [*en tē klēsei he eklēthē*]"? Before   *Beruf* answering this question, we must first examine the

19

problem arising from the strategic use of the term *klēsis*—or, better yet, from the word's translation into the German *Beruf*—in one of the most definite works in the social sciences in our century, Max Weber's *Protestant Ethic and the Spirit of Capitalism* (1904). You are certainly familiar with Weber's thesis, the one concerning what he calls the "spirit of capitalism," meaning the mentality that makes of profit a good, independently of hedonistic or utilitarian motives—that it originates from a Calvinist and Puritan professional ascesis emancipated from its religious foundation. This means that the capitalist spirit is a secularization of the Puritan ethic of the profession. What specifically interests us is that this modern concept of profession is in turn constructed out of the Pauline passage on *klēsis* that we have just read, transforming the messianic vocation in question into the modern conception of *Beruf*, as both vocation and worldly profession.

We witness a turning point in the process of secularization of messianic *klēsis* in the Lutheran translation of *klēsis* by *Beruf* in several passages of the letters and specifically in the passage that concerns us, 1 Corinthians 7:17–22. It is through the Lutheran version that a term originally signifying the vocation that only God or the Messiah addressed to man acquires the modern sense of a "profession." Shortly after Luther, the Calvinists and the Puritans invested it with an entirely new ethical meaning. According to Weber, the Pauline text does not convey any positive valuation of worldly professions, but only an attitude of "eschatological indifference." This is a consequence of awaiting the imminent end of the first Christian communities: "Since everyone was awaiting the coming of the Lord, then let everyone remain in the estate [*Stand*] and the secular occupation [*Hantierung*] in which the call [*Ruf*] of the Lord has found him, and continue to labor as before" (Weber, 31). Luther, who at first shared Paul's eschatological indifference, at a certain point, especially after the experience of the peasant revolts, gradually leans toward a new understanding of the importance of an individual's concrete profession being that of a command placed in him by God to fulfill the duties that correspond with the worldly position imposed upon him. "The individual should remain once and for all in the station and calling in which God had placed him, and should restrain his worldly activity within the limits imposed by his established station in life" (Weber, 85).

Weber frames the problem of the exact meaning of the term *klēsis* in the Pauline text in this particular context and dedicates a long note to it. "Luther," he writes,

> translates two apparently quite distinct concepts as *Beruf*. Firstly the Pauline *klēsis* in the sense of the calling of God to eternal salvation. In this category belong: 1 Corinthians 1:26; Ephesians 1:18; 4:1, and 4:4; 2 Thessalonians 1:11; Hebrews 3:1; 2 Peter 1:10. All these cases relate to the *purely* religious concept of the calling *Berufung*] which comes from God by means of the gospel preached by the apostle. The term *klēsis* has nothing whatever to do with secular "callings" in the present-day sense. (Weber, 55)

According to Weber, the connection between the "purely" religious usage of the term "calling" and the modern term *Beruf* is constituted precisely on the basis of our passage, 1 Corinthians 7. It is useful to quote Weber's reflections on this passage, for they betray a difficulty he is unable to resolve:

> The translation of a passage in the First Letter to the Corinthians forms a bridge between those two seemingly quite distinct uses of the word "Beruf" by Luther. In Luther (in the usual modern editions), the context in which this passage is located is as follows: 1 Corinthians 7:17: "Only as the Lord hath distributed to each man, as God hath called each, so let him walk. . . . Was any man called being circumcised? let him not remove the mark of circumcision. Hath any man been called uncircumcised? let him not be circumcised! Circumcision is nothing, and uncircumcision is nothing; but the keeping of the commandments of God. Let each man abide in that calling wherein he was called (*en tē klēse he eklēthē*—as Professor Merx tells me, this is unquestionably a Hebraism—the Vulgate translates it as *in qua vocatione vocatus est*). Wast thou called being a bond-servant? care not for it." . . . In his exegesis of this chapter, Luther, even in 1523, had followed the older German versions by translating *klēsis* in verse 20 as "Ruf" . . . and had at that time

interpreted this as "Stand" (estate or condition). It is in fact evident that the word *klēsis* in this—and *only* this—passage corresponds at least approximately to the Latin "status" and our "Stand" (in German), i.e., state, estate, or condition, as in married state, the condition of a servant, etc. In verse 20 Luther, following the older German translations, even in 1523 in his exegesis of this chapter, renders *klēsis* with *Beruf*, and interprets it with *Stand* ["status"]. . . . But of course not as Brentano . . . assumes, in the modern sense of *Beruf as profession*. (Weber, 56–57)

What does it mean that the term *klēsis* may and may not have the same meaning as the modern *Beruf*? Is it correct to interpret the Pauline concept of the call, like Weber does, as an expression of "eschatological indifference" toward worldly conditions? In addition, how exactly does the passage in question carry out the transition from the religious meaning of vocation to that of a profession? The determining moment obviously occurs in verse 20, in the *en tē klēse he eklēthē* that Weber, in accepting a suggestion from Merx, interprets as a Hebraism. In truth, this hypothesis harbors no philological bearing and only reflects a purely semantic difficulty in comprehension. From a syntactic-grammatical point of view, the phrase is in fact perspicuous, and Jerome renders it without any difficulty as *in qua vocatione vocatus est*. In an even more literal fashion, he could have written *in vocatione qua vocatus est*, "in the calling whereby he was called." The Greek anaphoric pronoun *he* (Lat. *qua*) is a perfect rendering of the meaning of the formula, of its peculiar tautegorical movement that comes from the call and returns back to it. According to the proper meaning of each anaphora, *he* actually signals a taking up of the previously mentioned term (here, *klēsis*). This anaphoric movement is constitutive of the meaning of Pauline *klēsis* and thus makes *klēsis* a technical term in his messianic vocabulary. *Klēsis* indicates the particular transformation that every juridical status and worldly condition undergoes because of, and only because of, its relation to the messianic event. It is therefore not a matter of eschatological indifference, but of change, almost an internal shifting of each and every single worldly condition by virtue of being "called." For Paul, the *ekklēsia*, the messianic community, is literally all *klēseis*, all messianic vocations. The messianic vocation does not, however, have any specific content; it is nothing but the repetition of those same factical or juridical conditions *in which* or *as which* we are called. Inasmuch as *klēsis* describes this immobile dialectic, this movement *sur place*, it can be taken for both the factical condition and the juridical status that signifies "vocation" as much as it does *Beruf.*

According to the apostle, this movement is, above all, a nullification: "Circumcision is nothing, and the foreskin is nothing." That which, according to the law, made one man a Jew and the other a *goy*, one a slave and another a free man, is now annulled by the vocation. Why remain in this nothing? Once again, *mene-tō* ("remaining") does not convey indifference, it signifies the immobile anaphoric gesture of the messianic calling, its being essentially and foremost a *calling of the calling.* For this reason, it may apply to any condition; but for this same reason, it revokes a condition and radically puts it into question in the very act of adhering to it.

This is what Paul says just a bit further on, in a remarkable passage that may be his most rigorous definition of messianic life (1 Cor. 7:29–32): "But this I say, brethren, time contracted itself, the rest is, that even those having wives may be as not [*hōs mē*] having, and those weeping as not weeping, and those rejoicing as not rejoicing, and those buying as not possessing, and those using the world as not using it up. For passing away is the figure of this world. But I wish you to be without care." *Hōs mē*, "as not": this is the formula concerning messianic life and is the ultimate meaning of *klēsis.* Vocation calls for nothing and to no place. For this reason it may coincide with the factical condition in which each person finds himself called, but for this very reason, it also revokes the condition from top to bottom. *The messianic vocation is the revocation of every vocation.* In this way, it defines what to me seems to be the only acceptable vocation. What is a vocation, but the revocation of each and every concrete factical vocation? This obviously does not entail substituting a less authentic vocation with a truer vocation. According

Vocation and Revocation

to what norm would one be chosen over the other? No, the vocation calls the vocation itself, as though it were an urgency that
works it from within and hollows it out, nullifying it in the very
gesture of maintaining and dwelling in it. This, and nothing less
than this, is what it means to have a vocation, what it means to
live in messianic *klēsis*.

At this point, the *hōs mē* shows itself as a technical term essential to Pauline vocabulary and must be understood in its specificity on both the syntactic-grammatical and semantic levels. We
should take note that in the Synoptic Gospels, the particle *hōs*
serves an important function as an introductory term for messianic comparisons (for example, in Matt. 18:3: "unless you [man]
. . . become as the children [*hōs ta paidia*]"; or in the negative, in
Matt. 6:5: "thou shalt not be as the hypocrites"). What is the
meaning of this comparison, and what is the meaning of any comparison in general? Medieval grammarians did not interpret the
comparative as an expression of identity or simple resemblance,
but rather, in the context of the theory of intensive magnitudes,
they interpreted the comparative as an (intensive or remissive) tension that sets one concept against another. To use our previous
example, the concept *man* is thus set against the concept *children*
in a way that does not presume any identification between the two
terms. The Pauline *hōs mē* seems to be a special type of tensor, for
it does not push a concept's semantic field toward that of another
concept. Instead, it sets it against itself in the form of the *as not*:
weeping as not weeping. The messianic tension thus does not tend
toward an elsewhere, nor does it exhaust itself in the indifference
between one thing and its opposite. The apostle does not say:
"weeping *as* rejoicing" nor "weeping as [meaning =] not weeping,"
but "weeping *as not* weeping." According to the principle of messianic *klēsis*, one determinate factical condition is set in relation to
itself—the weeping is pushed toward the weeping, the rejoicing
toward the rejoicing. In this manner, it revokes the factical condition and undermines it without altering its form. The Pauline passage on the *hōs mē* may thus conclude with the phrase "*paragei gar
to schēma tou kosmou toutou* [for passing away is the figure, the way
of being of this world]" (1 Cor. 7:31). In pushing each thing toward

itself through the *as not*, the messianic does not simply cancel out this figure, but it makes it pass, it prepares its end. This is not another figure or another world: it is the passing of the figure of this world.

ℸ An apocalyptic parallel to the Pauline *hōs mē* is discernable in 4 Ezra (or 2 Esdras) 16:42–46:

Qui vendit, quasi qui fugiet;
et qui emit, quasi qui perditurus;
qui mercatur, quasi qui fructum non capiat;
et qui aedificat, quasi non habitaturus;
qui seminat, quasi qui non metet;
et qui vineam putat, quasi non vindemiaturus;
qui nubunt, sic quasi filios non facturi;
et qui non nubunt, sic quasi vidui.

[Let him that sells be as one who will flee;
let him that buys be as one who will lose;
let him that does business be as one who will not make a profit;
and let him that builds a house be as one who will not live in it;
let him that sows be as one who will not reap;
so also him that prunes the vines, as one who will not gather the grapes;
let them that marry, as those who will have no children;
and them that do not marry, as those who are widowed.]

A more attentive analysis nevertheless demonstrates that this seeming closeness (*hōs mē, quasi non*) veils profound differences. Not only does Ezra contrast different verbs while Paul almost always negates the same verb, but, as Wolbert observes (Wolbert, 122), Ezra distinguishes between those verb tenses (present and future) that Paul merges into a single present. In Paul, the messianic nullification performed by *hōs mē* is completely inherent to *klēsis* and does not happen to it in a second time (like it does in Ezra), nor does it add anything to it. In this way, the messianic vocation is a movement of immanence, or, if one prefers, a zone of absolute indiscernability between immanence and transcendence, between this world and the future world. This will be important in understanding the structure of messianic time.

From this perspective, the passage 1 Corinthians 7:29–32 can be read as though it were implicitly opposed—perhaps even knowingly—to the passage in Ecclesiastes (3:4–8) in which *Qoheleth* clearly separates the

times Paul melds together: "A time to weep, and a time to laugh; a time
to mourn, and a time to dance . . . a time to seek and a time to lose; a
time to keep, and a time to throw away . . . a time for war and a time
for peace." Paul defines the messianic condition by simply superimpos-
ing, in the *hōs mē*, the times *Qoheleth* divides.

In order to render the messianic instance of an *as not* in every
klēsis, the urgency revoking every vocation which
Chrēsis   adheres to it, Paul uses a peculiar expression that gave
his interpreters much to ponder: *chrēsai*, "make use."
Let us now reread 1 Corinthians 7:21: "Art thou called being a
slave? care not for it: but if thou mayest be made free, use it
rather." Contra Luther, who refers *chrēsai* to freedom and not, as
implied by the formulas *ei kai* ("but if") and *mallon* ("rather"), to
slavery, we would do well to hear in this line, as do the majority
of interpreters, "But if thou mayest be made free, use your *klēsis* as
slave." *Use*: this is the definition Paul gives to messianic life in the
form of the *as not*. To live messianically means "to use" *klēsis*; con-
versely, messianic *klēsis* is something to use, not to possess.

We may now make better sense of the meaning of the antitheses in verses 30–31:"those buying as not possessing, and those
using [*chrōmenoi*] the world as not using it up [*katachrōmenoi*]."
They make an explicit reference to property (*dominium*) under
Roman law: *ius utendi et abutendi*. (The meaning is confirmed in
the reading of the L manuscript: *parachrōmenoi*, to make use of, in
the technical-juridical sense.) Paul contrasts messianic *usus* with
dominium; thus, to remain in the calling in the form of the *as not*
means to not ever make the calling an object of ownership, only
of use. The *hōs mē* therefore does not only have a negative content;
rather, for Paul, this is the only possible *use* of worldly situations.
The messianic vocation is not a right, nor does it furnish an identity; rather, it is a generic potentiality [*potenza*] that can be used
without ever being owned. To be messianic, to live in the Messiah,
signifies the expropriation of each and every juridical-factical
property (circumcised/uncircumcised; free/slave; man/woman)
under the form of the *as not*. This expropriation does not, however, found a new identity; the "new creature" is none other than the
use and messianic vocation of the old (2 Cor. 5:17: "So if anyone

is in the Messiah, the new creature [*kainē ktisis*]: everything old has passed away; see, everything has become new").

(•) It is against this backdrop of a messianic vocation as conceived by Paul, that the Franciscan claim to a *usus* opposed to property acquires its meaning. In their faith to a principle of *altissima paupertas* that went against the prescriptions of the Curia, factions of spiritual Franciscans were not limited in refusing all forms of property. With regard to the Franciscans, and as Bartolus of Saxoferrato's juridical astuteness made clear in his speaking of a *novitas vitae* to which civil law remained inapplicable, they implicitly put forth the idea of a *forma vivendi* that was entirely subtracted from the sphere of the law. *Usus pauper* is the name they gave to this form of life's relation to worldly goods. Contrary to those who believed that, in the final analysis, use could be referred back to a "right of usage" (*ius in usu, usum habere*) and was therefore equivalent to a *potestas licita utendi rem ad utilitatem suam* (as is the case, for example, in usufruct), Olivi confirms that "use and right are not the same thing: we may use something without having a right over it or over its usage, just as the slave uses his owner's thing without being an owner or an usufructuary" (Lambertini, 159).[1] Even though the Pauline text most often referred to by the Franciscans is 1 Timothy 6:8 ("if we have food and clothing, we will be content with these"), many passages in the *quaestio di altissima paupertate* on Olivi's distinction between *usus* and *dominium* can be read as true and proper glosses of 1 Corinthians 7:30–31: "dicendum quod dare et emere et ceteri contractus," he writes, "in apostolos erant solo nomine et solo ritu exteriori non autem in rei veritate [One should say that when it comes to the apostles, the acts of selling and buying and other types of contracts existed only in name and as external ritual, but not in the reality (truth) of the thing]" (Lambertini, 161). In elaborating on the trend, already present in the writings of Francis, to conceive of the order as a messianic community and dissolve the rule that was conceived of as a form of life in the gospel (the first rule begins *haec est vita evangeli Jesu Christi*), for Olivi as for Angelo Clareno, what mattered was to create a space that escaped the grasp of power and its laws, without entering into conflict with them yet rendering them inoperative. As we shall see, the Pauline strategy with regard to the law, of which our passage 1 Corinthians 7 on the *as not* forms an integral part, may be read from an analogous perspective.

1. *Translator's note.* Pierre Jean Olivi, 1248–98, philosopher of the Middle Ages, who was an early leader of the "Spiritual" reform movement in the Franciscan order.

ℸ It will help us here to compare the Pauline *as not* with a juridical institution as it permits for certain analogies. I am speaking of the institution of the *fictio legis*, correctly defined as a creation without precedent in Roman civil law (Thomas, 20). The "fiction" (which should not be confused with a presumption, which refers to an uncertain fact) consists in substituting a truth with an opposite accession, from which juridical consequences may be derived (*fictio est in re certa contrariae veritatis pro veritate assumptio*). Depending on whether the accession is negative or positive, it expressed in the formula *ac si-non* / *ac si, perinde ac si non* / *perinde si* [as if not / as if, just as if not / just as if]. One example of the *fictio legis* is the *Lex cornelia* (81 B.C.E.), on the validity of the testimony of Roman citizens who died in captivity. According to Roman law, captivity implied the loss of status of free citizen and, therefore, the loss of the capacity to make a testament. In order to remedy the patrimonial consequences of this principle, the *Lex cornelia* established that in the case of a Roman citizen who had fallen into slavery but made a testament one had to act "as though he had not been made a prisoner" (or, in the equivalent positive formulation, "as though he had died a free citizen," *atque se in civitate decessit*). The *fictio* consists in acting as if the slave were a free citizen and in deducing from this fiction the validity of a juridical act that would otherwise be null. This fiction of nonexistence could be pushed at times to the extent of annulling a legal provision (*ac si lex lata non esset*) or a particular juridical act so that, without ever contesting its reality (*pro infecto*), it could be considered as though it had never happened.

In the *as not*, in a characteristic gesture, Paul pushes an almost exclusively juridical regulation to its extreme, turning it against the law. What does it actually mean to remain a slave in the form of the *as not*? Here, the juridical-factical condition invested by the messianic vocation is not negated with regard to juridical consequences that would in turn validate a different or even opposite legal effect in its place, as does the *fictio legis*. Rather, in the *as not*, the juridical-factical condition is taken up again and is transposed, while remaining juridically unchanged, to a zone that is neither factual nor juridical, but is subtracted from the law and remains as a place of pure praxis, of simple "use" ("use it rather!"). Factical *klēsis*, set in relation to itself via the messianic vocation, is not replaced by something else, but is rendered inoperative. (Further on, we will see that Paul uses a specific term to signify this deactivation, rendering ineffective.) In this fashion, *klēsis* is laid open to its true use. This is the reason that the slave, as defined by Paul, is invested with a messianic vocation through the extraordinary hapax: *hyper doulos,* "super-slave, slave to the second power."

In his footnote on the meaning of the term *klēsis* in Paul, Weber is forced to take into account a passage by Dionysius of Halicarnassus, a passage that in **Klēsis and Class** his eyes constitutes the only text in Greek literature where *klēsis* "corresponds at least approximately to the Latin 'status' and our 'Stand' (in German)" (Weber, 57). In this passage, Dionysius derives the Latin word *classis* from the Greek term *klēsis,* which indicates that part of the citizenry called to arms (*klaseis kata tas Hellēnikas klēseis paranomasantos*). Even though modern philologists doubt this etymology, what interests us is that it allows us to relate messianic *klēsis* to a key concept in Marxian thought. It has often been noted that Marx was the first to substitute the Gallicism *Klasse* for the more common *Stand* (the term that Hegel would still habitually use in his political philosophy). That this substitution has a strategic function for Marx is proven in the fact that Hegelian doctrine of *Stände* is already under scrutiny in his "Critique of the Hegelian Concept of the State" (1841–42). While the Marxian use of the term is not always consistent, what is certain is that Marx invests the concept of "class" with a meaning that goes beyond his critique of Hegelian philosophy to designate the great transformation introduced into the political fabric by the domination of the bourgeoisie. In fact, the bourgeoisie represents the dissolution of all *Stände*; it is radically *Klasse* and no longer *Stand*: "the bourgeois revolution undermined all *Stand* and its privileges"; "By the mere fact that it is a *class* and no longer an *estate* [*Stand*], the bourgeoisie . . . " (Marx and Engels, 5: 90). So long as the system of the *Stand* remains intact, what cannot be brought to light is the split produced by the division of labor between the personal life of each individual and the life of that same individual inasmuch as it is subsumed to a certain condition of labor and the profession:

In the *Stand* (and even more in the tribe) this is as yet concealed: for instance, a nobleman always remains a nobleman, a *roturier* [commoner] always a *roturier*, a quality inseparable from his individuality irre-

spective of his other relations. The difference between the private individual and the class individual, the accidental nature of the conditions
of life for the individual, appears only with the emergence of the class,
which is itself a product of the bourgeoisie. (Marx and Engels, 5: 78)

Class therefore represents the split between the individual and
his social figure, for his social figure is divested of the meaning
Stand covered it up with, now revealing itself as mere accident
(*Zufälligkeit*). The class, the proletariat, incarnates this split in itself
and lays bare, as it were, the contingency of each and every figure
and social condition; nevertheless, it alone is capable of abolishing
this division and of emancipating itself along with society as a
whole. It is helpful here to reread the famous passage in the
"Contribution to the Critique of Hegel's Philosophy of Right" in
which Marx presents the redemptive function of the proletariat:

Where, then, is the positive possibility of a German emancipation?
Answer: In the formation of a class with *radical chains*, a class of civil
society which is not a class of civil society, an estate [*Stand*] which is the
dissolution of all estates [*Stände*], a sphere which has a universal character by its universal suffering and claims no *particular right* because no
particular wrong but wrong generally [*das Unrecht schlechtin*] is perpe-
trated against it; which can no longer invoke a historical but only a
human title; which does not stand in any one-sided antithesis to the
consequences but in an all-round antithesis to the premises of the
German state; a sphere, finally, which cannot emancipate itself without
emancipating itself from all other spheres of society and thereby emancipating all other spheres of society, which, in a word, is the *complete loss*
of man [*der völlige Verlust des Menschen*] and hence can win itself only
through the complete rewinning of man. This dissolution of society as
a particular estate [*Stand*] is the proletariat. (Marx and Engels, 3: 186)

Benjamin's thesis, that the Marxian concept of a "classless society"
is a secularization of the idea of messianic time, is obviously pertinent to us here. We will therefore attempt to take Dionysius's
etymology seriously for a short moment in bringing together the
function of messianic *klēsis* for Paul with the function of class for
Marx. Just as class represents the dissolution of all ranks and the
emergence of a split between the individual and his own social

condition, so too does messianic *klēsis* signify the hollowing out and nullification of all juridical-factical conditions through the form of the *as not*. From this perspective, the semantic indeterminacy between *klēsis*-calling and *klēsis-Beruf* (which so preoccupied Weber) can be read in terms of the arbitrariness marking each social condition for the messianic and for Marx's proletariat. The *ekklēsia*, inasmuch as it is a community of messianic *klēseis*—that is, inasmuch as it has become aware of this arbitrariness and lives under the form of the *as not* and usage—permits more than just one analogy with the Marxian proletariat. Just as he who is called is crucified with the Messiah and dies to the old world (Rom. 6:6) in order to be resuscitated to a new life (Rom. 8:11), so too is the proletariat only able to liberate itself through autosuppression. The "complete loss" of man coincides with his complete redemption. (From this perspective, the fact that the proletariat ends up being identified over time with a determinate social class—the working class that claims prerogatives and rights for itself—is the worst misunderstanding of Marxian thought. What for Marx served as a strategic identification—the working class as *klēsis* and as historical figure contingent on the proletariat—becomes, to the opposite end, a true and proper substantial social identity that necessarily ends in losing its revolutionary vocation.)

Marx's secularization of the messianic seems to me to be accurate and precise, up to this point. But can we really speak of a "society without *klēseis*" in Paul, in the same way that Marx speaks of a "classless society?" This is a legitimate question, for, if it is true that factical *klēseis* abide as such ("Let every man abide"), then they are nevertheless null and void of meaning ("Circumcision is nothing, and the foreskin is nothing"; "he that is called in the Lord, being a slave, is the Lord's freeman"). Several answers to this question are, of course, possible. Two are actually prefigured in Stirner's opposition between revolt (*Empörung*) and revolution (*Revolution*), and by Marx's vast critique of Stirner in *The German Ideology*. According to Stirner (or at least in Marx's presentation of Stirner's thought), revolution consists in "a transformation of the existing condition [*Zustand*], or *status*, of the state or society;

hence it is a *political* or *social* act" that has the creation of new institutions as its goal. Revolt, however, is "an uprising of individuals . . . without regard for the institutions that develop out of
it. . . . It is not a struggle against what exists, for if it prospers what
exists will collapse of itself; it is only the setting free of me from
what exists" (Marx and Engels, 5: 377). Commenting on these
affirmations, Marx cites a passage from George Kuhlmann's book,
which has an unmistakenly messianic title, *The New World; or, The
Kingdom of the Spirit upon Earth*: "Ye shall not tear down nor
destroy that which ye find in your path, ye shall rather go out of
your way to avoid it and pass by it. And when ye have avoided it
and passed it by, then it shall cease to exist of itself, for it shall find
no other nourishment" (Marx and Engels, 5: 539). While Marx
succeeds in ridiculing Stirner's theses, they still represent one possible interpretation, an interpretation which we will call the ethi-
cal-anarchic interpretation of the Pauline *as not*. The other interpretation, Marx's, which does not distinguish revolt from revolution, a political act from individual and egoistic need, runs into a
problem that is expressed by the aporia of the party, in the party's
being identical to class while simultaneously differing from it.
(This means that the Communist Party is not distinguishable from
the working class, except to the extent that it manages to grasp the
totality of the historical course of the working class.) If political
action (revolution) coincides perfectly with the egoistic act of the
singular individual (revolt), then why is something like a party
even necessary? Lukács's response to this problem in *History and
Class Consciousness* is well known: the problem of organization is
the problem of "class consciousness," for which the party is simultaneously the universal bearer and catalyst. But in the end, this
amounts to affirming that party is distinct from class, like consciousness from man, with all the aporias implied. (As an Averoist
aporia, the party becomes something like the intellectual agent of
medieval philosophers, which has to carry over into actuality the
potentiality of mens' intellect. As a Hegelian aporia, it is expressed
in the question: what is consciousness, if to it is attributed the
magical power to transform reality . . . in itself?) That Lukács ends

on this basis, by making "right theory" the decisive criterion for a definition of the party, once again demonstrates the proximity between the crux of this problem and that of messianic *klēsis*. In the same way, once the *ekklēsia,* the community of messianic vocations, wishes to impart to itself an organization distinct from the community while pretending to coincide with it, the problem of correct doctrine and infallibility (that is, the problem of dogma) becomes crucial.

A third interpretation is also possible. This is the anarchic-nihilistic interpretation attempted by Taubes in Benjamin's steps, which plays on the absolute indiscernability between revolt and revolution, worldly *klēsis* and messianic *klēsis.* One consequence of this is the impossibility of distinguishing something like an awareness of the vocation from the movement of its tension and revocation in the *as not.* This interpretation has Paul's explicit affirmation on its side, when Paul says that he does not recall seizing hold of himself, but only of being seized, and from this being seized, straining forward toward *klēsis* (Phil. 3:12–13). In this instance, vocation coincides with the movement of the calling toward itself. As you can see, many interpretations are possible, none of which, may be correct. The only interpretation that is in no way possible is the one put forth by the Church, based on Romans 13:1, which states that there is no authority except from God, and that you should therefore work, obey, and not question your given place in society. What happens to the *as not* in all of this? Doesn't the messianic vocation become reduced to a sort of mental reserve, or, in the best of cases, to a kind of Marranism *ante litteram?*

ℸ In the early 1920s, in a course entitled "Introduction to the Phenomenology of Religion," Heidegger read Paul and briefly commented on the passage 1 Corinthians 7:20–31, which concerns *klēsis* and the *hōs mē.* According to Heidegger, what is essential in Paul is not dogma or theory, but factical experience, the way worldly relations are lived (*Vollzug,* the carrying out, the way of living). For Paul, this way of living is determined through the *hōs mē*:

What is now at stake is a new fundamental comportment in regard to the *hōs mē.* This comportment has to be explicated according to the structure of how it is carried out [*vollzugsmässig*]. Whatever the meaning of real life, though this meaning is actual, it is lived *hōs mē, as if not* (*als ob nicht*). . . . Noteworthy is 1 Corinthians 7:20. A person should remain in the calling he is in, the *genesthai* is a *menein*. . . . Here, a particular context of meaning is indicated: the relations to the surrounding environment do not receive their meaning from the significance of the content toward which they are directed, but rather the reverse, from this original carrying-out (*Vollzug*), the relation and the meaning of lived significance is determined. Schematically said: something remains unchanged but is radically changed nevertheless. . . . That which is changed is not the meaning of the relation and even less so its content. Thus, the Christian does not leave the world. If someone is called to be a slave he should not fall into the tendency of believing that an increase of his freedom could gain anything for his being. The slave should remain a slave. It makes no difference what worldly significance he might hold. The slave as a Christian is free of all bonds, as a Christian the freeman will become a slave before God. . . . These directions of meaning, toward the surrounding world, toward one's calling, and toward that which one is, in no way determine the facticity of the Christian. Nevertheless, these relations are there, they are maintained, and thus first appropriated [*zugeeignet*] in an authentic manner. (Heidegger 1995, 117–19)

This passage is important because in it we find more than just a simple anticipation of what would become in *Being and Time* the dialectic of the proper (*Eigentlichkeit*) and the improper (*Uneigentlichkeit*). What is essential to this dialectic is that the proper and the authentic are not "something which floats above falling everydayness; existentially, it is only a modified way in which such everydayness is seized upon" (Heidegger 1962, 224). This means that the authentic does not have any other content than the inauthentic. It is through his reading of the Pauline *hōs mē* that Heidegger seems to first develop his idea of the appropriation of the improper as the determining trait of human existence. The Christian way of life is in fact not determined by worldly relations or by their content, but by the way, and only by the way, in which they are lived and are appropriated in their very impropriety. Nonetheless, for Paul, what is at stake is not appropriation, but use, and the messianic subject is not only *not* defined by propriety, but he is also unable to seize hold of himself as a whole, whether in the form of an authentic decision or in Being-toward-death.

Adorno ends *Minima Moralia* with an aphorism, in the form of a seal that bears the messianic title *Zum Ende*, "Finale." In it, philosophy is defined as follows: "The only philosophy   As If which can be responsibly practiced in face of despair is the attempt to contemplate all things as they would present themselves from the standpoint of redemption" (Adorno, 247). Taubes noted that when this text, which he found "wonderful, but finally empty" (Taubes, 74), is compared with Benjamin and Karl Barth, it shows itself to be nothing other than an aestheticization of the messianic in the form of the *as if*. This is why, Taubes adds, the aphorism concludes with the thesis, "The question of reality or unreality of redemption becomes almost an indifferent one." I have often questioned whether this accusation of an "aestheticization of the messianic"—which implies the renunciation of redemption in exchange for the appearance of redemption—is justified, given that the author of *Aesthetic Theory* pushes his mistrust of beautiful appearances to the point of defining beauty as *der Bann über den Bann*, "the spell over spells." Whatever the outcome, this point interests us for it allows us to bring into perspective the distance separating the Pauline *as not* from every *as if* and from the *als ob* in particular. Beginning with Kant, the *als ob* reveled in its overwhelming success in modern ethics. You are familiar with Hans Vaihinger's book *The Philosophy of "As If."* Even though all the vices of Neo-Kantianism can already be found in it, its main thesis on the centrality of fiction to modern culture—by which he intends not only the sciences and philosophy but also law and theology—is nevertheless right on the mark. Vaihinger defines fiction (or the "fictive activity" of thought) as "the production and use of logical methods, which, with the help of accessory concepts—where the improbability of any corresponding objective is fairly obvious—seek to attain the objects of thought" (Vaihinger, 17). The problem that concerns us is, of course, the status of being of this "fiction," for which language is itself, so to speak, the archetype. It would be asking too much, however, to expect Vaihinger to raise this issue. His reconstruction of the importance of fiction—which one should not confuse with a

hypothesis!—in modern science is also of interest. But what truly
fails is the way in which he attempts to resolve the *als ob* with practical reason and the Kantian conception of the idea with the *focus
imaginarius* by means of a kind of glorification of Pharisaism.
With a glaring absence of tact, Vaihinger flattens out Kant into the
likes of Friedrich Karl Forberg. Forberg was a mediocre theologian
to whom Vaihinger attributes the invention of a "religion of As-
if," which supposedly has the merit of clearly presenting "at least
in its basic principles, Kant's As-if doctrine" (Vaihinger, 321).
Unfortunately, Forberg is the inventor *ante litteram* of the social-
democratic theory of the ideal as infinite progress. This theory will
be the very target of Benjamin's critique in his *Theses on the
Philosophy of History*. Listen to why:

The kingdom of truth will almost certainly never come, and in the final
aim set before itself by the republic of scholars will, in all likelihood,
never be attained. Nevertheless, the unquenchable interest in truth that
burns in the breast of every thinking man will demand, for all eternity,
that he should combat error with all his power and spread truth in every
direction, i.e. behave exactly *as if* error must some day be completely
extirpated and we might look forward to a time when truth will reign in
undisputed sovereignty. This indeed is characteristic of a nature like that
of man, designed to be forever approximating to unattainable ideals. . . .
It is true that in all this you cannot scientifically demonstrate that it
must be so. Enough that your heart bids you act *as if* it were so.
(Vaihinger, 322)

There are still people today—although really only a small group,
who seem to have almost become respectable these days—who are
convinced that one can reduce ethics and religion to acting *as if*
God, the kingdom, truth, and so on existed. At the same time, the
as if has become a highly popular nosological figure verging on a
common condition. All of the people whose cases cannot be clearly ascribed to psychoses or neuroses are called *as if* personalities, or
borderline personalities, because their "problem" consists in the
fact that they have no problem, so to speak. They live *as if* they
were normal, as if the reign of normality existed, as if there were
"no problem" (this is the idiotic formula that they learn to repeat

on every occasion), and this alone constitutes the origin of their discomfort, their particular sensation of emptiness.

The fact remains that the question of the *as if* is infinitely more serious than Vaihinger imagines it to be. Eight years before Vaihinger's book, the far more interesting author Jules de Gaultier published his masterpiece *Bovarysm*, in which the problem of fiction is restored to the rank to which it is due, that is, to the level of the ontological. According to Gaultier, the "faculty of believing one is different from what one is," which constitutes the essence of man, the essence of the animal who has no essence, is shown in Flaubert's characters in a pathological way. Because he is not anything in himself, man can only be if he acts as if he were different from what he is (or what he is not). Gaultier was an avid reader of Nietzsche and understood that every nihilism implied an *as if,* making the problem lie in the way in which one dwells in the *as if.* The Nietzschean overcoming of nihilism has to contend with this fundamental Bovarysm and know how to correctly seize hold of it (hence the problem of the artist in Nietzsche).

Let us turn now to Adorno and to Taubes's plaint that accuses him of an aestheticization of the messianic. Were I to assume the role of the accused in this trial, I would proceed by reading the final aphorism of *Minima Moralia* with the beginning of *Negative Dialectics*: "philosophy lives on because the moment to realize it was missed." The fact of having missed the moment of its realization is what obliges philosophy to indefinitely contemplate the appearance of redemption. Aesthetic beauty is the chastisement, so to speak, of philosophy's having missed its moment. Only in this vein may we truly speak of an *als ob* in Adorno. This is why aesthetic beauty cannot be anything more than the spell over spells. There is no satisfaction in it, for the *as if* is the condemnation that the philosopher has already inflicted on himself.

At a certain point in his work, Benjamin Whorf, a linguist acutely aware of the way structures of language determine structures of thought, speaks of a spe- **Impotential** cial verbal category of the Hopi language, which he defines as the category of "impotential." This modal category is

particularly difficult to express in the languages Whorf calls SAE
languages (Standard Average European languages) and corresponds to a kind of "teleological ineffectiveness" (Whorf, 121). "If
a Hopi is reporting on a train of events in which a man ran away
from his pursuers but was eventually captured by them, he will use
the impotential, and say *ta'.qa as wa.'ya* 'the man ran away' (implying that 'ran away' cannot here be held to mean 'escaped'). If the
man ran away and escaped, the statement would be simply *ta'.qa
wa.'ya*" (Whorf, 122).

The whole of Adorno's philosophy is written according to
impotential meaning that the *as if* can only be taken as a warning
signal at the heart of this intimate modality of his thought.
Philosophy had been realizing itself, but the moment of its realization was missed. This omission is at one and the same time
absolutely contingent and absolutely irreparable, thus impotential. Redemption is, consequently, only a "point of view." Adorno
could never even conceive of restoring possibility to the fallen,
unlike Paul, for whom "power [*potenza*] is actualized in weakness"
(2 Cor. 12:9). Despite appearances, negative dialectics is an
absolutely non-messianic form of thought, closer to the emotional tonality of Jean Améry than that of Benjamin.

You are familiar with the wicked joke Duns Scotus borrows
from Avicenna to prove contingency: "Those who deny contingency should be tortured until they admit that they could
also have not been tortured." Jean Améry endured this terrible
proof, forced to acknowledge the senseless cruelty of contingency. From that moment on, what happened was absolutely
irreparable and resentment the only suitable emotional
response. In his extraordinary testimony *Au-delà de la faute et
de l'expiation* (*Beyond Guilt and Atonement*)—the title of
which demonstrates a kind of ethical justification of resentment that finds a parallel in the subtitle of *Minima Moralia*,
"Reflections from Damaged Life [*beschädigten Leben*]," likewise betraying something akin to resentment—Améry
explains how the poems he had memorized by Hölderlin lost
their ability to save and transcend the world. The "spell on

spells" may even aptly describe poetry; for Améry and Adorno, all gestures that could claim to lift the spell are absent.

Is there something like a messianic modality that would allow us to define its specificity in relation to Adorno's impotential and Améry's resentment? This modality,   Exigency
which is rarely ever thematized as such in the history
of philosophy, is exigency. So essential to philosophy, it could even be said to make it coincide with the possibility of philosophy itself. Let us attempt to inscribe this concept into the table of modal categories alongside possibility, impossibility, necessity, and contingency. In the essay written in his youth on Dostoevsky's *Idiot*, Benjamin says that the life of Prince Mishkin must remain unforgettable, even if no one remembers it. This is exigency. Exigency does not forget, nor does it try to exorcise contingency. On the contrary, it says: even though this life has been completely forgotten, there is an exigency that it remain unforgettable.

In "Primary Truths" (*De veritatibus primis*), Leibniz defines the relation between possibility and reality as follows: *omne possibile exigit existere*, every possibility demands [*esige*] to exist, to become real. Despite an unconditional respect for Leibniz, I do not think that this formulation is correct. In order to define what is truly an exigency, we should invert the formulation and write: *omne existens exigit possibilitatem suam*, each existent demands [*esige*] its proper possibility, it demands that it become possible. Exigency consists in a relation between what is or has been, and its possibility. It does not precede reality; rather, it follows it.

I imagine Benjamin had something like this in mind when, referring to the life of the idiot, he spoke
of the exigency to remain unforgettable.   The Unforgettable
This does not simply mean that something forgotten should now reappear in our memory and be remembered. Exigency does not properly concern that which has not been remembered; it concerns that which remains unforgettable. It refers to all in individual or collective life that is forgotten with each instant and to the infinite mass that will be forgotten by both. Despite the efforts of historians, scribes, and all sorts

of archivists, the quantity of what is irretrievably lost in the history of society and in the history of individuals is infinitely greater than what can be stored in the archives of memory. In every instant, the measure of forgetting and ruin, the ontological squandering that we bear within ourselves far exceeds the piety of our memories and consciences. But the shapeless chaos of the forgotten is neither inert nor ineffective. To the contrary, it is at work within us with a force equal to that of the mass of conscious memories, but in a different way. Forgetting has a force and a way of operating that cannot be measured in the same terms as those of conscious memory, nor can it be accumulated like knowledge. Its persistence determines the status of all knowledge and understanding. The exigency of the lost does not entail being remembered and commemorated; rather, it entails remaining in us and with us as forgotten, and in this way and only in this way, remaining unforgettable.

From this stems the inadequacy in trying to restore to memory what is forgotten by inscribing it in the archives and monuments of history, or in trying to construct another tradition and history, of the oppressed and the defeated. While their history may be written with different tools than that of the dominant classes, it will never substantially differ from it. In trying to work against this confusion, one should remember that the tradition of the unforgettable is not exactly a tradition. It is what marks traditions with either the seal of infamy or glory, sometimes both. That which makes each history historical and each tradition transmissible is the unforgettable nucleus that both bear within themselves at their core. The alternatives at this juncture are therefore not to forget or remember, to be unaware or become conscious, but rather, the determining factor is the capacity to remain faithful to that which having perpetually been forgotten, must remain unforgettable. It demands [*esige*] to remain with us and be possible for us in some manner. To respond to this exigency is the only historical responsibility I feel capable of assuming fully. If, however, we refuse to respond, and if, on both the collective and individual levels, we forgo each and every relation to the mass of the forgotten that accompanies us like a silent *golem*, then it will reappear within us in a destructive and perverse way, in the form Freud called the return of the repressed, that is, as the return of the impossible as such.

What does all of this have to do with Paul? For Paul, the redemption of what has been is the place of an exigency for the messianic. This place does not involve a point of view from which we could see a world in which redemption had taken place. The coming of the Messiah means that all things, even the subjects who contemplate it, are caught up in the *as not*, called and revoked at one and the same time. No subject could watch it or act *as if* at a given point. The messianic vocation dislocates and, above all, nullifies the entire subject. This is the meaning of Galatians 2:20, "It is no longer I that live [*zō oukēti egō*], but the Messiah living in me." He lives in him precisely as the "no longer I," that dead body of sin we bear within ourselves which is given life through the spirit in the Messiah (Rom. 8:11). The whole of creation was subjected to caducity (*mataiotēs*), the futility of what is lost and decays, but this is why it groans as it awaits redemption (Rom. 8:20–22). The thing in the spirit to correspond with this creature's continuously lost lament is not a well-formed discourse able to calculate and register loss, but "unspeakable groanings" (*stenagmois alalētois*) (Rom. 8:26). This is why the one who upholds faith in what is lost cannot believe in any identity or worldly *klēsis*. The *as not* is by no means a fiction in the sense intended by Vaihinger or Forberg. It has nothing to do with an ideal. The assimilation to what has been lost and forgotten is absolute: "We are made as the filth of the world, the offscouring of all things" (1 Cor. 4:13). Pauline *klēsis* is a theory of the interrelation between the messianic and the subject, a theory that settles its differences once and for all with presumed identities and ensuing properties. In this sense, that which is not (*ta mē onta*) is stronger than that which is.

Karl Barth's thesis that there is no place for the *as if* in the messianic except when "hope is the *Aufhebung* of the *as if*," and that "we now *truly* see . . . that which we nevertheless do not see" (Barth, 298), is substantially correct, even if it lags behind Pauline exigency. Just as Kafka intuited in his extraordinary parable on parables ("*Von den Gleichnissen*"), the messianic is the simultaneous abolition and realization of the *as if,* and the subject wishing to indefinitely maintain himself in similitude (in the *as if*), while contemplating his ruin, simply loses the wager. He who upholds himself in the messianic vocation no longer knows the *as if,* he no longer has similitudes at his disposal. He knows that in messianic time the saved world coincides with the world that is irretrievably lost, and that, to use Bonhoeffer's words, he must now really live in a world without God. This means that he may not disguise this world's being-without-God in any way. The saving God is the God who abandons him, and the fact of representations (the fact of the *as if*) cannot pretend to save the appearance of salvation. The messianic subject does not contemplate the world as though it were saved. In Benjamin's words, he contemplates salvation only ☞ to the extent that he loses himself in what cannot be saved; this is how difficult it is to dwell in the calling.

⊙ The term parable comes from the Greek *parabole* (Luther's translation is *Gleichnis*). This term serves such an

Parable and Kingdom   important function in the Gospels in its referring to Jesus' discourse, inasmuch as he "speaks in parables" (Matt. 13:10), that from it (through the Latin *parabolare*) comes the verb "to speak" in Romance languages (meaning Provençal, French, and Italian; the Spanish *hablar* comes from *fabulari*). The Hebrew precedent is *mashal,* meaning "comparison, proverb." An implicit link between the structure of parable and the messianic kingdom is already found in Matthew 13:18–19, where "the word of the kingdom" (*logos tēs basileias*) is what makes it necessary to speak in parables. The parable of the sower explained in this passage treats the *logos* so that the seed represents language itself (in the exegesis of Mark 4:13, "He that soweth, soweth the *logos*"). In the series of parables that follow, the messianic kingdom is compared to a field in which good seed and weeds are sown together; to a grain of mustard; to yeast; to treasure hidden in a field; to a merchant in search of a pearl; to a net cast to the water. On this subject Eberhard Jüngel observed that "the kingdom of God comes into language in the parable as a parable" (Jüngel, 295), so that both the difference and closeness between the kingdom of God and this world become exposed together. In the parable, the difference between the *signum* and *res significa* thus tends to annul itself without completely disappearing. In this sense, we can say that like the parable of the sower in Matthew, messianic parables are always parables on language, that is, on the representation of the kingdom in which not only are the kingdom and the terms of the parable placed next to one another (*para-ballō*), but the discourse on the kingdom and the kingdom itself is also placed side by side, so that the understanding of the parable coincides with the *logos tēs basileias*. In the messianic parable *signum* and *res significa* approximate each other because language itself is what is signified. This is undoubtedly the meaning—and unavoidable ambiguity—of Kafka's parable and of every parable in general. If what has to happen in the parable is a passage beyond language, and if, according to Kafka, this is only possible by becoming language ("if you only followed the parables, you yourselves would become parables"), then everything hangs on the moment and manner in which the *as* becomes abolished.

From this perspective, what is decisive is that Paul rarely ever uses parables in the technical sense, and that, as we have just seen, the *as not* defining Paul's messianic *klēsis* does not compare two distinct terms but puts each being and each term in a tension with itself. The messianic event, which, for Paul, has already happened with the resurrection, does not express itself as a parable in a parable, but is present *en tō nun kairō*, as the revocation of every worldly condition, released from itself to allow for its use.

§ The Third Day

Aphōrismenos

Aphōrismenos is the past participle of *aphorizō* and means "separated." Jerome translates it as *segregatus*. This term is clearly an important one for Paul given that, already in the Letter to the Galatians, he uses a form of this verb to characterize his vocation: "he who separated me from the womb of my mother, and having called me through his grace" (Gal. 1:15). This term nevertheless points to an unavoidable problem: how is it possible that Paul, who proclaims universalism and announces the messianic end of all separation between Jews and pagans, refers to himself as one who is "separated"? In Ephesians 2:14–15, Paul says, word for word, that the Messiah "has made both one and has broken down the wall of separation [*to mesotoichon tou phragmou*]." This phrase is powerful, for it puts a fundamental point of Judaism into question. (The author of the letter of Aristeas, who clearly was not a fanatic, defines Jews as follows: "Our lawgiver . . . fenced us about with impregnable palisades and with walls of iron, to the end that we should mingle in no way with any of the other nations [*ethnē*]" (Aristeas, 157). The messianic announcement means that these walls have come down, that a division no longer exists between men, or between men and God. Why then does Paul continue to define himself as "separated"? Did he not, at the moment of the meeting at Antioch, severely reproach Peter precisely because he was "separated" (*aphōrizen heauton*) from the non-Jews (Gal.

2:12)? Separating oneself means questioning the "truth of the messianic proclamation" (*tēn alētheian tou euaggeliou*) to the point that Paul cannot refrain from intervening: "If you, though a Jew, live like a non-Jew, and not like a Jew [*ethnikōs kai ouchi Ioudaikōs*], how can you compel the non-Jews to live like Jews [*Ioudaizein*]" (Gal. 2:14)? He nevertheless cites Isaiah 52:11 elsewhere: "Come out from them, and separate yourselves [*aphoristhēte*]" (2 Cor. 6:17).

To understand the exact meaning of the term *aphōrismenos* thus entails correctly situating a fundamental problem, that of universalism, or Paul's supposed universalism and the "Catholic" vocation of the messianic community. But first, one observation concerning Paul's autobiography. Paul's autobiography is present in the letters not only in a direct fashion, as in the long *excursus* in the Letter to the Galatians, but also indirectly, through allusions that one has to be able to recognize. The term *aphōrismenos* is one of these hidden allusions. In defining himself as "separated," Paul evokes his past as a "then," a *pote*, that must have still been burning in his memory: "then . . . I savagely persecuted God's community" (Gal. 1:13). *Aphōrismenos* is nothing more than the Greek translation of the Hebrew term *parush* or the Aramaic *pᵉrish*, that is, "Pharisee" (the Greek calque *pharisaios* comes from the Aramaic). In the Letter to the Philippians, when he lays claim to his Judaism with regard to the circumcised, Paul says that he was "circumcised on the eighth day, a descendant of the people of Israel, of the tribe of Benjamin, a Hebrew born of Hebrews; as to the law, a Pharisee [*kata nomon Pharisaios*]" (Phil. 3:5).

Paul was therefore a Pharisee, one who was separated. Whatever the origins of this sect—or rather, of this Jewish movement—that historians trace back to the Pharisee Hasidim of the Maccabean era, Pharisees were certainly separated ones who, in distinguishing themselves from the masses while being essentially laypeople, insisted on scrupulous attention to rules of sacerdotal purity. This is how they "separate" themselves—not only and as much from the pagans, but also and above all from the '*am-ha'aretz*, the people of the earth, meaning, the ignorant farmers who do not follow the law. (In this sense, in Kafka's apologue "Before the Law," the "peasant" can be read as an *'am-ha'aretz*, and the gatekeeper as a *parush*, a Pharisee.) Pharisees became a dominant class in Palestine around the end of the first century B.C.E., and if Paul says, "as to the law, a Pharisee" (Phil. 3:6), it is because the Pharisaic ideal constituted an integral code of law in followers' lives. Pharisaism distinguished itself from other factions in Judaism in that, according to the Pharisees, the law did not solely consist in the Torah in the strict sense, that is, as written law, but also as the oral Torah, that is, in tradition conceived as a "dividing wall" or a "fence" surrounding the Torah that prevents contact with any impurity.

In defining himself as *aphōrismenos*, one who is "separated," Paul thus alludes, in an ironic, albeit cruelly ironic fashion to his separation of times past, his segregation as a Pharisee. He refers to it and negates it in the name of another separation that is no longer a separation according to the *nomos*, but a separation according to the messianic proclamation (*eis euaggelion theou*). This is how one should read the phrase *to mesoitochon tou phragmou* in the passage just cited from Ephesians 2:14, which is translated as "the wall of separation," but literally means "the dividing wall of the fence." This is an overt allusion to the "dividing partition" and to the fence surrounding the Torah that constituted the Pharisaic ideal. The wall that the messianic proclamation brings down, the one announced in *aphōrismenos*, is the same wall that the Pharisee had once maintained around the Torah in order to protect it from the *'am-ha'retz* and the goyim, the non-Jews.

☞ If this is true, meaning that if the separation in the messianic aphorism resumes and divides the separation of the *parush*, then *aphōrismenos* implies something like a separation to the second power, a separation which, in its very separateness, divides and traverses the divisions of Pharisaic laws. But this also means that the messianic aphorism partakes in a complex structure that we must actually grasp if we want to understand correctly the meaning of the separations traced out by Paul in his letters. All of Paul's grapplings with the law, and not just in the Letter to the Romans, are actually scanned by a series of divisions, among which the division *sarx / pneuma*, "flesh / breath," occupies a central position. What is the meaning and the strategic function of this division, a division that Paul actively sets against the partitions of the law?

Paul actually starts by stating that the law operates primarily in instituting divisions and separations. In so doing, he seems to take the etymological meaning of the Greek term *nomos* seriously, since he uses the term to designate the Torah as well as laws in general, in that *nomos* derives from *nemō*, "to divide, to attribute parts." As you may recall, in the beginning of the passage on vocation in 1 Corinthians 7:17, in his referring to the varying conditions in which men find themselves divided, Paul says *hōs emerisen ho kyrios*, "in the part which the Lord has attributed to him." In addition, in Ephesians 2:14, the "wall of separation" that the Messiah abolished coincides with the *nomos ton entolōn*, the "law of the commandments," which divided men into "foreskin" and "circumcised."

The Divided People

The principle of the law is thus division. The fundamental partition of Jewish law is the one between Jews and non-Jews, or in Paul's words, between *Ioudaioi* and *ethnē*. In the Bible, the concept of a "people" is in fact always already divided between *am* and *goy* (plural *goyim*). *Am* is Israel, the elected people, with whom Yahweh formed a *berit*, a pact; the goyim are the other peoples. The Septuagint translates *am* with *laos* and *goyim* with *ethnē*. (A fundamental chapter in the semantic history of the term "people" thus begins here and should be traced up to the contemporary usage of the adjective *ethnic* in the syntagma *ethnic conflict*. It would be equally interesting to question the reason why the Septuagint refrains from using that other Greek term for a people, the term that enjoys such prestige in our philosophical-political tradition: the *dēmos*. In both cases, it is plain to see that the term "people" is always already divided, traversed by an originary theological-political fault.)

Even if the whole of the *'am* is called Israel, different denominations are nevertheless also possible. The term *yehudi* (Greek

Ioudaios), which originally designated the inhabitants of the kingdom of Juda, progressively extends to all the members of the *am*
(above all when the non-Jews speak of it). There is also the term
ivri (the Greek is *Hebraios*), which initially had a juridical over-
tone to it, and in rabbinical literature specifically designated
lashon ha-qodesh, Hebrew as a holy tongue, but was then extended to the whole of Israel. In Paul's case, he uses all three terms:
Israel, Hebraios, Ioudaios. One could say that the name itself
divides, that the law constituting Israel as *am* is the principle of
incessant division.

The fundamental division of the law is, nevertheless, that of
Jews and non-Jews, which Paul crudely renders in the antithesis
circumcision/foreskin. Prophets may of course direct their message
toward all peoples, but even in Isaiah 49:6, the "slave of the lord"
whom the prophet announces is defined as *berit 'am,* a "covenant"
of Israel, and *or goyim,* simply meaning a "light" for the non-Jews.
This oppositive sense of the term *ethnē* is found as many as twen-
ty-three times in Paul. The same opposition is also rendered in the
letters via the terms *Ioudaios/Hellēn* (the non-Jews whom Paul was
involved with were Greeks, or people who spoke Greek). This is
why, in Romans 11:13, Paul defines himself as *ethnōn apostolos,*
apostle of the non-Jews, and in Ephesians 3:1 he can say, "I, Paul,
a prisoner of the Messiah for you *ethnē.*" And, when, in the discussion with Peter in Antioch, which, contrary to what Jerome
thought, was absolutely not a farce, Paul says, "Why do you want
to make the *ethnē* live like Jews [*ioudaizein*]?" we should read this
accordingly.

The problem then becomes the following: what is Paul's strategy when confronting this fundamental division? How, from the
messianic perspective, does he manage to neutralize the partitions
of the law? This problem obviously cannot be separated from the
Pauline critique of the law, which is at the center of the Letter to
the Romans. The aporias of the Pauline critique of the law culmi-
nate in the messianic *theologoumena* of Romans 3:31 ("Do we then
abolish the law by this faith? By no means! On the contrary, we
uphold the law") and 10:4 ("the Messiah is the *telos* of the law").

We will attempt to unfold these aporias, which are cosubstantial with the messianic event, by commenting on the word *euaggelion* at a later moment. The Messiah is actually the instance par excellence for a conflict with the law. The Kabbalists will resolve this conflict by distinguishing two aspects of the Torah: the Torah of Beriah, the law of creation, the law of the world that is not yet redeemed, and the Torah of Atzilut, the law that precedes creation, which the Messiah must restore. For now we should note that in the Letter to the Romans, the partitions of the *nomos* traverse even the interior of man, which is divided as it undergoes the law's effect ("I do not do the good I want, but the evil I do not want, this I do"; Rom. 7:19). But even the law divides itself, for he who is divided by the law sees in his members "another law" that struggles against the "law of the breath of life" (Rom. 7:23).

How does Paul tackle these divisions? And how should one come to understand the messianic law of the breath? Should one perhaps oppose one law to another law, a law that is similar to the preceding one but more universal? And what happens to the law's fundamental partitions in the messianic?

Confronting these partitions, Paul puts another division to work, one that does not coincide with the preceding ones but that is not exterior to them either. The messianic aphorism works on the divisions of the law themselves, imposing upon them a further cut. This cut is that of *sarx* / *pneuma*, the cut of "flesh/breath."

Let us take the fundamental division of the law to be that of the Jew/non-Jew. The criteria for how this division works is both clear (circumcised/foreskin) and exhaustive, for it divides all "men" into two subsets, without leaving a remainder [*resto*] or remnant. Paul cuts this division in two via a new division, that of the flesh/breath. This partition does not coincide with that of the Jew/non-Jew, but it is not external to it either; instead, it divides the division itself.

In the German edition of Benjamin's *Passagenwerk*, line N. 7a, I, we read, "a line divided according to the cut of Apollo [*nach dem apoll(i)nischen Schnitt*]" that "perceives its own

The Cut of Apelles

division as beyond itself." The sentence does not make sense, for there is never any "cut of Apollo" in Greek mythology or elsewhere. The problem of course lies in the misreading of *apellnischen Schnitt* (the "i" is by no means necessary), which is actually the "cut of Apelles." Some of you will recall the story Pliny mentions concerning a contest between Apelles and Protogenes. The classical tradition abounds with these kinds of artistic upsets (X manages to fool the birds that come to eat the grapes he has just painted, while Y fools the painter himself in painting a veil that the painter tries to lift, etc.). Here, however, the contest is about a line. Protogenes draws such a fine line that it seems not to have been drawn by the paintbrush of any human being. But Apelles, using his brush, divides his rival's line in two with an even finer line, cutting it lengthwise in half.

In this sense, the messianic aphorism can be seen as a cut of Apelles that does not have any object proper to itself but divides the divisions traced out by the law. The subset "Jews" is thus divided into "apparent Jews," or Jews according to the flesh (*Ioudaios . . . en tō phanerō en sarki*), and "hidden Jews," or Jews according to the breath (*en tō cryptō Ioudaios . . . en pneumati*; Rom. 2:28–29). The same thing happens to the non-Jews (even if Paul does not explicitly say so). This means that "the [true] Jew is not the apparent one and that [true] circumcision is not that of the flesh" (Rom. 2:28–29). Under the effect of the cut of Apelles, the partition of the law (Jew/non-Jew), is no longer clear or exhaustive, for there will be some Jews who are not Jews, and some non-Jews who are not non-Jews. Paul states it clearly: "Not all of those of Israel are Israel" (Rom. 9:6); and, further on, citing Hosea, "I will call my own people a non-people" (Rom. 9:25). This means that messianic division introduces a remnant [*resto*] into the law's overall division of the people, and Jews and non-Jews are constitutively "not all."

This "remnant" is not any kind of numeric portion or substantial positive residue, that would entail a whole homogeneous to the former divisions, in itself harboring the capacity to surpass differences without our understanding precisely how. To the contrary, from an epistemological point of view, it consists in cutting the polarized Jew/non-Jew partition so that one could move on to a logic of an intuitionist sort, or better yet, a logic like that of Nicholas of Cusa in his *De non aliud*, in which the A/non-A opposition admits a third term which then takes on the form of a double negation: non non-A. There are grounds for evoking this logical paradigm in Paul's text, especially in the passage 1 Corinthians 9:20–23, in which he defines his position with regard to the division Jew (*hypo nomon*, "under the law") / non-Jew (*anomoi*, "without law") according to the unusual expression, "as without law, not without the law of God, but in the law of the Messiah" (*hōs anomos, mē ōn anomos theou all'ennomos christou*). He who keeps himself in the messianic law is not-not in the law.

The division of the law into Jew/non-Jew, in the law / without law, now leaves a remnant on either side, which cannot be defined either as a Jew, or as a non-Jew. He who dwells in the law of the Messiah is the non-non-Jew. This works, more or less, according to the following schema:

JEW		NON-JEW	
Jew according to the breath	Jew according to the flesh	non-Jew according to the breath	non-Jew according to the flesh
NON-NON-JEW		NON-NON-JEW	

What is significant in this "division of divisions"? Why do I think that the Pauline aphorism is so important? First and foremost, because it forces us to think about the question of the universal and particular in a completely new way, not only in logic, but also in ontology and politics. You are aware that Paul was always considered to be the apostle of universalism and that the Church, in intending to found itself on his doctrine, claimed for itself the title "Catholic," meaning universal. Hence the subtitle of a recent book on Paul, *The Foundation of Universalism*, which tries to demonstrate precisely how "a universal thought, proceeding on the basis of the worldly proliferation of alterities (the Jew, the Greek, women, men, slaves, free men, and so on) *produces* a

Sameness and an Equality (there is no longer either Jew, or Greek, and so on)" (Badiou, 109). But is this really accurate? And is it really possible to think a universal as "the production of the Same" in Paul?

The messianic cut of Apelles clearly never adds up to a universal. The Jew "according to the breath" is not a universal, because he cannot be a predicate of all Jews; in the same way, the "non-Jew according to the flesh" cannot be a universal either. But this does not mean that the non non-Jews can only be part of the Jews or the non-Jews. Rather, they represent the impossibility of the Jews and *goyim* to coincide with themselves; they are something like a remnant between every people and itself, between every identity and itself. At this point one can measure the distance that separates the Pauline operation from modern universalism—when something like the humanity of man, for example, is taken as the principle that abolishes all difference or as the ultimate difference, beyond which further division is impossible. This is how, in the book just referred to, Badiou is able to think about Paul's universalism as "benevolence with regard to customs and opinions" or as an "indifference that tolerates differences," which then becomes "that which must be traversed in order for universality itself to be constructed" (Badiou, 98–99).

Despite the legitimacy of concepts such as "tolerance" or "benevolence," which in the end, pertain to the State's attitude toward religious conflict (one can see here how those who declare their wanting to abolish the state are often unable to liberate themselves from a point of view of the state), these concepts are certainly not messianic. For Paul, it is not a matter of "tolerating" or getting past differences in order to pinpoint a sameness or a universal lurking beyond. The universal is not a transcendent principle through which differences may be perceived—such a perspective of transcendence is not available to Paul. Rather, this "transcendental" involves an operation that divides the divisions of the law themselves and renders them inoperative, without ever reaching any final ground. No universal man, no Christian can be found in the depths of the Jew or the Greek, neither as a principle nor as an end; all that is left is a remnant and the impossibility of the Jew or the Greek to coincide with himself. The messianic vocation separates every *klēsis* from itself, engendering a tension within itself, without ever providing it with some other identity; hence, Jew *as non*-Jew, Greek *as non*-Greek.

In referring to a book by Robert Antelme, Blanchot once wrote that man is the indestructible that can be infinitely destroyed (Blanchot, 30). Think about the paradoxical structure implied by this formulation. If man, the indestructible, can be infinitely destroyed, this means that there is no human essence to destroy or recover, that man is a being who is infinitely missing himself and is already divided against himself. But if man is that which may be *infinitely* destroyed, this also means that something other than this destruction, and within this destruction, remains, and that man is this remnant.

You see why it makes no sense to speak of universalism with regard to Paul, at least when the universal is thought of as a principle above cuts and divisions, and the individual as the ultimate limit of each division. In this sense, there is neither beginning nor end in Paul, only Apelles' cut, the division of division, and then a remnant.

The theory of the remnant developed by Paul in Romans 11:1–26 should be read in this light, precisely when he takes his formulation of the problem of the **Remnant** *am/goyim*, Jew/non-Jew to an extreme. He begins by asking, "Has God rejected his people?" and quickly follows with the answer, "By no means!" And he makes a claim about his Judaism in the flesh: "I myself am an Israelite, from the seed of Abraham, of the tribe of Benjamin." God did not reject his chosen people, but, as was the case in the time of Elijah, in facing the prophet's accusations against Israel, he reserved seven thousand men for himself, "so that, in the time of the now [*en tō nyn kairō*, the technical expression of messianic time] a remnant is produced, chosen by grace" (Rom. 11:5).

In Paul's Greek, "remnant" is *leimma*. Paul does not invent this concept, but, characteristically, he is merely reviving it from the prophetic tradition. The term is a technical one in the language of the prophets and performs an important function in Isaiah, Amos, and particularly in Micah. The corresponding terms in Hebrew are *she'ar* and *she'erit* (in the Septuagint, *kataleimma* and *hypoleimma*). Something like a paradox is found in these prophets, for they address themselves to the elected people, to Israel, as though they were a whole, while announcing that only a remnant will be saved. The exemplary passage, which Paul even cites, is the messianic prophecy of Isaiah 10:20–22 "On that day, the remnant of Israel, the survivors of the house of Jacob, will no more lean on the one who struck them. . . . A remnant will return, the remnant of Jacob, to the mighty God. For though your people, oh Israel, were like the sand of the sea, only a remnant will return." The idea of a messianic remnant is already contained in what Yahweh announces to Isaiah as the son's name: *Shear Yashuv*, literally meaning "a remnant will return." (Return and salvation are so closely bound together in Judaism that the Septuagint translates *yashuv* as *sōthēsetai*, "will be saved.") Messianic salvation, the work of the divine, has as its remnant a subject: "from Jerusalem a remnant shall go out, from Mount Zion a band of survivors" (Isa. 37:32). But a remnant even figures in matters of election and calling: Isaiah cries, "Listen to me, house of Jacob and all the remnant of Israel" (Isa. 46:3), words that reverberate deeply in the Pauline text, "you, seized in your mother's womb, taken from your mother's breast." In the same manner, in Micah 4:7, the messianic proclamation pertains to a remainder: "In that day, says the Lord, I will assemble the lame, and gather those who have been driven away, and those whom I have afflicted. Of the lame I will make a remnant, of those cast off a strong nation." Even Amos, who announces the entire destruction of God's people, nevertheless aporetically proposes a remnant: "Hate evil and love good. Follow justice at the gate, it may be that the eternal, the god of hosts, will take pity on the remnant of Jacob" (Amos 5:15).

How should we conceive of this "remnant of Israel"? The problem is misunderstood from the very start when the remnant is taken as a numeric remainder or portion, as is the case with several theologians who understand it as that portion of the Jews who survived the eschatological catastrophe, or as a kind of bridge between ruin and salvation. It is even more misleading to interpret the remnant as outright identical to Israel, in the sense of its being an elected people that survived the final destruction of peoples. A closer reading of the prophetic texts shows that the remnant is closer to being a consistency or figure that Israel assumes in relation to election or to the messianic event. It is therefore neither the all, nor a part of the all, but the impossibility for the part and the all to coincide with themselves or with each other. *At a decisive instant, the elected people, every people, will necessarily situate itself as a remnant, as not-all.*

This is the messianic-prophetic concept of the remnant that Paul resumes and develops, and this is also the ultimate meaning of his aphorism, his division of divisions. For him, the remnant no longer consists in a concept turned toward the future, as with the prophets; it concerns a present experience that defines the messianic "now." "In the time of the now a remnant is produced [*gegonen*]."

An unusual dialectic is found here, a dialectic that brings three elements together without any mediation. First there is the all (*pas, panta*). **The All and the Part** Taubes has already noted that the entire First Letter to the Corinthians is constructed in the form of a fugue around the word *pas* (in the Greek Bible, the term *pas* is unquestionably the most frequently used term after *kyrios,* "Lord," with circa seven thousand occurrences). In Paul, *pas,* "all," is the expression proper to the eschatological *telos.* At the end of time, God will be "all in all" (*panta en pasin;* 1 Cor. 15:28—this formula, which in itself unites both its summational and distributive meanings, will be used again by the pantheists). In this same sense, Paul specifies that, in the end, "all of Israel will be saved" (Rom. 11:26).

Next is the part (*meros*) that defines the secular world, the time under the law. Everything here is divided, everything is *ek merous,* "in part." Remember the famous passage 1 Corinthians 13:9–13,

"For we know only in part [*ek merous*], and we prophecy only in part; but when fulfillment comes [*to teleion*], that which is in part will be made inoperative . . . now we see in a mirror, in enigmas, but then we will see face to face. Now I know only in part, then I will know fully as I am fully known. Now faith, hope, and love dwell [*menei*] in these three; and the greatest of these is love."

Finally, the messianic remnant, which does not go beyond the part, but, as we have seen, results from the part's division, is intimately linked to this division. In this sense, the fact that the messianic world is nothing other than the secular world, means that it is still in some way partial. And in 1 Corinthians 12:27, Paul clearly reminds the members of the messianic community of this: "You are the body of Christ and members in part [*ek merous*]." Nevertheless, the remnant is precisely what prevents divisions from being exhaustive and excludes the parts and the all from the possibility of coinciding with themselves. The remnant is not so much the object of salvation as its instrument, that which properly makes salvation possible. In Romans 11:11–26, Paul describes the remnant's soteriological dialectic with clarity. The "diminution" (*hēttēma*) that makes Israel a "part" and a remnant is produced for the salvation of the *ethnē*, the non-Jews, and foreshadows its *plērōma*, its fullness as the all, since, in the end, when the *plērōma* of the people will have come, then "all of Israel will be saved." The remnant is therefore both an excess of the all with regard to the part, and of the part with regard to the all. It functions as a very peculiar kind of soteriological machine. As such, it only concerns messianic time and only exists therein. In the *telos*, when God will be "all in all," the messianic remnant will not harbor any particular privilege and will have exhausted its meaning in losing itself in the *plērōma* (1 Thess. 4:15: "we, who remain alive, unto the coming of the Lord shall not overtake them which are asleep"). But in the time of the now, the only real time, there is nothing other than the remnant. This does not properly belong either to an eschatology of ruin or salvation, but rather, to use Benjamin's words, it belongs to an unredeemable, the perception of which allows us to reach salvation. The only possible meaning of Kafka's aphorism, in which there is salvation, but "not for us," is found here. As remnant, we, the living who remain *en tō nyn kairō*, make salvation possible, we are its "premise" (*aparchē*; Rom. 11:16). We are already saved, so to speak, but for this reason, it is not as a remnant that we will be saved. The messianic remnant exceeds the eschatological all, and irremediably so; it is the unredeemable that makes salvation possible.

If I had to mark out a political legacy in Paul's letters that was immediately traceable, I believe that the concept of the remnant would have to play a part. More specifically, it allows for a new perspective that dislodges our antiquated notions of a people and a democracy, however impossible it may be to completely renounce them. The people is neither the all nor the part, neither the majority nor the minority. Instead, it is that which can never coincide with itself, as all or as part, that which infinitely remains or resists in each division, and, with all due respect to those who govern us, never allows us to be reduced to a majority or a minority. This remnant is the figure, or the substantiality assumed by a people in a decisive moment, and as such is the only real political subject.

ℸ The messianic concept of the remnant undoubtedly permits more than one analogy to be made with the Marxian proletariat—in the latter's noncoinciding with itself as class and in its necessarily exceeding the state and social dialectic of *Stände*—which underwent "no *particular wrong* but *wrong absolutely* [*das Unrecht schlechtin*]." This concept also enables a better understanding of what Deleuze calls a "minor people," a people that is constitutively positioned as a minority. (This notion most certainly has older origins, since I remember that José Bergamín, having lived through the Spanish civil war, used to say, almost like an adagio, *el pueblo es siempre minoria*, "the people is always a minority.") In a somewhat analogous fashion, in a 1977 interview with Jacques Rancière, Foucault spoke of the pleb as a nondemarcatable element absolutely irreducible to power relationships, not simply external to them but marking their limit in some manner: "The pleb does not exist in all probability, but there is something of the pleb, nevertheless (*il y a de la plèbe*). Something of pleb is in bodies, in spirits, in individuals, in the proletariat, but, with each dimension, form, energy, and irreducibil-

ity, differs in each and every instance. This part of pleb does not represent some exteriority with regard to power relationships as much as it
represents their limit, their ruin, their consequence" (Foucault, 421).

Years later, Rancière himself returned to this Foucauldian concept so as
to develop it into the concept of a people, understood as the "part of
those who have no part," meaning a supernumerary party, the bearer of
a wrong which establishes democracy as a "community of dispute." But
everything here depends on how one interprets "wrong" and "dispute."
If democratic dispute is understood for what it truly is, that is, the possibility of *stasis* or of civil war, then this definition is pertinent. If, however, following what Rancière seems to think, the wrong for whom the
people are the cipher is not "absolute" (as it still was in Marx), but, by
definition, can be "processed" (Rancière, 39), then the line between
democracy and its consensual, or postdemocratic, counterfeit (which
Rancière goes so far as to overtly critique) tends to dissolve.

§ The Fourth Day

Apostolos

The term *apostolos*, which, according to our reading, grammatically depends upon *aphōrismenos*, harbors a particular significance for Paul. *Apostolos* defines the specific function of *aphōrismenos* not only in the greeting of almost all the Letters but elsewhere as well. The meaning, which comes from the Greek verb *apostellō*, to send forth, harbors no ambiguity. The apostle is an emissary, and in this case, not an emissary of men but an emissary of the Messiah Jesus and the will of God for the messianic announcement. (This the case in the two Letters to the Corinthians and the Letters to the Galatians, Ephesians, and the Colossians.) The Hebrew antecedent invoked in lexicons, the *shaliaḥ*, is essentially a juridical notion. The *shaliaḥ* is a mandatory, a man sent on a specific assignment. Whatever the nature of this assignment (a contract, a marriage, etc.), the rabbinic maxim "A man's emissary is like the man himself," is applicable to the *shaliaḥ*. (As with Roman law, the effects of mandatory's acts fall on the mandatory.) In Judaism, this originally juridical figure acquires a religious meaning (to the extent that one can make a distinction in Judaism between religion and the law); the communities of Palestine thus sent *sheluḥim* to those of the Diaspora. Nevertheless, even when the assignment had a religious character to it, it was always a specific assignment and bore a figure without much pretense; hence the *humor* of the joke that circulated centuries later concerning the Sabbatai Sevi: "he left a *shaliaḥ* and returned a *mashiaḥ*."

59

Why does Paul define himself as an apostle and not, for example, a prophet? What difference is there between apostle and prophet? Paul himself plays on this difference, quickly altering a citation from Jeremiah in Galatians 1:15–16. When Jeremiah says, "I made you a prophet at your mother's breast," Paul, having just defined himself as an "emissary [*apostolos*] not from human beings nor through a human being, but through Jesus Messiah and God the father," cancels out "prophet" and simply writes, "who from my mother's womb had set me apart."

You are undoubtedly familiar with the importance of the
Nabi
prophet, the *nabi*, in Judaism and in Antiquity in general. The persistent legacy of this figure in Western culture is less well known; it extends to the threshold of modernity, where it does not completely vanish. Aby Warburg marked out Nietzsche and Jacob Burckhardt as two opposite kinds of *nabi*, the former turned toward the future, and the latter toward the past; and I remember that Michel Foucault, in his lecture on February 1, 1984, at the Collège de France, delineated four figures of "veridiction" or truth-telling in Antiquity: the prophet, the sage, the expert, and the parrhesiast, tracing out their legacy in the history of modern philosophy.[1] (This is an interesting exercise I suggest undertaking.)

What is a prophet? He is first and foremost a man with an unmediated relation to the *ruaḥ Yahweh* (the breath of Yahweh), who receives a word from God which does not properly belong to him. Prophetic discourse opens with the formula "Thus speaks, or spoke, Yahweh." As an ecstatic spokesperson for God, the *nabi* is clearly distinct from the apostle, who, as an emissary with a determinate purpose, must carry out his assignment with lucidity and search on his own for the words of the message, which he may consequently define as "my announcement" (Rom. 2:16; 16:25). Nevertheless, in Judaism, prophecy is not an institution whose functions and figures could be clearly delineated; rather, it is something like a force or a tension that is in constant struggle with other forces that seek to limit it in its modalities, primarily in its

1. *Translator's note.* The word parrhesiast comes from *parrhesia*, which refers to frankness or freedom of speech. For more on this term, see the lectures by Foucault which were also given as lectures at the University of California, Berkeley, in Fall 1983, published as Michel Foucault, *Fearless Speech.*

time. The rabbinic tradition thus tends to enclose any legitimate prophecy within the limits of an ideal past, ending with the first destruction of the Temple in 587 B.C.E. Affirmations are thus read along the lines: "The second time has five less things than the first: fire, the Ark, and the oil of unction, *urim* and *tummim* and the holy breath [that is, the prophetic spirit]," or "After the death of the last prophets Haggai, Zechariah, and Malachi, the holy breath took leave of Israel; but the heavenly messages reached the *bat kol* [literally, the 'daughter of the voice,' meaning an echo or a remnant of prophecy]." But strangely enough, along with this closure of prophecy from the outside, so to speak, is corresponding limitation that works it from within, as if it contained within itself the intimation of its own closure and insufficiency. Thus, for example, in Zechariah 13:2, one reads, "On that day . . . I shall rid the land of the prophets and the unclean spirit. And if anyone continues to prophesy, his parents, father and mother, shall say to him, 'You shall not live, because you have spoken a lie in the name of the Lord.' When he prophesies, his father and mother shall pierce him through. On that day, every prophet will be ashamed to relate his vision." (The archetype for the curse of the poet at the beginning of Baudelaire's *Fleurs du mal* is easily recognizable here; the Pauline affirmation "I am not ashamed of my announcement" should be understood in reference to passages like these.)

However one understands this closure, the prophet is essentially defined through his relation to the future. In Psalm 74:9 we read, "We see no signs, no prophet any more, and there is no one among us who knows how long." "How long": each time the prophets announce the coming of the Messiah, the message is always about a time to come, a time not yet present. This is what marks the difference between the prophet and the apostle. The apostle speaks forth from the arrival of the Messiah. At this point prophecy must keep silent, for now prophecy is truly fulfilled. (This is how one should read its innermost tension toward closure.) The word passes on to the apostle, to the emissary of the Messiah, whose time is no longer the future, but the present. This is why Paul's technical term for the messianic event is *ho nyn kairos*, "the time of the now"; this is why Paul is an apostle and not a prophet.

But the apostle must be distinguished from another figure, with
whom he is often confused, just as messianic
Apocalyptic   time is confused with eschatological time. The
most insidious misunderstanding of the messian-
ic announcement does not consist in mistaking it for prophecy,
which is turned toward the future, but for apocalypse, which contemplates the end of time. The apocalyptic is situated on the last
day, the Day of Wrath. It sees the end fulfilled and describes what
it sees. The time in which the apostle lives is, however, not the
eschaton, it is not the end of time. If you want to formulate the difference between messianism and apocalypse, between the apostle
and the visionary, I think you could say, using a phrase by Gianni
Carchia, that the messianic is not the end of time, but *the time of
the end* (Carchia, 144). What interests the apostle is not the last
day, it is not the instant in which time ends, but the time that contracts itself and begins to end (*ho kairos synestalmenos estin*; 1 Cor.
7:29), or if you prefer, the time that remains between time and its
end.

The Jewish apocalyptic tradition and rabbinic tradition recognized a distinction between two times or two worlds (*'olamim*):
the *'olam hazzeh*, which designates the duration of the world from
creation to its end, and the *'olam habba*, the world to come, the
atemporal eternity that comes after the end of the world. In the
Greek-speaking Jewish communities, it follows that two *aiones* or
two *kosmoi* are marked out: *ho aiōn touto, ho kosmos outos* ("this
eon, this world,") and *ho aiōn mellōn* ("the coming eon"). Both of
these terms appear in the Pauline text, but messianic time, the
time in which the apostle lives, the only time that concerns him,
is neither the *'olam hazzeh* nor the *'olam habba*, neither chronological time nor the apocalyptic *eschaton*. Once again, it is a remnant, the time that remains between these two times, when the
division of time is itself divided, whether it be divided by a messianic caesura or Apelles' cut.

This is why it is of utmost importance that we rectify the frequent misunderstanding that occurs when messianic time is flatly
identified with eschatological time, thus making the specificity of

what constitutes messianic time unthinkable. Around the second half of the 1960s—following Hans Blumenberg's book on *The Legitimacy of the Modern Age* (1966) and before it, the book by Karl Löwith on *Meaning and History: Theological Implications of the Philosophy of History* (1948)—extensive debate on the theme secularization and modernity took place in Germany. Even though these authors' positions differ, and in certain regards are even opposed to one another, they share a common presupposition, that of the irreconcilable antithesis between modernity and eschatology. For both, the Christian conception of a time oriented toward eschatological salvation and, hence, toward a final end, was obsolete and ultimately antithetical to modernity's handling of its own conception of its history and time. Without entering into this debate, I would simply like to note that Blumenberg and Löwith both mistake messianism for eschatology, the time of the end for the end of time. What is essential in Paul, messianic time, thus escapes them, in that it puts into question the very possibility of a clear division between the two *'olamim*.

How should this time be represented? On first glance, things seem simple. First, you have secular time, which Paul usually refers to as *chronos*, which spans from creation to the messianic event (for Paul, this is not the birth of Jesus, but his resurrection). Here time contracts itself and begins to end. But this contracted time, which Paul refers to in the expression *ho nyn kairos*, "the time of the now," lasts until the *parousia*, the full presence of the Messiah. The latter coincides with the Day of Wrath and the end of time (but remains indeterminate, even if it is imminent). Time explodes here; or rather, it implodes into the other eon, into eternity.

If we try to represent this schema in a line, we would end up with something like this:

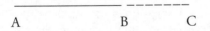

A   B   C

A is creation, B is the messianic event, the resurrection of Jesus, and C is the *eschaton*, when time moves into eternity. This representation has the advantage of clearly showing that messianic time, *ho nyn kairos*, does not coincide either with the end of time and the future eon or with secular chronological time; nevertheless, it is not outside of chronological time either. Messianic time is that part of secular time which undergoes an entirely transformative contraction (in our sketch this heterogeneity is inadequately represented by dotted lines). It would probably be more exact if we took recourse to Apelles' cut, representing messianic time as a caesura which, in its dividing the division between two times, introduces a remainder [*resto*] into it that exceeds the division:

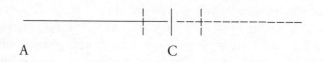

A   C

In this schema, messianic time is presented as a part of the secular eon that constitutively exceeds *chronos* and as a part of eternity that exceeds the future eon, while being situated in the position of a remainder [*resto*] with regard to the division between the two eons.

But can we speak of having truly understood messianic time in this fashion? A general problem arises here regarding our representations of time, which are of a spatial order. It has often been noted that these spatial representations—point, line, segment—generate a kind of falsification that makes unthinkable the lived experience of time. The confusion between *eschaton* and messianic time is a flagrant example of this: if you represent time as a straight line and its end as a punctual instant, you end up with something perfectly *representable*, but absolutely *unthinkable*. Vice-versa, if you reflect on a real experience of time, you end up with something *thinkable*, but absolutely *unrepresentable*. In the same manner, even though the image of messianic time as a segment situated between two eons is clear, it tells us nothing of the experience of the time that remains, a time that begins to end. Where does this gap between representation and thought, image and experience come from? Is another representation of time possible, one that would avoid this misunderstanding?

In attempting to respond to this question, I will avail myself of a concept that does not come from the sciences or from philosophy, but from the   Operational Time work of a linguist who is perhaps the most philosophical linguist of our century: Gustave Guillaume. Even though he worked alongside Meillet and Benveniste, his reflections on language remained particularly marginal in twentieth-century linguistics and have only recently begun to be explored in their depths. Guillaume looks at language [*lingua*] from the point of view of the Aristotelian distinction between potential and act, and thus is able to come up with an original perspective, already implicit in the Saussurean distinction between *langue* and *parole*, yet far more complex. Guillaume's book *Temps et verbe* (Time and Verb) is the book that interests us the most. It reunites two studies that were published in 1929 and 1945 respectively. The concept that I am referring to is that of *temps opératif,* "operational time," which appears in both of his works. According to Guillaume, the human mind experiences time, but it does not possess the representation of it, and must, in representing it, take recourse to constructions of a spatial order. It follows that grammar represents verbal time as an infinite line comprised of two segments, past and future, separated by the cutting of the present:

past	present	future

This representation, which Guillaume even calls a time-image, is inadequate precisely because it is too perfect. It presents time as though it were always already constructed, but does not show time in the act of being constructed in thought. In order to truly understand something, Guillaume says, considering it only in its constructed or achieved state is not enough; you also have to represent the phases through which thought had to pass constructing it. Every mental operation, however quick, has to be achieved in a certain time, which, while short, is no less real. Guillaume defines "operational time" as *the time the mind takes to realize a time-image*. An astute study of linguistic phenomena shows that languages do not organize their own verbal systems according to the previous linear schema (whose defect lies in its being too perfect), but rather by referring the constructed image back to the operational time in which it is constructed. In this way, Guillaume is able to complicate the chronological representation of time by adding a projection in which the process of forming the time-image is cast back onto the time image itself. In so doing, he comes up with a new representation of time, that of chronogenetic time, which is no longer linear but three-dimensional. The schema of chronogenesis thus allows us to grasp the time-image in its pure state of potentiality (time *in posse*), in its very process of formation (time *in fieri*), and, finally, in the state of having been constructed (time *in esse*), taking into account all of the verb forms of a language (aspects, modalities, and tenses) according to a unitary model.

(•)   It becomes clear why one would want to introduce the concept of operational time into the science of language. Not only does this allow Guillaume to restore time in a spatial representation that is completely deprived of time, as are all images; in addition, the idea that language could refer itself back to the operational time of its own becoming already provides it with the basis—and with that, the principle for an additional intrication—for one of the most ingenious creations of twentieth-century linguistics, Benveniste's theory of enunciation. Through shifters, what Benveniste calls *indicateurs de l'énonciation*, language refers to its own taking place, to a pure instance of discourse in action. This capacity to refer to the pure presence of the enunciation goes hand in hand, according to Benveniste, with *chronothèse*, time-positing (literally, "chronothesis"), itself the origin of our representation of time. In this way, an axial point of reference is established with regard to our representation of time. But if each mental operation, each "thought in action of language" as Guillaume says, implies an operational time, then even referring to the instance of discourse in action would imply a certain time, and chronothesis, or time-positing, would contain within itself another time that introduces a disjointedness and delay in the "pure presence" of the enunciation. Because Benveniste makes enunciation the very foundation of subjectivity and consciousness, this lapse and delay would then be a part of the structure of the subject. To the extent that thought is always "in the action of language" and, for this reason, necessarily implies an operational time in itself, then—no matter how great its speed and ability to soar over things—thought could never coincide perfectly with itself and the self-presence of consciousness consequently would always take on the form of time. Among other things, this would explain why the thought of time and the representation of time could never coincide. For in order to form the words in which thought is expressed—and in which a certain time-image is realized—thought would have to take recourse to an operational time, which cannot be represented in the representation in which it is still implicated.

We may now attempt to develop the paradigm of operational time beyond the confines of linguistics and apply it to our problem of messianic time. In every representation we make of time and in every discourse by means of which we define and represent time, another time is implied that is not entirely consumed by representation. It is as though man, insofar as he is a thinking and speaking being, produced an additional time with regard to chronological time, a time that prevented him from perfectly coinciding with the time out of which he could make images and representations. This ulterior time, nevertheless, is not another time, it is not a supplementary time added on from outside to chronological time. Rather, it is something like a time within time—not ulterior but interior—which only measures my disconnection with regard to it, my being out of synch and in noncoincidence with regard to my representation of time, but precisely because of this, allows for the possibility of my achieving and taking hold of it. We may now propose our first definition of messianic time: messianic time is *the time that time takes to come to an end*, or, more precisely, the time we take to bring to an end, to achieve our representation of time. This is not the line of chronological time (which was representable but unthinkable), nor the instant of its end (which was just as unthinkable); nor is it a segment cut from chronological time; rather, it is operational time pressing within the chronological time, working and transforming it from within; it is the time we need to make time end: *the time that is left us* [*il tempo che ci resta*]. Whereas our representation of chronological time, as the time *in which* we are, separates us from ourselves and transforms us into impotent spectators of ourselves—spectators who look at the time that flies without any time left, continually missing themselves—messianic time, an operational time in which we take hold of and achieve our representations of time, is the time *that* we ourselves are, and for this very reason, is the only real time, the only time we have.

It is because messianic *klēsis* is caught up in this operational time that it can take on the form of the *as not*, the constant revocation of every vocation. The passage on the *hōs mē* that we commented on at length in 1 Corinthians 7 begins, "This I say, brethren, time contracted itself" [*ho kairos synestalmenos estin: systellō* signifies the act of brailing up sails as well as the way in which an animal gathers himself before lunging]. It continues, "the rest is [*to loipon*, as was noted, not only signifies 'finally' or 'besides,' but also marks out messianic time as the time remaining] that even those having wives may be as not having, and those weeping as not weeping." But for this very reason, messianic time is the time that we have, par excellence ("Therefore, whilst we have time [*hōs kairon echomen*] let us work good"; Gal. 6:10). Paul twice uses the expression *ton kairon exagorazomenoi*, "buying up time" (Eph. 5:16 and Col. 4:5) to convey the temporal condition of messianic time.

Kairos and *chronos* are usually opposed to each other, as though they were qualitatively heterogeneous, which is more or less the case. But what is most important in our case is not so much—or not only—the opposition between the two, as much as the relation between them. What do we have when we have *kairos*? The most beautiful definition of *kairos* I know of occurs in the *Corpus Hippocraticum*, which characterizes it in relation to *chronos*. It reads: *chronos esti en ho kairos kai kairos esti en hō ou pollos chronos*, "*chronos* is that in which there is *kairos*, and *kairos* is

Kairos and Chronos

that in which there is little *chronos*." Look at the extraordinary interlacing of these two concepts, they are literally placed within each other. *Kairos* (which would be translated banally as "occasion") does not have another time at its disposal; in other words, what we take hold of when we seize *kairos* is not another time, but a contracted and abridged *chronos*. The Hippocratic text continues with these words: "healing happens at times through *chronos*, other times through *kairos*." That messianic "healing" happens in *kairos* is evident, but this *kairos* is nothing more than seized *chronos*. The pearl embedded in the ring of chance is only a small portion of *chronos*, a time remaining [*restante*]. (Hence the pertinence of the rabbinic apologue, for which the messianic world is not another world, but the secular world itself, with a slight adjustment, a meager difference. But this ever so slight difference, which results from my having grasped my disjointedness with regard to chronological time, is, in every way, a decisive one.)

   Let us now take a closer look at the structure of messianic time in Paul. As noted, Paul decomposes the messianic event into two times: resurrection and *parousia*, the second coming of Jesus at the end of time. Out of *Parousia* this issues the paradoxical tension between an *already* and a *not yet* that defines the Pauline conception of salvation. The messianic event has already happened, salvation has already been achieved according to believers, but, nevertheless, in order to truly be fulfilled, this implies an additional time. How should we interpret this unusual scission, since it seems to introduce a constitutive delay or deferment into the messianic? The problem is crucial, for on it hangs the correct solution to the antinomies that characterize the interpretations of messianism in our time. According to Scholem—who holds a view fairly widespread in Judaism—the messianic antinomy is defined as "a life lived in deferment" (*Leben im Aufschub*), in which nothing can be achieved: "So-called Jewish existence," he writes, "possesses a tension that never finds true release" (Scholem 1971, 35). Equally aporetic is the position that thinks of messianic time as a kind of border zone, or even "a *transitional time* between two periods, that is, two *parusie*, the first which determines the beginning of the new eon, and the second the end of the antique eon," and as such, makes it belong to both eons. What is at risk here is a delay implicit in the concept of "transitional time," for, as with every transition, it tends to be prolonged into infinity and renders unreachable the end that it supposedly produces.

The Pauline decomposition of presence finds its true meaning from the perspective of operational time. As operational time, as the amount of time needed to end representations of time, the messianic *ho nyn kairos* can never fully coincide with a chronological moment internal to its representation. The end of time is actually a time-image represented by a final point on the homogeneous line of chronology. But as an image devoid of time, it is itself impossible to seize hold of, and, consequently, tends to infinitely defer itself. Kant must have been thinking of a time like this when, in "The End of All Things," he speaks of an idea of the end of time that is "contranatural" and "perverse" and "comes from us when we misunderstand the final end" (Kant, 200). Giorgio Manganelli also seems to allude to a similar kind of inadequate representation of the end when he makes his great heresiarch say that we do not realize that the world has already ended, because the end "generates a kind of time, in which we dwell, that in itself prevents us from experiencing it" (Manganelli, 19). The fallacy lies in changing operational time into a supplementary time added onto chronological time, in order to infinitely postpone the end. This is why it is important that one correctly understand the meaning of the term *parousia*. It does not mean the "second coming" of Jesus, a second messianic event that would follow and subsume the first. In Greek, *parousia* simply means presence (*par-ousia* literally signifies to be next to; in this way, being is beside itself in the present). *Parousia* does not signal a complement that is added to something in order to complete it, nor a supplement, added on afterward, that never reaches fulfillment. Paul uses this term to highlight the innermost uni-dual structure of the messianic event, inasmuch as it is comprised of two heterogeneous times, one *kairos* and the other *chronos*, one an operational time and the other a represented time, which are coextensive but cannot be added together. Messianic presence lies beside itself, since, without ever coinciding with a chronological instant, and without ever adding itself onto it, it seizes hold of this instant and brings it forth to fulfillment. The Pauline decomposition of messianic presence is similar to the one in Kafka's extraordinary *theologoumenon*, in which the Messiah does not come on the day of his arrival, but only on the day after; not on the last day but on the very last day. ("Er [the Messiah] wird erst einen Tag nach seiner Ankunft kommen, er wird nicht am letzten Tag kommen, sondern am allerletzten"; Kafka, 90). I found a perfect parallel in an Islamic text that reads, "My coming and the hour [messianic time] are so close to one another that the hour of my coming risks arriving before me" (Casanova, 69). The Messiah has already arrived, the messianic event has already happened, but its presence contains within itself another time, which stretches its *parousia*, not in order to defer it, but, on the contrary, to make it graspable. For this reason, each instant may be, to use Benjamin's words, the "small door through which the Messiah enters." The Messiah always already had his time, meaning he simultaneously makes time his and brings it to fulfillment.[2]

The rabbinic commentary known as the *Genesis Rabbah* provides an instructive reflection on the fallacy (common nowadays) of taking operational time (the time that time takes to end) for supplementary time (which is added onto time indefinitely). These reflections concern Saturday, which, for Judaism as well as for the Church Fathers, constituted a kind of small-scale model for messianic time and referred in particular to the interpretation of Genesis 2:2, "And on the seventh day God completed his work which he had made; and on the seventh day he rested from all his work." In order to avoid this paradoxical coincidence of fulfillment and interruption, the Septuagint amends the first clause, writing "sixth day" (*en tē hēmera tē ektē*) instead of "seventh," so that the conclusion of the work of creation becomes another day (*tē hēmera tē hebdomē*). But the author of *Genesis Rabbah* instead says, "Man, who knows not times, moments and hours, takes

2. *Translator's note*. The Italian plays on the expression *fare suo tempo*, meaning that something "has its time." The Italian reads: "Il messia fa già sempre il suo tempo—cioè, insieme, fa suo il tempo e lo compie."

something from profane time and adds it to holy time; but the holy one, blessed be his name, who knows times, moments, and hours, will enter on Saturday only by a hairsbreadth" (*Genesis Rabbah*, vol. 1, chap. 10, sec. 9). Saturday—messianic time—is not another day, homogeneous to others; rather, it is that innermost disjointedness within time through which one may—by a hairsbreadth—grasp time and accomplish it.

(•)   Now is the time for us to bring up the theme of the millenary kingdom, or the messianic *Zwischenreich*, in Paul.
Millenary Kingdom   According to a notion that most certainly has Jewish origins, but which also has roots in the Christian tradition, a messianic kingdom will take place on earth, after the *parousia* and before the end of time, that will last for a thousand years (hence the term *Chiliasm*). But even if Eusebius, and later on Jerome, had been accusing Papias of circulating this "Jewish tale," the idea is nevertheless present in the Apocalypse and in pseudo-Barnabas, as well as in Justin, Tertullian, Irenaeus, and at least to a certain degree, Augustine, before it reappears fully in the twelfth century with Joachim of Flora.

For what concerns Paul, the question essentially comes down to the interpretation of 1 Corinthians 15:23–27 and 1 Thessalonians 4:13–18. Against the Chiliastic reading of these passages, Wilcke noted that "for Paul, the *basileia Christi* was equivalent to a new eon, and therefore to something present, distinct from the divine eschatological kingdom" (Wilcke, 99), and that "in Pauline eschatology . . . there is no place for a messianic interim-kingdom on earth, instead, at the end of time, the latter flows directly into the eternal kingdom of God without any intermediate stages" (Wilcke, 156). Bultmann, for his part, wrote that "the primitive Christian community is aware of its being situated 'between two times,' that is, it finds itself at the end of the old eon and at the beginning, or at least just before the beginning, of a new eon. As a consequence, this community understands its present as a very particular kind of 'between.' In 1 Cor. 15:23–27 a very clear rendering of this occurs. Rabbinic theory holds that the messianic kingdom is situated between the old and new eons. For Paul, this kingdom is the present found between resurrection and parusia" (Bultmann, 691).

Correctly understanding the problem of the kingdom (and, in a parallel fashion, its secularized equivalent, the Marxian problem of the transitional phase between prehistory and history) depends on the meaning of this "between." This would mean that millenarian interpretations are both right and wrong. They are wrong if they try to identify the messianic kingdom literally, meaning according to a certain span of chronological time situated between *parousia* and the end of time. They are right, since, in Paul, messianic time, as operational time, implies an actual transformation of the experience of time that may even interrupt secular time here and now. The kingdom does not coincide with any chronological instant but is between them, stretching them into *paraousia*. This is the reason for its particular "nearness," which corresponds in Paul, as we shall see further on, with the nearness of the word of faith. It is therefore important that one does not take *entos hymōn* in the passage in Luke 17:21 ("the kingdom of God is *entos hymōn*") to mean "within yourselves," as the common translations would have it, but "close at hand, within the range of possible action," meaning nearby (Rüstow, 214–17).

Paul defines this innermost relation of messianic time to chronological time, that is, to the time spanning from creation to resurrection, via two fundamental notions. *Typos* The first is that of *typos*, meaning figure and prefiguration, or foreshadowing. The determining passage is 1 Corinthians 10:1–11, when Paul recalls a series of episodes in Israel's history: "For I would not, brothers, have you ignorant, that our fathers were all under the cloud, and all passed through the sea; and were all immersed into Moses in the cloud and in the sea; and did all eat the same spiritual meat; and did all drink the same spiritual drink: for they drank of that spiritual Rock that . . . was the Messiah. But with many of them God was not well pleased: for they were overthrown in the desert." At this point Paul adds, "In these things they became figures [*typoi*] to us to the intent we should not lust after evil things, as they also lusted." A few lines later he uses the same image: "Now these things happened unto them by way of figure [*typicōs*]; and they were written for us, for our admonition, upon whom the ends of the ages are come to face each other" [*ta telē tōn aiōnōn katēntēken; antaō*—from *anti*— means "to be face to face, to confront each other"].

Erich Auerbach has shown the importance of this "figural" conception of the world (Jerome translates *typoi* in 1 Cor. 10:6 with *in figura*) in the Christian Middle Ages, when it becomes the grounds for a general theory of allegorical interpretation. Through the concept of *typos*, Paul establishes a relation, which we may from this point on call a typological relation, between every event from a past time and *ho nyn kairos*, messianic time. If follows that in Romans 5:14, Adam, through whom sin has entered the world, is defined as *typos tou mellontos*, the "figure of the future," meaning, the figure of the Messiah through whom grace will abound for men. (In Hebrews 9:24, the man-made temple is defined as the *antitypos* of the heavenly temple, which could also imply a symmetrical relation with regard to *typos*.) What matters to us here is not the fact that each event of the past—once it becomes figure—announces a future event and is fulfilled in it, but is the transformation of time implied by this typological relation. The problem here does not simply concern the biunivocal correspondence that binds *typos* and *antitypos* together in an exclusively hermeneutic relationship, according to the paradigm that prevailed in medieval culture; rather, it concerns a tension that clasps together and transforms past and future, *typos* and *antitypos*, in an inseparable constellation. The messianic is not just one of two terms in this typological relation, *it is the relation itself*. This is the meaning of the Pauline expression "for us, upon whom the ends of the ages [*aiōnōn*, the *olamin*] are come to face each other." The two ends of the *olam hazzeh* and the *olam babba* contract into each other without coinciding; this face to face, this contraction, is messianic time, and nothing else. Once again, for Paul, the messianic is not a third eon situated between two times; but rather, it is a caesura that divides the division between times and introduces a remnant, a zone of undecidability, in which the past is dislocated into the present and the present is extended into the past.

One of the theses (the eighty-third, to be exact) Scholem wanted to offer Benjamin on his twentieth birthday in 1918 reads, "Messianic time is time of inversive *waw*" (Scholem 1971, 295). The Hebrew system of verbs distinguishes between verb forms not so much according to tense (past and future) but according to aspect: complete (which is usually translated by the past), and incomplete (usually translated by the future). If, however, you put a *waw* (which is, for this reason called inversive or conversive) before a complete form, it changes it into an incomplete, and vice-versa. According to Scholem's astute suggestion (which Benjamin may have recalled years later), messianic time is neither the complete nor the incomplete, neither the past nor the future, but the inversion of both. This conversive movement is perfectly rendered in the Pauline typological relation as an area of tension in which two times enter into the constellation the apostle called *ho nyn kairos*. Here, the past (the complete) rediscovers actuality and becomes unfulfilled, and the present (the incomplete) acquires a kind of fulfillment.

The second notion through which Paul expresses messianic time, and which complements *typos*, is recapitulation. Paul does not use the substantive **Recapitulation** *anakephalaiōsis*, but the corresponding verb *anakephalaioomai*, which literally means "to recapitulate." The determining passage is Ephesians 1:10. Having just laid out the divine project of messianic redemption (*apolytrōsis*), Paul writes, "as for the economy of the *pleroma* of times, all things are recapitulated in him, things in heaven and things on earth [*eis oikonomian tou plērōmatos tōn kairōn, anakephalaiōsasthai ta panta en tō christō, ta epi tois euranois kai ta epi tēs gēs en autō*]." This short verse is laden with meaning to the point that one could say that several fundamental texts in Western culture—such as the doctrine of apocastasis in Origen and Leibniz; repetition or retrieval [*Gjentagelse*] in Kierkegaard; the eternal return in Nietzsche; and repetition [*Wiederholung*] in Heidegger—are the consequences of an explosion of the meaning harbored within.

What Paul says here is that insofar as messianic time aims toward the fulfillment of time—(*plērōma ton kairōn*; note that it says *kairoi* and not *chronoi*! cf. Gal. 4:4: *plērōma tou chronou*)—it effectuates a recapitulation, a kind of summation of all things, in heaven and on earth—of all that has transpired from creation to the messianic "now," meaning of the past as a whole. Messianic time is a summary recapitulation of the past, even according to the meaning of the adjective in the juridical expression "summary judgment."

This recapitulation of the past produces a *plērōma*, a saturation and fulfillment of *kairoi* (messianic *kairoi* are therefore literally full of *chronos*, but an abbreviated, summary *chronos*), that anticipates eschatological *plērōma* when God "will be all in all." Messianic *plērōma* is therefore an abridgment and anticipation of eschatological fulfillment. It is not by chance that recapitulation and *plērōma* are found beside each other: this juxtaposition is found also in Romans 13:9–10, when Paul says that each commandment (*entolē*) "is recapitulated [*anakephalaioutai*] in the phrase "Love your neighbor as yourself," and straightaway adds, "Love . . . is the *plērōma* of the law." If the Pauline recapitulation of the law contains something more than Hillel's motto, from which it supposedly derives (responding to the goy who asks him to teach him the whole of the Torah, Hillel says, "What you would not like others to do unto you, do not even do it unto your neighbor"), this is because Paul does not intend it only as a practical maxim, but as a *messianic* recapitulation, something inseparable from the messianic fulfillment of times.

What is decisive here is that the *plērōma* of *kairoi* is understood as the relation of each instant to the Messiah—each *kairos* is *unmittelbar zu Gott* [immediate to God], and is not just the final result of a process (as is the case with the model Marxism inherited from Hegel). Just as Ticonius intuited in the chapter *de recapitulatione* in his *Regulae*, each time is the messianic now (*totum illud tempus diem vel horam esse*), and the messianic is not the chronological end of time, but the present as the exigency of fulfillment, what gives itself "as an end" (*licet non in eo tempore finis, in eo tamen titulo futurum est*) (Ticonius, 110).

In this sense, recapitulation is nothing else than the other facet of the typological relation established by messianic *kairos* between present and past. The fact that we are not only dealing with a prefiguration, but with a constellation and a quasi unity between the two times, is implicit in the idea that the entire past is summarily contained, so to speak, in the present; this is how the pretense of a *remnant* as all finds an ulterior foundation. The three things that "remain" in 1 Corinthians 13:13 ("three things now remain: faith, hope, love") are not states of mind, but three arches that bend to sustain and fulfill the messianic experience of time. What is undoubtedly at stake is only summary recapitulation, for God is not yet "all in all," as he will be in the *eschaton* (when repetition is no longer). Yet this recapitulation is all the more significant for it is precisely through it that the events of the past acquire their true meanings and thus may be saved. (The passage in Ephesians 1:13–14, of which the previous verse is a part, is entirely devoted to setting out the "announcement of salvation," *euaggelion tēs sotērias*.)

What happens at this point is similar to the panoramic vision that the dying supposedly have of their lives, when the whole of their ### Memory and Salvation existence passes before their eyes in a flash—a vertiginous abbreviation. In messianic recapitulation, something like a memory is also at stake, but this particular memory only concerns the economy of salvation (yet couldn't this be said to be the case for every memory?). In this case, memory shows itself as a propaedeutic and anticipation of salvation. And just as the past frees itself only in memory from the distant strangeness of what has been lived—thereby becoming my past for the very first time—so too, in the "economy of the plenitude of times," men appropriate their history, and what once happened to the Jews is recognized as a figure and reality for the messianic community. And just as the past becomes possible again in some fashion through memory—that which was fulfilled becomes unfulfilled and the unfulfilled becomes fulfilled—so too in messianic recapitulation do men ready themselves to forever take leave of the past in eternity, which knows neither past nor repetition.

This is why the widespread view of messianic time as oriented solely toward the future is fallacious. We are used to hearing that in the moment of salvation one has to look to the future and to eternity. To the contrary, for Paul recapitulation, *anakephalaiōsis*, means that *ho nyn kairos* is a contraction of past and present, that we will have to settle our debts, at the decisive moment, first and foremost with the past. This obviously does not imply attachment or nostalgia; quite the opposite, for the recapitulation of the past is also a summary judgment pronounced on it.

ℵ This double orientation of messianic time also allows us to understand Paul's particular formula that expresses messianic tension: *epekteinomenos*. After evoking his past as a Pharisee and Jew according to the flesh, he writes, "Brothers, I for my part do not consider myself as having seized hold of myself. Just one thing: forgetting what lies behind, but straining forward [*epekteinomenos*] to what lies ahead" (Phil. 3:13). The two contrasting prepositions *epi* (on) and *ek* (from), prepositions that go before a verb that means "to be in a tension toward something," clearly convey the double movement in the Pauline gesture. The tension toward what lies ahead is produced on and out of what lies behind. "Forgetting the past, only on and out of this straining toward the future." This is why Paul, caught in this double tension, can neither seize hold of himself nor be fulfilled; he can only seize hold of his own being seized: "It is not that I have already seized hold of it or have already reached fulfillment, but I strive to seize hold because the Messiah once seized hold of me" (Phil. 3:12).

I would now like to provide you with something like a concrete example, a kind of a small-scale

The Poem and Rhyme

model of the structure of messianic time that we have been attempting to grasp in the Pauline text. This model may perhaps surprise you, but I think that the structural analogy furnished by this example is pertinent. It concerns the poem—or, better yet, that poetic structure that represents—in modern poetry and more particularly, in its origins in Romance lyric, the convention of rhyme.

Rhyme, which appears infrequently in classical poetry, is developed in Latin Christian poetry starting from the fourth century and eventually becomes an essential component in the fashioning of Romance lyric. Among the various verse forms, I will concentrate on one of the best known sestinas, "Lo ferm voler qu'el cor m'intra" ("The firm will which enters my heart"), by Arnaut Daniel. Before we begin our reading, I would like to make one observation on the temporal structure of lyric poetry in general, especially in metrical schemes, as they appear in the sonnet, the canzone, the sestina, and so on. From this perspective, a poem is something that will necessarily finish at a given point: it will end after fourteen lines in the sonnet, but may be prolonged by three more lines, if the sonnet has a coda.

The poem is therefore an organism or a temporal machine that, from the very start, strains toward its end. A kind of eschatology occurs within the poem itself. But for the more or less brief time that the poem lasts, it has a specific and unmistakable temporality, it has its own *time*. This is where rhyme, which in the sestina consists in repeated and often rhyming end words, comes into play.[3]

What is peculiar to the sestina is that the status of the repeated end words changes, in the sense that the return of homophony as in typically rhymed poems, the final syllables is replaced by the reappearance of the six end words in the six stanzas, in a complex but equally regulated order. At the end, the tornada recapitulates the end words by dispersing them within its three lines.

Let us look at our example:

> *Lo ferm voler qu'el cor m'intra*
> *no' m pot ges becs escoissendre ni ongla*
> *de lauzengier qui pert per mal dir s'arma;*
> *e pus no l'aus batr'ab ram ni ab verja,*
> *sivals a frau, lai on non aurai oncle,*
> *jauzirai joi, en vergier o dins cambra.*
>
> *Quan mi sove de la cambra*
> *on a mon dan sai que nulhs om non intra*
> *—ans me son tug plus que fraire ni oncle—*
> *non ai membre no.m fremisca, neis l'ongla,*
> *aissi cum fai l'enfas devant la verja:*
> *tal paor ai no 'l sia prop de l'arma.*

3. *Translator's note.* For a discussion on temporality and the sestina, with a discussion of Arnaut Daniel, see Shapiro (1980).

Del cors li fors, non de l'arma,
e cossentis m'a celat dins sa cambra,
que plus mi nafra 'l cor que colp de verja
qu'ar lo sieus sers lai ont ilh es non intra:
de lieis serai aisi cum carn e ongla
e non creirai castic d'amic ni d'oncle.

Anc la seror de mon oncle
mon amei plu ni tan, per aquest'arma,
qu'aitan vezis cum es lo detz de l'ongla,
s'a lieis plagues, volgr'esser de sa cambra;
de me pot far l'amors qu'ins el cor m'intra
miels a son vol c'om fortz de frevol verja.

Pus floric la seca verja
ni de n'Adam foron nebot e oncle
tan fin'amors cum selha qu'el cor m'intra
mon cug fos anc en cors no neis en arma:
on qu'eu estei, fors en plan o dins cambra;
mos cors no.s part de lieis tan cum ten l'ongla.

Aissi s'empren e s'enongla
mos cors en lieis cum l'escors'en la verja,
qu'ilh m'es de joi tors e palais e cambra;
e non am tan paren, fraire ni oncle,
qu'en Paradis n'aura doble joi m'arma,
si ja nulhs hom per ben amar lai intra.

Arnaut tramet son cantar d'ongl'e et d'oncle
a Gran Desiei, qui de sa verj'a l'arma,
son cledisat qu'apres dins cambra intra.

[The firm will that enters into my heart
Can never be torn away from me with beak or nail
By a false flatterer who, through evil talk, loses his soul.
And since I don't dare to bat them with branch or rod,
At least on the sly, where I don't have any uncle,
I'll enjoy my joy in an orchard or in a chamber.

Whenever I remember the chamber
Where, to my damage, I know that no man enters
(Instead everyone's worse to me than a brother or an uncle),
I don't have a member that doesn't tremble—nor a nail—
Just like a child standing before the rod;
Such fear I have that it [she] may be too much for my soul.

If only I were hers with body—not with soul—
And she'd consent to hiding me inside her chamber!
For my heart wounds me more than a blow from a rod,
Since this serf of hers, where she lies, doesn't enter.
I'll always be close to her, like her flesh to her nails,
And I don't heed the reproach of a friend or an uncle.

I never loved the sister of my uncle
More or as much—upon my very soul!—
For as close as stands the finger to its nail
(If it pleased her), I would like to be to her chamber.
This love can handle me as it enters my heart
More at its will than a tough man with a frail rod.

After the flourishing of the Dry Rod
And from Lord Adam issued nephews and uncles,
A fine love like that which into my heart enters
I don't think ever existed in a body or even a soul.
Wherever she may be—outside in the square or in her chamber—
My body doesn't leave her as far as extends a nail.

And so my body clings with its nails
And is attached to hers like the bark around a rod;
For to me she's a tower of joy, a palace, a chamber,
And I don't love as much any brother, parent, or uncle;
For in Paradise double joy will await my soul
If ever any man, through loving well, enters there.

Arnaut sends his song of the Uncle-Nail
For the pleasure of her who arms him with her rod,
His Desired One, whose value enters into the chamber.]
                                   (Wilhelm, 116–17)

As you can see, the order that governs the repetition of rhyming
end words is what is called *retrogradatio cruciata*, or cruciform ret-

rogradation, an alternation between inversion and progression, in which the last rhyming end word of one stanza becomes the first end word of the next stanza, the first line's end word slides into the place of the second in the next stanza, the next to last slides to the place of the third, and the second to the forth, and so on, in such a way that the movement continues through the six stanzas. The seventh stanza, if there were one, would repeat the same order as the first. What interests us is not so much the numerological intrication, at least not for the time being, but the temporal structure that is at work in the sestina. The sequence of thirty-nine lines (36 + 3), could ideally unfurl itself according to a sequence that was perfectly homologous with linear chronological time; however, the thirty-nine lines are scanned and animated through the play of alternating and rhyming end words, in such a way that each of them uses and recalls the one in the preceding stanzas (or it recalls itself as another). At the same time, it announces its own repetition to come in the lines that follow. Through this complicated to-and-fro directed both forward and backward, the chronological sequence of linear homogeneous time is completely transformed into rhythmic constellations themselves in movement. It is not that there is another time, coming from who-knows-where, that would substitute for chronological time; to the contrary, what we have is the same time that organizes itself through its own somewhat hidden internal pulsation, in order to make place for the time of the poem. Then, at the very end, when the movement of cruciform retrogradation is fulfilled and the poem seems condemned to repeat itself, the *tornada* returns to and recapitulates the rhyming end words in a new sequence, simultaneously exposing their singularity along with their secret connectedness.

By now you will have perfectly understood why I suggested looking at the sestina as a miniature model of messianic time. The sestina—and, in this sense, every poem—is a soteriological device which, though the sophisticated *mēchanē* of the announcement and retrieval of rhyming end words (which correspond to typological relations between past and present), transforms chronological time into messianic time. Just as this time is not other to chronological time or eternity, but is the transformation that time undergoes when it is taken for a remnant, so too is the time of the sestina the metamorphosis that time undergoes insofar as it is the time of the end, the *time that the poem takes to come to an end.*

What is most surprising is that the structural analogy does not seem fortuitous, at least in the case of the sestina. Contemporary scholars have rediscovered the importance of numerological relations within medieval poetry. The overt connection between the sestina and the number six has since been related to the number's meaning in the story of creation (Durling and Martinez, 270). In a distich, Honorius of Autun had already highlighted the significance of the sixth day, in which both creation and the fall of man take place, as well as the sixth age of the world, in which man's redemption is fulfilled: *sexta namque die Deus hominem condidat sexta aetate, sexta feria, sexta hora eum redimit* ["God destroyed man on the sixth day and redeemed him on the sixth age, sixth holiday, and sixth hour"]. In Dante the "sixth hour" explicitly refers to Adam's six hours in Paradise (*Paradiso* 26.141–42, "de la prim'ora a quella che seconda / come 'l sol muta quadro, l'ora sesta": "from the first hour, to that which cometh next / as the sun changes quarter, to the sixth"), and his use of the sestina in the *rime petrose* is also tinged with soteriological meaning (Adam is the type for the Messiah). The movement through the six stanzas of the sestina repeats the movement of the six days of creation and together articulates their relation to Saturday (the tornada) as a cipher of the messianic fulfillment of time. One could say, as does the author of *Genesis Rabbah*, that Saturday is not considered to be a day homogeneous to others. Rather, it is the recapitulation and messianic abbreviation of the story of creation (in three lines the *tornada* recapitulates the internal structure of the poem). This is why the sestina cannot really end: its end is missed, just as the seventh stanza is missed.

These thoughts may perhaps shed some light on the problem of the origins of rhyme in European poetry—a problem on which scholars are far from reaching even a shadow of agreement. Eduard Norden's book, *Die antike Kunstprosa*, previously referenced with regard to Paul's style, contains a long and especially interesting appendix on the history of rhyme. According to Norden, who disregards the old issue of the people having "invented" or introduced rhyme into modern Western poetry (according to Wilhelm Meyer, rhyme has Semitic origins), rhyme is born from classical rhetoric, specifically from homeoteleuton (or homoioteleuton), which defines the figure we call parallelism. So-called "Asianic" rhetoric, to which Norden dedicates a large part of his analyses, segments periods into short *commata* or *cola*, which are then articulated and connected with each other through the repetition of the same syntactic structure.[4] It is precisely in the context of this parallel repetition of *cola* that we see something like rhyme appear for the first time, where corresponding parts of the phrase are also linked through the consonance of the final syllables of the end words (homeoteleutons).

This is an interesting theory, and yet it harbors a certain irony, since it makes prose come from an institution often associated exclusively with poetry. It fails, however, to tell us anything about the reasons why a completely secondary rhetorical figure in prose is transposed and absolutized into a fundamental poetic institution. I have already said that rhyme appears in Latin Christian poetry at the end of the imperial era, and progressively develops up the threshold of modernity, where it takes on its present importance. In George Lote's noteworthy book *Histoire du vers français*, among the best cited examples of rhymed poetry is a piece by Augustine, an author, as you know, who was particularly attuned to the problem of time. In this poem, directed against the Donatists, true rhymes appear exactly at the point where Augustine reworks the evangelical parable that makes the parallel between the kingdom of the heavens and a fishing net (Lote, 38). When Lote wants to cite a work of poetry in which rhyme has already become a recognized formal organizing principle, the example he gives is the *hora novissima* of the messianic event (Lote, 98):

> *Hora sub hac novissima*
> *mundi petivit infima,*

4. *Translator's note.* In Eduard Norden's study of rhyme, he discerns between various Greek styles and, using 4 Maccabees as an example, calls one style "Asianic" since it differs from styles known to be from Alexandria.

promissus ante plurimis
propheticis oraculis.

About this latest (or last)
hour of the world,
he reached for the lowest things,
promised before by many prophetic oracles.

Moreover, scholars have remarked that Christian Latin poetry organizes its relation to Scripture according to a typological structure. Sometimes, as is the case for the epanaleptic distich found in Sedulius and Rabanus Maurus, this typological structure is translated into a prosodic structure where *typos* and *antitypos* are related to one another through the parallelism of two hemistichs (the first half of line A corresponding with the second half of line B).

By now you will have perfectly understood the hypothesis I am about to put forth, which should be taken more as an epistemological paradigm rather than as an historical-genealogical hypothesis: that rhyme issues from Christian poetry as a metrical-linguistic transcodification of messianic time and is structured according to the play of typological relations and recapitulations evoked by Paul. But also the Pauline text—especially if it is portioned in *stichoi* as it is in certain editions, that is to say, in syntagmatic units that do not differ greatly from *cola* and *commata* in classical rhetoric—reveals itself as being entirely animated according to an unprecedented play of inner rhymes, of alliterations and end words. Norden notes that Paul draws from the formal use of parallelism in Greek art, as well as from the semantic parallelism found in Semitic poetry and prose. Augustine, who read Paul in Latin, had already taken note of his use of "the figure designated by the Greek word *climax*, though some prefer the Latin *gradatio* . . . whereby words or ideas are linked one with another" (Augustine, 107). Jerome, who for his part is a shoddy and dubious exegete of Paul, nevertheless as a translator understands the rhyme value of homeoteleuton, which he attempts to preserve at all costs. Paul pushes to an extreme the use of parallelism, antitheses, and homophony in classical rhetoric and Hebrew prose. But, in breaking up a period into short and abrupt *stichoi*, articulated in and stressed by rhyme, he reaches unknown heights in Greek or even Semitic prose, as though he were responding to an inner exigency and an epochal motivation.

I will furnish you with a few examples. The first is the passage on the *hōs mē*, which we have commented on at length. Even a faithful translation could not do justice to the prosodic structure of the original:

> *kai oi klaiontes*
> *hōs mē klaiontes,*
> *kai oi chairontes*
> *hōs mē chairontes,*
> *kai oi agorazontes*
> *hōs mē katechontes,*
> *kai oi chrōmenoi ton kosmon*
> *hōs mē katachrōmenoi*
>
> [those weeping
> as not weeping,
> those rejoicing
> as not rejoicing,
> those buying
> as not possessing,
> those using the world
> as not using it up]

Moreover, in the same First Letter to the Corinthians (15:42–44), we find:

> *speiretai en phtorai*
> *egeiretai en aphtarsiai,*
> *speiretai en atimiai*
> *egeiretai en doxē,*
> *speiretai en astheneiai*
> *egeiretai en dynamei,*
> *speiretai sōma psychicon*
> *egeiretai sōma pneumatikon*
>
> [it is sown in corruption
> it is raised in incorruption,
> it is sown in dishonor
> it is raised in glory,

    it is sown in weakness
    it is raised in power,
    it is sown a natural body
    it is raised a spiritual body]

And in the Second Letter to Timothy 4:7–8, when the apostle's life seems to rhyme with itself once it reaches its end (Jerome seems to have noticed this, since his translation even further multiplies the rhyme: *bonum certamen certavi / cursum consummavi / fidem servavi*, "I have fought a good fight / I have finished my course / I have kept the faith"), we read:

    ton kalon agōna ēgōnismai,
    ton dromon teteleka,
    tēn pistin tetērēka
    loipon apokeitai moi
    ho tēs dikaiosynēs stephanos.

I would like to end our exegesis of messianic time with the following hypothesis: rhyme, understood in the broad sense of the term as the articulation of a difference between semiotic series and semantic series, is the messianic heritage Paul leaves to modern poetry, and the history and fate of rhyme coincide in poetry with the history and fate of the messianic announcement. One example is enough to prove beyond a doubt that this is to be taken quite literally and show that this is not a question of secularization, but of a true theological heritage unconditionally assumed by poetry. When Hölderlin, on the threshold of a new century, elaborates on his doctrine of the leave-taking of the gods—specifically of the last god, the Christ—at the very moment in which he announces this new atheology, the metrical form of his lyric shatters to the point of losing any recognizable identity in his last hymns. The absence of the gods is one with the disappearance of closed metrical form; atheology immediately becomes a-prosody.

The Fifth Day

Eis euaggelion theou

In an author's choice of terminology, hierarchies of a grammatical nature harbor no significance, and a particle, adverb,
Eis   and occasionally a punctuation mark can rise to the status of a *terminus technicus*, as may a substantive. Martin
Puder has highlighted the strategic importance of the adverb *gle-
ichwohl* (nevertheless) in Kant. In this vein, one could just as well
highlight the determining function of Heidegger's uses of the
adverb *schon* (already) and the hyphen, in expressions like *In-der-
Welt-sein* or *Da-sein*, the hyphen being the most dialectical of
punctuation marks, uniting only to the extent that it separates.

It comes as no surprise then that in Paul the Greek preposition
eis, which signals a general movement toward something, can take
on a terminological quality. Paul actually uses it to convey the
nature of faith, in expressions like *pisteuein eis*—or *pistis eis*—*christon Iēsoun* (which then becomes our "to believe in," "faith in," via
Jerome's translation). But because we will be analyzing this specific Pauline usage of the term later on, paying close attention to the
term that follows it, *euaggelion*, we will postpone our analysis until
then.

Euaggelion (like the Hebrew *besora*—which appears in the verbal forms *bsr* and *euaggelizesthai* in the Bible and
Euaggelion   the Septuagint) means the "announcement" and

"joyful message" announced by the *euaggelos*, the messenger of joy. The term signifies both the act of announcing, and at the same time, the content of the announcement. This is why, twice in the Letter to the Romans (2:16; 16:25), Paul uses the formula "according to my announcement" (*kata ton euaggelion emou*), allowing for a perfect indeterminacy between the two meanings. It is only later on, once a scriptural canon begins to form, that the term *euaggelion* becomes identified with a written text. This is why Origen (first half of the third century) feels compelled to note a difference in specific reference to the Pauline formula *kata ton euaggelion emou*: "For among Paul's writings," he notes, "we do not have a book called 'gospel' [*euaggelion*] in the usual sense, but everything which he preached and said was *euaggelion*, the gospel" (Origen 1989, 38). Rabbi Meir's quip, which plays on Greek and Hebrew words, calling the Christian *euaggelion* the *'avon gillayon*, "the book [or scroll] of sin," occurs in this same period and is only comprehensible if at that time *euaggelion* also designated a book.

Just as the apostle differs from the prophet, so does the temporal structure implied by his *euaggelion* differ from the temporal structure of prophesy. The announcement does not refer to a future event, but to a present fact. "*Euaggelion*," Origen writes, "is either a discourse [*logos*] which contains the presence [*parousia*] of a good for the believer, or a discourse which announces that an awaited good is present [*pareinai*]" (Origen 1989, 39). The underlying connection between announcement-faith-presence (*euaggelion-pistis-parousia*) is conveyed perfectly in this definition and is precisely what we must attempt to understand. The problem regarding the meaning of the term *euaggelion* is inseparable from the problem in the meaning of the term *pistis*, "faith," and the implied *parousia*. What is a *logos* that can enact a presence for whomever hears it and believes?

Taken this way, the entire Letter to the Romans is no more than a paraphrase of the term *euaggelion*, which appears in the incipit, and at the same time it itself coincides with the content of the message announced. The letter is thus the impossibility of distinguishing between the announcement and its content. When modern theological lexicons note that in Paul "the *euagelion*, under-stood as the promise of salvation, unites both the theological con-ception of a *word which promises* with a *good which is the object of the promise*," the meaning of this coincidence is what must be thought through. Coming to grips with the *euaggelion* thus neces-sarily means entering into an experience of language in which the text of the letter is at every point indistinguishable from the announcement and the announcement from the good announced.

Pistis, faith, is the name Paul gives to this zone of indistinction. Immediately following the greeting of the Letter to the Romans, Paul defines the essential relation between *euaggelion* and *pistis* in the following terms: "the announcement is power [*dynamis*] for the salvation of he who believes [*panti to pisteuonti*]" (Rom. 1:16). This definition seems to imply that inasmuch as the announce-ment entails *dynamis*, potentiality—(*dynamis* signifies power as much as it does possibility)—it needs the complement of faith ("whoever believes") for it to be effectual. Paul is perfectly aware of the typical Greek opposition—which pertains both to cate-gories of language and thought—between potentiality (*dynamis*) and act (*energeia*). He even refers to it several times (Eph. 3:7: "according to the *energeia* of his *dynamis*"; and Phil. 3:21: "accord-ing to the *energeia* of *dynasthai*"). Paul often couples faith with *energeia*, being in act, so that with regard to potentiality, faith is *energumen* (*energoumenē*) par excellence, the principle of actuality and operativity (Gal. 5:6: "*pistis di' agapēs energoumenē*, faith oper-ative in love"; Col. 1:29: "according to his [the Messiah's] *energeia*, the one operating [*energoumenē*] in my power"). But for Paul, this principle is not external to the announcement; rather, it is pre-cisely that within it which makes potentiality active [*ne mette in atto la potenza*] (Gal. 3:4: "that which makes potentiality operative [*energon dynameis*] among you, comes from the hearing of faith [*euaggelizetai tēn pistin*]"), while at the same time, it may also be presented as the very content of what is announced (Gal. 1:23: "Now he [Paul] announces the faith [*euaggelizetai tēn pistin*]"). What has just been announced is the same faith that realizes the power of the announcement. Faith is the announcement's being in act, its *energeia*.

The *euaggelion* is therefore not merely a discourse, a *logos* that says something about something independent of the site of its enunciation and the subject who *Plērophoria* hears it. To the contrary, for "our announcement was not produced only in a discourse [*en logō*], but also in power and in much *plērophoria*" (1 Thess. 1:5). *Plērophoria* is not limited to meaning a "conviction," in the sense of an inner state of mind, nor, as one scholar has suggested, "the abundance of divine activity." Etymologically speaking, the meaning is self-evident: *pleros* signifies "full, fulfilled," and *phoreō*, frequentative of *pherō*, means "assiduously carrying" or in the passive, "to be transported violently." In this sense, the compound therefore signifies bringing to fullness, or in the passive, to be transported in fullness, to fully adhere to something without any gap left over. Understood this way it means being convinced (not in the psychological sense, but in the ontological sense, according to the meaning Michelstädter ascribes to the term *persuasion*). The announcement is not a *logos* empty in-itself but that may nevertheless be believed and verified; it is born—*egenēthē*—in the faith of the one who utters it and who hears and lives in it exclusively. The reciprocal interlacing of announcement, faith, and *plērophoria* is repeated in Romans 4:22, when the apostle seems to approximate an awareness of a particular performative power implicit in the promise (*epaggelia*). (Thus, in the greeting, Paul highlights the etymological connection between *epaggelia* and *euaggelion*: *euaggelion ho proepēggeilato*, "the announcement which had been pre-announced," meaning, promised; Rom. 1:2.) Faith consists in being fully persuaded of the necessary unity of promise and realization: "[Abraham] being fully persuaded that he who promised is equally capable of doing." The announcement is the form the promise assumes in the contraction of messianic time.

In this sense, understanding the meaning of the term *euaggelion* implies an equal understanding of the terms *pistis* and *epaggelia*. Yet one has to take into account that the *Nomos* Pauline treatment of faith and promise is so tightly interwoven with a critique of the law that the difficulties and apo-

rias implied in these terms coincide fully with the difficulties and
aporias that arise in his critique of the *nomos*, and it is only in
working through the latter that one may enter into the former.
The aporetic quality of the Pauline treatment of the law was recognized by the most ancient of commentators, especially Origen,
the first to systematically comment on the Letter to the Romans.
Two centuries of enigmatic silence precede him, barely broken by
a few citations that were not always in his favor. After Origen
came the endless flowering of commentary on Paul: in Greek, by
John Chrysostom, Didymus the Blind, Theodorus of Cyrene,
Theodore of Mopsuestia, Cyril of Alexandria, and so forth; and in
Latin, the first being Marius Victorinus, who, even though he was
an exceedingly boring writer (Hadot never forgave himself for
having dedicated twenty years of his life to him), nevertheless
played a central role as mediator between Greek and Christian cul-
tures. Origen, an unparalleled theorist of interpretation, tells us he
was taught by a rabbi to compare the writings of Scripture to a
plethora of rooms in a house, each locked by key, one key to each
keyhole. But because someone entertained himself by jumbling up
the keys, they no longer belonged to the door in which they were
found. When Origen confronts the obscure quality of the Pauline
treatment of the law in the Letter to the Romans, he feels compelled afterward to complicate the rabbinical apologue and com-
pares the text to a palace filled with magnificent rooms, each room
containing additional hidden doors. When the apostle composes
his writings, he enters one door and exits via another, without ever
being seen (*per unum aditum ingressus per alium egredi*, is how
Rufinus badly translates it; the original is lost; Origen 2001, 308).
This is why, Origen says, we cannot understand the text and are
given the impression that Paul contradicts himself when he speaks
of the law. A century later, Ticonius—a profoundly interesting figure, whose *Book of Rules* (*Liber regularum*) goes far beyond being
the first treaty on the interpretation of Scripture—claims to provide "keys and lamps" (Ticonius, 3) with which to open and illu-
minate the secrets of tradition, dedicating the longest of his *regulae* precisely to the aporias found in the Pauline treatment of the

law and the seeming contradictions between promise and law found therein.

The terms pertaining to this problem are well known. In the Letter to the Romans as well as in the Letter to the Galatians, Paul sets *epaggelia* and *pistis* on the one side against *nomos* on the other. What matters to him is to situate faith, promise, and law with respect to the decisive problem concerning the criteria of salvation, according to his affirmation in Romans 3:20—"By works of the law there shall be no flesh justified before God"—and 3:28: "Therefore we conclude that a man is justified by faith without works of the law." Paul pushes his formulations here to the point of almost sounding strongly antinomial, affirming that "what things soever the law says, it says . . . in order that every mouth be stopped and all the world become guilty before God," and that the law is given, not for salvation but for "the knowledge [*epignōsis*, "a posteriori knowledge"] of sin (Rom 3:19–20).

This is how promise becomes opposed to law in the following verse, and even more explicitly, in the Letter to the Galatians, how Abraham is played against Moses, so to speak. **Abraham and Moses** "For the promise that he should be the heir of the world was not to Abraham or to his seed, through the law, but through the justice of faith" (Rom. 4:13). The promise made to Abraham precedes Mosaic law genealogically since, according to Jewish chronology, Mosaic law comes four hundred years after the promise and is thus unable to revoke it. "The law, which was four hundred and thirty years after, cannot disannul a pact of God, making the promise inoperative. For if the inheritance be of the law, it is no more of the promise; but God gave it to Abraham by promise. Wherefore then the law? It was added because of transgressions, till the seed should come to whom the promise was made" (Gal. 3:17–19).

The antagonism here between *epaggelia-pistis* and *nomos* seems to find its footing in the opposition of two completely heterogeneous principles; however, the issue is not so straightforward. First of all, Paul repeatedly seeks to reaffirm the sanctity and goodness of the law without any lingering strategic cunning ("Wherefore the law is holy, and the commandment is holy, and just and good"; Rom. 7:12). In addition, in the majority of instances Paul seems to neutralize these antitheses in order to articulate a far more complex relation between promise, faith, and law. This is why in Romans 3:31 he softens his usual antinomial gesture, even if it is in the form of a rhetorical question: "Do we then make the law inoperative through faith? Let it not be! We hold the law firm." In Galatians 3:11–12, the apostle seems to aporetically exclude any hierarchical relation between faith and law: "But that no man is justified by the law in the sight of God, it is evident: for, 'The just shall live by faith.' And the law is not of faith, but 'He who puts these precepts into practice shall live through them.'" The citation that fuses Habakkuk 2:4 ("The just shall live by his faith") with Leviticus 18:5 (God tells Moses, "speak to the Israelites and among them . . . put my laws and my precepts into practice and follow them, and he who will have put them into practice will live in them") does not imply an opposition or hierarchical subordination of law to faith as much as it does an even tighter interrelation of the two, just as Ticonius noted, as though each implicated and confirmed the other in reciprocal fashion (*invicem firmant*).

Let us attempt to unravel the terms of this aporia, which has been commented on at length, by taking an even closer look at the Pauline text. It is well known that in the Septuagint's and Paul's Judeo-Greek, *nomos* can be read as a generic term with many meanings. More than once, however, Paul goes to great lengths to specify the way in which *nomos* is set against *epaggelia* and *pistis*. At stake is the law in its prescriptive and normative aspect, which he refers to as *nomos tōn entolōn*, "the law of the commandments" (Eph. 2:15)—(in the Septuagint, *entolē* is the translation of the Hebrew word *miswa*, a legal precept; remember the 613 *miswoth* that every Jew must observe!)—or even as the *nomos tōn ergōn*, the "law of works" (Rom. 3:27–28), meaning the law of acts carried out in the execution of precepts. The antithesis therefore concerns *epaggelia* and *pistis*, on the one hand, and on the other, not just the Torah itself, but its normative aspect. This is why, in an important passage (Rom. 3:27), Paul is able to set the *nomos pisteōs*, the law of faith, against the *nomos tōn ergōn*, the law of works. Rather than being an antinomy that involves two unrelated and completely heterogeneous principles, here the opposition lies within the *nomos* itself, between its normative and promissive elements. There is something in the law that constitutively exceeds the norm and is irreducible to it, and it is this excess and this inner dialectic that Paul refers to by means of the binomial *epaggelia / nomos* (the first corresponding to faith, the second to works). This is how, in 1 Corinthians 9:21, having stated that he made himself *hōs anomos*, "as without law," along with those who are without law (meaning *goyim*), he immediately rectifies this affirmation specifying that he is not *anomos theou*, "outside God's law," but *ennomos christou*, "in the law of the Messiah." The messianic law is the law of faith and not just the negation of the law. This, however, does not mean substituting the old *miswoth* with new precepts; rather, it means setting a non-normative figure of the law against the normative figure of the law.

If this is this case, how should this non-normative aspect of the law be understood? And what relation is there between these two figures of the *nomos?* Let us begin **Katargein** by answering the second question, starting with a lexical observation. In order to convey the relation between *epaggelia-pistis* and *nomos*—and, more generally, the relation between the messianic and the law—Paul constantly uses one verb, which gives us substance for reflection, since I happened to make a discovery on this subject that was particularly surprising for a philosopher. The discovery concerns the verb *katargeō*, a true key word in the Pauline messianic vocabulary (twenty-six of the twenty-seven occurrences in the New Testament are in the Letters!). *Katargeō* is a compound of *argeō*, which in turn derives from the adjective *argos*, meaning "inoperative, not-at-work (*a-ergos*), inactive." The compound therefore comes to mean "I make inoperative, I deactivate, I suspend the efficacy" (or as Henri Estienne's *Thesaurus græcæ linguæ* suggests, *reddo aergon et inefficacem, facio cessare ab opere suo, tollo, aboleo*). As Estienne has already noted, the verb is essentially New Testament, and as we have seen, openly Pauline. Up until Paul, it is rarely used (it is found in Euripides, in the context of "hands left idle," and in Polybus, in a passage the *Suda lexicon* glosses as *anenergēton einai*, "to be inoperative"). After Paul it appears frequently in the Greek Fathers (146 occurrences in John Chrysostom alone) that obviously derives from Paul and because of this is only indirectly helpful in understanding Pauline usage. Before Paul, in a context undoubtedly familiar to him, is the noteworthy usage of the form *argeō* in the Septuagint, a translation of the Hebrew word that signifies rest on Saturday (see, for example, 2 Macc. 5:25). It is certainly not by chance that the term used by the apostle to express the effect of the messianic on works of the law echoes a verb that signifies the sabbatical suspension of works.

You can find the twenty-six occurrences of the verb in the Pauline text listed in New Testament lexicons; I will limit myself to one relevant sampling. But first, one consideration on the general meaning of the term. As we have seen, this term (which is prudently rendered by Jerome as *evacuari*, "to empty out") does not mean "to annihilate, to destroy"—or, as one recent lexicon suggests, "to make perish": the latter states, "In addition to uttering the powerful '*Let it be!*' the creator utters the equally powerful '*Let it perish!*' [*katargeō* being the negative equivalent of *poieō*]." Even the most elementary knowledge of Greek would have shown that the positive equivalent of *katargeō* is not *poieō*, but *energeō*, "I put to work, I activate." This is especially evident since Paul himself plays on this connection in an important passage, which in turn will furnish us with our first illustration: "For when we were in the flesh, the passions of sin were enacted [*enērgeito*] through the law in our members to bring forth fruit unto death. But now we are de-activated [*katergēthēmen*, 'made inoperative'] from the law" (Rom. 7:5–6). The etymological opposition with *energeō* clearly demonstrates that *katergeō* signals a taking out of *energeia*, a taking out of the act. (In the passive, it means no longer being in the act, being suspended.) As we have seen, Paul is clearly familiar with the typically Greek opposition *dynamis/energeia*, potentiality/act, which he uses more than once. In this opposition, the messianic enacts an inversion that is completely analogous with what Scholem describes as the conversive *waw*. Just as the latter made the unfulfilled fulfilled and the fulfilled unfulfilled, here potentiality passes over into actuality and meets up with its *telos*, not in the form of force or *ergon*, but in the form of *astheneia*, weakness. Paul formulates this principle of messianic inversion in the potential-act relation in a well-known passage. Just as he asks the Lord for liberation from the thorn lodged in his flesh, he hears, "Power [or potentiality] realizes itself in weakness [*dynamis en astheneia teleitai*]" (2 Cor. 12:9). This is repeated in the next verse: "when I am weak, then am I powerful."

How should we understand the *telos* of a power realized in weakness? Greek philosophy was well versed in the principle according to which privation (*sterēsis*) and im-potentiality (*adynamia*) maintain a kind of potentiality ("each thing is powerful either through having something or through the privation of this same thing"; "every potentiality is im-potentiality of the same [potentiality] and with respect to the same"; *Metaphysics* 1019b9–10, 1046a32). According to Paul, messianic power does not wear itself out in its *ergon*; rather, it remains powerful in it in the form of weakness. Messianic *dynamis* is, in this sense, constitutively "weak"—but it is precisely through its weakness that it may enact its effects—"God has chosen weak things of the world to shame the things which are mighty" (1 Cor. 1:27).

Astheneia

There is another aspect to this messianic inversion of the potential-act relation. Just as messianic power is realized and acts in the form of weakness, so too in this way does it have an effect on the sphere of the law and its works, not simply by negating or annihilating them, but by de-activating them, rendering them inoperative, no-longer-at-work [*non-piu-in-opera*]. This is the meaning of the verb *katargeō*: just as, in the *nomos*, the power of the promise was transposed onto works and mandatory precepts, so does the messianic now render these works inoperative; it gives potentiality back to them in the form of inoperativity and ineffective-

ness. The messianic is not the destruction but the deactivation of
the law, rendering the law inexecutable [*l'ineseguibilità della legge*].

The Pauline affirmations which state that, on the one hand, the
Messiah "will render all rule, authority, and power inoperative
[*katargēsē*]" (1 Cor. 15:24), and on the other, that the Messiah constitutes "the *telos* of the law" (Rom. 10:4), can only be fully understood in this light. The question has been raised—with little
accompanying thought—as to whether or not *telos* means "end"
or "fulfillment." Only to the extent that the Messiah renders the
nomos inoperative, that he makes the *nomos* no-longer-at-work
and thus restores it to the state of potentiality, only in this way
may he represent its *telos* as both end and fulfillment. The law can
be brought to fulfillment only if it is first restored to the inoperativity of power. As the highly original pericope in 2 Corinthians
3:12–13 states, the Messiah is *telos tou katargoumenou*, "fulfillment
out of that which has been de-activated," taken out of the act—
namely, at one and the same time, deactivation and fulfillment.

From this stems the ambiguity of the gesture in Romans 3:31,
which makes for the stumbling block of every reading of the
Pauline critique of the law: "Do we then make the law inoperative
[*katargoumen*] through faith? No, we hold the law firm [*his-
tanomen*]." The first commentators were quick to point out that
the apostle seems to contradict himself in this passage (*contraria
sibi scribere*, "he alleges against himself"; Origen 2001, 233); after
having declared many times that the messianic renders the law
inoperative, it seems that Paul affirms the contrary. In truth, the
apostle is merely elucidating the meaning of his *terminus technicus*, taking it back to its etymological root. That which is deacti-
vated, taken out of *energeia*, is not annulled, but conserved and
held onto for its fulfillment.

John Chrysostom analyzes this double meaning of Pauline
katargein in an extraordinary passage. When the apostle uses this
verb (for example, in the expression *gnōsis katargēsthētai*; 1 Cor.
13:8), what he is actually referring to in *katargēsis* is not the
destruction of being *(aphanisis tes ousias)*, but the progression
toward a better state.

This is the meaning of *katergeitai*, and he made it clear to us in the words which follow. After you heard him say *katergeitai*, he did not wish you to think of this as complete dissolution but as an increase and advancement to something better. So after he had said *katergeitai*, he went on to add: "Our knowledge is imperfect and our prophesying is imperfect. When the perfect comes, then the imperfect will be rendered inoperative [*katargēthēsai*]." So the imperfect no longer exists, but the perfect does. . . . This is because the rendering inoperative [*katargēsis*] is a fulfillment [*plērōsis*] and advancement to something better [*pros to meizon epidosis*]. (Chrysostom, 55)

Messianic *katargēsis* does not merely abolish; it preserves and brings to fulfillment.

At this point, I must return to the discovery I alluded to concerning the posthumous life of the verb *katargein* in the philosophical tradition. How does Luther translate *Aufhebung* this Pauline verb, whether in Romans 3:31 or wherever else the verb occurs in the Letters? Luther uses *Aufheben*—the very word that harbors the double meaning of abolishing and conserving (*aufbewahren* and *aufhören lassen*) used by Hegel as a foundation for his dialectic! A closer look at Luther's vocabulary shows that he is aware of the verb's double meaning, which before him occurs infrequently. This means that in all likelihood the term acquires its particular facets through the translation of the Pauline letters, leaving Hegel to pick it up and develop it. It is because of the word's having been used by Luther to convey the antinomial gesture in Pauline *katargēsis* in Romans 3:31 (*heben wir das Gesetz auff / durch den glauben? Das sey ferne / sondern wir richten das Gesetz auff*) that the German verb then took on this double meaning—which was a "delight" for "speculative thought" (Hegel, 107). This is how a genuinely messianic term expressing the transformation of the law impacted by faith and announcement becomes a key term for the dialectic. That Hegel's dialectic is nothing more than a secularization of Christian theology comes as no surprise; however, more significant is the fact that (with a certain degree of irony) Hegel used a weapon against theology furnished by theology itself and that this weapon is genuinely messianic.

(•)   If this genealogy of *Aufhebung* that I am putting forth is correct, then not only is Hegelian thought involved in a tightly knit hermeneutic struggle with the messianic—in the sense that all of its determining concepts are more or less conscious interpretations and secularizations of messianic themes—but this also holds for modernity, by which I intend the epoch that is situated under the sign of the dialectical *Aufhebung*.

In the *Phenomenology of Spirit*, the *Aufhebung* makes its appearance in the context of the dialectic of sense certainty and its expression in language via the "this" (*diese*) and the "now" (*jetzt*). Throughout the course of the *Aufhebung*, Hegel simply describes the movement of language itself in its possessing a "divine nature" that transforms sense certainty into a negative and a nothingness and conserves this nothingness, converting the negative into being. In the "this" and the "now," the immediate is thus always already *aufgehoben*, lifted and preserved. Inasmuch as the "now" has already ceased to be once it has been uttered (or written), the attempt to grasp the "now" always produces a past, a *gewesen*, which as such is *kein Wesen*, nonbeing. It is this nonbeing that is preserved in language and is posited as such, as it truly is, only at the end. The "Eleusinian mysteries" of sense certainty—the exposition of which initiates the *Phenomenology of Spirit*—show themselves to be nothing more than an exposition of the structure of linguistic signification in general. To use the language of modern linguistics, as language refers to its own taking place via shifters, the "this" and the "now," language produces the sensible expressed in it as a past and at the same time defers this sensible to the future. In this fashion, it is always already caught up in a history and a time. In each case what is presupposed by the *Aufhebung* is that what has been lifted is not completely eliminated, but rather persists somehow and can thus be preserved (*Was sich aufhebt, wird dadurch nicht zu Nichts*, "What is sublated, is not thereby reduced to nothing"; Hegel, 107).

What is demonstrated here is both the connection and difference between the problem of the *Aufhebung* and that of messianic time. While messianic time (as operational time) also introduces a disconnection and delay into represented time, this cannot be tacked onto time as a supplement or as infinite deferment. To the contrary, the messianic—the ungraspable quality of the "now"—is the very opening through which we may seize hold of time, achieving our representation of time, making it end. When the Torah is rendered inoperative in messianic *katargēsis*, it is not caught up in a deferment or in an infinite displacement; rather, the Torah finds its *plērōma* therein. We find a genuinely messianic exigency reemerge in Hegel in the problem of the *plērōma* of times and the end of history. Hegel, however, thinks the pleroma not as each instant's relation to the Messiah, but as the final result of a global process. His French interpreters—Koyré and Kojève, who are actually Russian, which comes as no surprise given the importance of the apocalypse in twentieth-century Russian culture—thus start off with the conviction that "in Hegelian philosophy, the 'system,' is only possible if history is over, if there is no more future and if time stops" (Koyré, 458). But what happens here, as is clearly the case in Kojève, is that both of these interpretations end up flattening out the messianic onto the eschatological, thus confounding the problem of messianic time with the problem of posthistory. The fact that the concept of *désœuvrement*—a good translation of Pauline *katargein*—first appears in twentieth-century philosophy precisely in Kojève, in his definition of the post-historical condition of man, the *voyou désœuvré* as the "*Shabbat* of man" (Kojève, 458), is enough to prove that the connection here to the messianic has not yet been completely neutralized.

Analogous conclusions could be drawn for the concepts of privative opposition, degree zero, and the surplus of the signifier in twentieth-century human sciences, as well as for the Degree Zero trace and the originary supplement in contemporary thought. In Trubetzkoy, the concept of privative opposition defines an opposition in which one of two terms is characterized by the existence of a mark, the other by the lack thereof. What is presupposed is that the unmarked term is not simply opposed to the marked one as an absence (a nothing) is opposed to a presence, but that nonpresence is in some manner equivalent to a zero-degree presence (meaning that presence is *lacking* in its absence). According to Trubetzkoy, this is shown when, once the opposition is neutralized, the marked term loses its value and the unmarked one remains as the only relevant one. Thus, the unmarked one takes on the role of archiphoneme, representing all distinctive traits common to both terms. (When Trubetzkoy speaks of "neutralization" he uses the term *Aufhebung*, and not by chance, since in the *Science of Logic* it implies the unity of opposites.) In the *Aufhebung*, the unmarked term—being a sign of lacking-a-sign—counts as an archiphoneme, a zero-degree signification, and the opposition is both lifted and preserved as the zero degree of difference. (It was Jakobson who, in Bally's steps, initiated systematic use of the terms "zero sign" and "zero phoneme" instead of "unmarked degree" and "archiphoneme." In this way, for Jakobson, even though the zero phoneme does not imply any differential factor, it works by opposing itself to the mere absence of phoneme. The philosophical grounds for this concept are found in the Aristotelian ontology of privation. In the *Metaphysics* [1004a16], Aristotle makes a point to distinguish privation [*sterēsis*] from mere absence [*apousia*], inasmuch as privation still implies a reference to the being or form deprived which manifests itself through its lack. This is why Aristotle writes that privation is a kind of *eidos*, a form.)

In 1957, Lévi-Strauss developed these concepts in his theory of the signifier's constitutive surplus in its relation to the signified. According to this theory, signification always exceeds the signifieds that could match up with it. This gap between the two then translates into the existence of free or floating signifiers in themselves void of meaning, yet with the sole function of conveying the gap between signifier and signified. What we have are therefore non-signs, or signs in the state of *décœuvrement* and *Aufhebung*, "with a *zero symbolic value*, that is, a sign marking the necessity of a supplementary symbolic content" (Lévi-Strauss, 64); they are set in opposition to the absence of signification without standing in for any particular meaning.

Beginning with *Speech and Phenomena* and *Of Grammatology* (1967), Derrida restored philosophical standing to these concepts, demonstrating their connectedness to Hegelian *Aufhebung* and developing them into an actual ontology of the trace and originary supplement. In his careful deconstruction of Husserlian phenomenology, Derrida critiques the primacy of presence in the metaphysical tradition and shows how metaphysics always already presupposes nonpresence and signification. This is the setting in which he introduces the concept of an "originary supplement," which is not simply added onto something but comes to supplement a lack and nonoriginary presence both of which are always already caught up in a signifying. "What we would ultimately like to draw attention to is that the for-itself of self-presence (*für-sich*)—traditionally determined in its dative dimension as phenomenological self-giving, whether reflexive or prereflexive—arises in the role of supplement as primordial substitution, in the form 'in the place of' (*für etwas*), that is, as we have seen, in the very operation of significance in general" (Derrida 1973, 88–89). The concept of the "trace" names the impossibility of a sign to be extinguished in the fullness of a present and absolute presence. In this sense, the trace must be conceived as "before being," the thing itself, always already as sign and *repraesentamen,* the signified always already in the position of signifier. There is no nostalgia for origins since there is no origin. The origin is produced as a retroactive effect of nonorigin and a trace, which thus becomes the origin of the origin. These concepts (or better yet, these nonconcepts, or even as Derrida prefers to call them, these "undecidables") call into question the primacy of presence and signification for the philosophical tradition, yet they do not truly call into question signification in general. In radicalizing the notion of *sterēsis* and zero degree, these concepts presuppose both the exclusion of presence and the impossibility of an extinguishing of the sign. They therefore presuppose that there is still signification beyond presence and absence, meaning that nonpresence still signifies something, it posits itself as an "arche-trace," a sort of archiphoneme between presence and absence. If there is no nostalgia for origins here, it is because its memory is contained in the form of signification itself, as *Aufhebung* and zero degree. In order for deconstruction to function, what must be excluded is not the fact that that presence and origin are *lacking* but that they are purely insignificant. "Therefore the sign of this excess must be absolutely excessive as concerns all possible presence-absence, all possible production or disappearance of beings in general, and yet, *in some manner* it must still signify. . . . The mode of inscription of such a trace in the text of metaphysics is so unthinkable that it must be described as an erasure of the trace itself. The trace is produced as its own erasure" (Derrida 1982, 65). In this instance, the arche-trace simultaneously shows its link to—and difference from—the Hegelian *Aufhebung* with its messianic theme. In this context, the movement of the *Aufhebung,* which neutralizes signifieds while maintaining and achieving signification, thus becomes a principle of infinite deferment. A signification that only signifies itself can never seize hold of itself, it can never catch up with a void in representation, nor does it ever allow anything to be an in-significance; rather, it is displaced and deferred in one and the same gesture. In this way, the trace is a suspended *Aufhebung* that will never come to know its own *plērōma.* Deconstruction is a thwarted messianism, a suspension of the messianic.

In our tradition, a metaphysical concept, which takes as its prime focus a moment of foundation and origin, coexists with a messianic concept, which focuses on a moment of fulfillment. What is essentially messianic and *historic* is the idea that fulfillment is possible by retrieving and revoking foundation, by coming to terms with it. When these two elements are split up, we are left with a situation like the one so clearly witnessed in Husserl's *Crisis of European Sciences,* that of a foundation which is part and parcel of an infinite task. If we drop the messianic theme and only focus on the moment of foundation and origin—or even the absence thereof (which amounts to the same thing)—we are left with empty, zero degree, signification and with history as its infinite deferment.

How should we think the state of the law under the effect of messianic *katargēsis?* What is a law that is simultaneously suspended and fulfilled? In answering this question, I found there to be nothing more helpful than the epistemological paradigms at the center of the work of a jurist who developed his conception of law and the sovereign state according to an explicitly anti-messianic constellation. But for this very reason, insofar as he is, in Taubes's words "an apocalypticist of counterrevolution," he cannot help but introduce some genuinely messianic *theologoumena* into it. According to Schmitt, whom you will have already identified without my naming him, the paradigm that defines the proper functioning and structure of the law is not the norm, but the exception.

The exception most clearly reveals the essence of the state's authority. The decision parts here from the legal norm, and (to formulate it paradoxically) authority proves that to produce law it need not be based on law [*die Autorität beweist, daß sie, um Recht zu schaffen, nicht Recht zu haben braucht*]. . . . The exception is more interesting than the normal case [*Normalfall*]. The normal [*das Normale*] proves nothing; the exception proves everything: The exception does not only confirm the rule [*Regel*]; the rule as such lives off the exception alone (Schmitt 1985, 13–15).

It is important to remember that in the exception, what is excluded from the norm does not simply have no bearing on the law; on the contrary, the law maintains itself in relation to the exception in the form of its own self-suspension. The norm is applied, so to speak, to the exception in dis-applying itself, in withdrawing itself from it. In this way, the exception is not a mere exclusion, but an *inclusive exclusion*, an *ex-ceptio* in the literal sense of the term: a seizing of the outside. In defining the exception, the law simultaneously creates and defines the space in which juridical-political order is granted value. In this sense, for Schmitt, the state of exception represents the pure and originary form of the enforcement of the law, and it is from this point only that the law may define the normal sphere of its application.

Let us take a closer look at the fundamental features of the law in the state of exception:

1. First and foremost, there is an absolute indeterminacy between inside and outside. This is what Schmitt conveys in the paradox of the sovereign. To the extent that the sovereign has the legitimate power to suspend the validity of the law, he is both inside and outside the law. If, in the state of exception, the law is in force in the form of its suspension, being applied in disapplying itself, then the law thus includes, so to speak, that which is rejected from itself. Or, if you prefer, this means that there is no "outside" of the law. In the state of sovereign autosuspension, the law thus meets up with the utmost limit of its enforcement and, in including its outside in the form of the exception, it coincides with reality itself.

2. If this is true, then in the state of exception it becomes impossible to distinguish between observance [*osservanza*] and transgression of the law. When the law is in force only in the form of its suspension, no matter what mode of behavior appears to be in line with the law in a normal situation—like walking peacefully down the street—this behavior might also imply a transgression—as, for example, in the case of a curfew. Vice versa, the transgression may even be conceived of as carrying out the law. In this sense, one could say that in the state of exception, the law, inasmuch as it simply coincides with reality, is absolutely unobservable [*ineseguibile*], and that unobservability [*ineseguibilità*] is the originary figure of the norm.

3. One corollary of this unobservability of the norm is that in the state of exception, the law is absolutely unformulatable [*infor-*

mulabile]. It no longer has, or does not yet have, the form of a prescription or a prohibition. This unformulability [*informulabilità*] is to be taken to the letter. Let us consider the state of exception at its extreme: the one established in Germany by the Decree for the Protection of the People and the State, on February 28, 1933, immediately following the acquisition of power by the Nazi party. This decree simply states: "The articles 114, 115, 117, 118, 123, 124, and 153 of the Constitution of the *Reich* are suspended until further orders" (the decree remained in force over the entire course of the Nazi regime). This laconic statement neither orders nor prohibits anything. But by simply suspending the articles of the Constitution pertaining to personal freedom, it becomes impossible to know or articulate what is licit and illicit. The concentration camps, where everything becomes possible, issue from the space that is opened up by the unformulability of the law. This means that in the state of exception, the law is not configured as of a new body of norms that spells out new prohibitions and new duties, but that the law enacts itself only by means of its unformulability.

Let us now compare the threefold articulation of the law in the state of exception with the state of the law in the horizon of messianic *katargēsis*.

Concerning the first point (on the indiscernability of an outside and inside of the law): as we have seen, the distinction between Jews and non-Jews, those who are within the law and those who are outside, no longer holds in the messianic. This does not mean that Paul simply extends the application of the law to the non-Jews; rather, he makes Jews and non-Jews, inside and outside the law, indistinguishable from each other by introducing a remnant. This remnant—the non-non-Jews—is neither properly inside nor outside, neither *ennomos* nor *anomos* (according to the way Paul defines himself in 1 Cor. 9:21); it is the cipher of messianic deactivation of the law, the cipher of its *katargēsis*. The remnant is an exception taken to its extreme, pushed to its paradoxical formulation. In his rendering of the messianic condition of the believer, Paul radicalizes the condition of the state of exception, whereby law is applied in disapplying itself, no longer having an inside or an outside. With regard to this law that applies itself in disapplying itself, a corresponding gesture of faith ensues, applying itself in disapplying itself, rendering law inoperative while carrying it to its fulfillment.

Paul calls this paradoxical figure of the law in the state of messianic exception *nomos pisteōs*, "the law of faith" (Rom. 3:27), as it can no longer be defined through works, the execution of the *miswoth*, but as a manifestation of "justice without law" (*dikaiosynē chōris nomou*; Rom. 3:21). This amounts, more or less, to "observing the law without law," especially if one takes into consideration the fact that in Judaism, justice is, par excellence, with him who observes the law. This is why Paul says that the law of faith is the suspension—literally, the "exclusion"—(*exekleisthē*; Rom. 3:27) of the law of works. Paul's formulation of this dialectical aporia, which affirms that faith is both deactivation (*katargein*) and preservation (*histanein*) of the law, is nothing more than the coherent expression of this paradox. Justice without law is not the negation of the law, but the realization and fulfillment, the *plērōma*, of the law.

As for the last two instances of the state of exception, the unobservability and unformulability of the law, they appear in Paul as the necessary consequences of the exclusion of works brought on by the law of faith. The entire critique of the *nomos* in Romans 3:9–20 is no more than a clear-cut enunciation of a real messianic principle of the unobservability of the law: "There is not a just one, not even one. . . . Now we know that whatever the law says applies to those who are under the law, so that every mouth may be silenced and the whole world held accountable to God. Because by works of law not one of all flesh will be justified before Him." The particular expression Paul uses in verse 12, "all *ēchreōthēsan*," which Jerome translates as *inutiles facti sunt*, literally means (*a-chreioō*) "they were made unable to use," and perfectly conveys the impossibility of use, the unobservability that characterizes the law in messianic time, which only faith may restore in *chrēsis*, in use. The well-known description of the division of the subject in

Romans 7:15–19 ("I know not what I do . . . for I do not do what I want . . . what I do not want, this I do") is a perfectly clear reading of the agonizing condition of a man faced with a law that has become entirely unobservable, and, as such, only functions as a universal principle of imputation.

Shortly before this, Paul's drastic abbreviation of Moses' commandment—which did not simply say, "Do not desire," but "Do not desire the woman, the house, the slave, the mule, and so on . . . of thy neighbor"—renders the commandment unobservable and equally impossible to formulate: "What shall we say then? Is the law sin? Let it not be! But I did not know sin except through law; for also I did not know lust except the law said, 'You shall not lust'" (Rom. 7:7). The law here is no longer *entolē*, a norm that clearly prescribes or prohibits something ("Do not desire" is not a commandment); instead, the law is only the knowledge of guilt, a trial in the Kafkaesque sense of the term, a perpetual self-accusation without a precept.

On the side of faith, the counterpart to this contraction of Mosaic law is the messianic recapitulation of the commandments; Paul refers to it in Romans 13: 8–9: "For the one who loves another has fulfilled the law. For the commandments, 'You must not commit adultery; you must not murder; you must not steal; you must not covet,' and every other commandment is summed up in this statement: 'You must love your neighbor as yourself.'" Once he divides the law into a law of works and a law of faith, a law of sin and a law of God (Rom. 7: 22–23)—and thus renders it inoperative and unobservable—Paul can then fulfill and recapitulate the law in the figure of love. The messianic *plērōma* of the law is an *Aufhebung* of the state of exception, an absolutizing of *katargēsis*.

The Mystery of *Anomia*

We should now turn to the enigmatic passage in 2 Thessalonians 2:3–9 on *katechōn*. In speaking of the *parousia* of the Messiah, Paul warns the Thessalonians of the anxiety that may be produced by the announcement of the Messiah's imminence:

Let no one deceive you in any way. Because it will not be unless the apostasy shall have come first, and the man of lawlessness, the son of destruction, is revealed. He opposes and exalts himself above every so-called god and object of worship. As a result, he seats himself in the sanctuary of God and declares himself to be God. Don't you remember that I repeatedly told you about these things when I was still with you? You know what it is that is now holding him back [*ho katechōn*], so that he will be revealed when his time comes. For the mystery of anomy (*anomia*) is already at work, but only until the person now holding him back [*ho katechōn*] is removed. Then the lawless one [*anomos*] will be revealed, whom the Lord will abolish with the breath of his mouth, rendering him inoperative by the manifestation of his presence [*parousia*]. The presence [*parousia*] of the former is according to the working of Satan in every power [*dynamis*].

If the identification of the "lawless one" with the Antimessiah (*antichristos*) from the Letter of John is generally accepted—even if this identification still harbors problems—the question remains of who or what the *katechōn* is (in the impersonal form in verse 6, and in the personal form in verse 7). An ancient tradition, which is already found in Tertullian, identifies the power which delays or maintains the end of time as the Roman Empire, which in this sense has a positive historical function. (This is why Tertullian says, "We pray for the permanence of the world [*pro statu saeculi*], for peace in things, for the delay of the end [*pro mora finis*].") This tradition culminates in the Schmittian theory that finds in 2 Thessalonians 2 the only possible foundation for a Christian doctrine of State power:

Essential to this Christian empire was that it never consisted in an eternal reign and that it always kept in mind its own end as well as the end of the present eon, and despite all this, that it was still capable of exerting a historical power. The decisive and historically powerful concept that grounded its continuity was the concept of the "arresting force," the *kat-echon*. "Empire" here means the historical power that is capable of arresting the coming of the Antichrist and the end of the current eon. A force *qui tenet*, according to the words of the apostle Paul in the second letter to the Thessalonians. . . . I do not believe that any other concept of history than the *kat-echon* is possible for an originary Christian faith.

The belief in an arresting force that can stave off the end of the world is the only link leading from the eschatological paralysis of every human action to such a great historical agency [*Geschichtsmächtigkeit*] as that of the Christian empire at the time of the Germanic kings. (Schmitt 1997, 29)

Things do not change much for those modern interpreters who link *katechōn* with God himself and take the delay of the *parousia* to be an expression of the divine plan of salvation ("the *katechōn*, understood correctly, is God himself. . . . It is not a matter of a worldly force that would delay the coming of the Antichrist, but of delaying the *parusia* implied in the divine temporal plan"; Strobel, 106–7).

As you can see, a great deal is at stake here. In a certain sense, every theory of the State, including Hobbes's—which thinks of it as a power destined to block or delay catastrophe—can be taken as a secularization of this interpretation of 2 Thessalonians 2. Yet the fact remains that despite its obscurity, this Pauline passage does not harbor any positive valuation of *katechōn*. To the contrary, it is what must be held back in order that the "mystery of *anomia*" be revealed fully. The interpretation of verses 7–9 is therefore decisive:

For the mystery of lawlessness is already at work [*energeitai*], but only until the person now holding it back [*ho katechōn*] gets out of the way. Then the lawless one [*anomos*] will be revealed, whom the Lord will destroy with the breath of his mouth, rendering him inoperative [*katargēsei*] by the manifestation of his presence [*parousia*]. The presence [*parousia*] of the former is according to the working of Satan in every power [*kat'energeian tou satana en pasē dynamei*].

Anomia should not be translated here, as it is in Jerome, by the generic "iniquity" or the even worse rendering "sin." *Anomia* can only mean "absence of law" and *anomos* the one outside the law (remember that Paul presents himself to the gentiles as being *hōs anomos*). Paul is thus referring to the condition of the law in messianic time, when the *nomos* is rendered inoperative and is in a state of *katargēsis*. This is why Paul's technical vocabulary concerning *energeia* and *dynamis*, being in the act (*energein*) and being inoperative (*katargēsis*) reappears in this instance. The *katechōn* is therefore the force—the Roman Empire as well as every constituted authority—that clashes with and hides *katargēsis*, the state of tendential lawlessness that characterizes the messianic, and in this sense delays unveiling the "mystery of lawlessness." The unveiling of this mystery entails bringing to light the inoperativity of the law and the substantial illegitimacy of each and every power in messianic time.

It is therefore possible to conceive of *katechōn* and *anomos* not as two separate figures (unlike John, Paul never mentions an *antichristos*), but as one single power before and after the final unveiling. Profane power—albeit of the Roman Empire or any other power—is the semblance that covers up the substantial lawlessness [*anomia*] of messianic time. In solving the "mystery," semblance is cast out, and power assumes the figure of the *anomos*, of that which is the absolute outlaw [*del fuorilegge assoluto*]. This is how the messianic is fulfilled in the clash between the two *parousiai*: between that of the *anomos*, who is marked by the working of Satan in every power [*potenza*], and that of the Messiah, who will render *energeia* inoperative in it. (An explicit reference is made here to 1 Corinthians 15:24: "Afterwards the end, when he delivers the kingdom to God and the Father, when he will render inoperative all rule, and all authority [*potestà*] and power"); 2 Thess. 2 may not be used to found a "Christian doctrine" of power in any manner whatsoever.

ℸ With this in mind, it may be helpful to look at the relation between Nietzsche and this Pauline passage. It is seldom asked why Nietzsche entitled his declaration of war on Christianity   Antichrist and Paul *The Anti-Christ*. And yet, in the Christian tradition, the Antichrist is precisely the figure that marks the end of time and the triumph of Christ over every power—including "this most admirable of all works of art in the grand manner" (Nietzsche, 85), which Nietzsche calls the Roman Empire. One cannot seriously believe that Nietzsche was unaware that the "man of lawlessness"—the precise figure through which he identified himself as an Antichrist—was a

Pauline invention. His gesture—of signing his declaration of war against Christianity in the name of a figure that belonged entirely to that tradition and played a specific role therein—must harbor some parodic intention. *The Anti-Christ* can therefore be read as a messianic parody in which Nietzsche, in cloaking himself in the garments of the Antimessiah, is actually only reciting a script written by Paul. We can then understand why, in the subtitle, the book already presents itself as a "curse" and concludes with the emanation of a "law" with messianic pretenses ("dated on the day of salvation") being nothing but a "curse of holy history." Not only is this identification between law and curse genuinely Pauline (Gal. 3:13: "The Messiah has redeemed us from the curse of the law [*ek tēs kataras tou nomou*]"), but the idea that the "man of lawlessness" is unable to do anything but enact this law-curse is itself a lucidly ironic reading of *katechōn* in 2 Thessalonians 6:7.

§ The Sixth Day

(Eis euaggelion theou)

At the beginning of this seminar I spoke of Buber's *Two Types of Faith*, in which the author opposes Jewish *emunah*, the immediate faith in the community in which one lives, to Pauline *pistis*, the act of recognizing something as true. In 1987, David Flusser, a professor at the Hebrew University of Jerusalem who was preparing an afterword for a newer German edition of this book, was strolling down a street in Athens when he saw the following written on a door: *Trapeza emporikēs pisteōs*. Wondering where this enigmatic formula with the word *pistis* came from, he stopped and realized that it was simply a part of the insignia of what is called the "Bank of Commercial Credit." Because of this, Flusser was able to confirm something he had known all along: that from a linguistic standpoint there was no real foundation for Buber's opposing *emunah* and *pistis*. Flusser notes, "The Greek *pistis* means precisely the same thing as the Hebrew *emunah*" (Buber, 211). The significance of a book like Buber's thus had to be found elsewhere, and as we shall see, Flusser did just this in a very cunning way.

If *pistis* does not mean "to recognize as true," and if this means that we cannot speak of two types of faith, how then should we understand the meaning of *pistis* in Paul's   Oath text? And, above all, what meaning does the family of the word *pistis* harbor in Greek? One of the most ancient meanings of the term *pistis* and the adjective *pistos* is as a synonym—or an attributive, in the case of *pistos* (trustworthy)—of the term *horkos*, oath, in expressions like *pistin kai horka poieisthai*, "to take an oath," or *pista dounai kai lambanein*, "to exchange oaths." In Homer, oaths, *horkia*, are *pista*, "trustworthy," par excellence. In ancient Greece, *horkos* designated both the oath and the object held at the time of the oath's pronouncement. This object had the power to kill off the perjurer (*epiorkos*) and thus made for the best guarantee of the oath's being fulfilled. Even the gods, who swore on the water of the Styx, were not exempt from the terrifying power of the *horkos*. The immortal who committed perjury lay lifeless on the ground for a year and was excluded from the presence of the gods for an additional nine years. The oath thus belongs to one of the most archaic areas of the law, the sphere French scholars call *pré-droit*, literally, prelaw, a prejuridical sphere in which magic, religion, and law are absolutely indiscernible from one another. (One could even define "magic" as the zone of indistinction between religion and law.) But this means that since *pistis* is tightly bound up in its origin with oath and only takes on the technical-juridical meaning of "guarantee" and "credit" later on, it then it comes from this same obscure prehistoric background. Even more significantly, this means that when Paul sets *pistis* against law, he does not intend to set a new and luminous element against the "antiquity of the *nomos*." Rather, he plays one element of prelaw against the other, or, at the very least, he tries to disentangle two elements that present themselves as being tightly interwoven at their origin.

One of the achievements of a great Sephardic linguist, perhaps the greatest linguist of the twentieth century, Émile Benveniste, entailed using purely linguistic data to reconstruct the originary features of this most ancient Indo-European institution, which the Greek called *pistis* and the Latin *fides*, and which he defined as *fidélité personnelle*, "personal loyalty." "Faith" (or trust) is the credit that one enjoys in another, the result of placing our trust in him, having consigned something like a pledge to him that links us in a relation of loyalty. For this reason faith is just as much the trust that we *grant* someone, the faith we place in someone, as it is the trust we enjoy on behalf of someone, the faith or the credit that we *possess*. In this light, the long-standing problem of the two symmetrical meanings of the term "faith," as active and passive, objective and subjective, "a (provided) guarantee" and "inspired confidence," which Eduard Fränkel had highlighted in a well-known essay, can be explained without a glitch:

> The one who holds the *fidēs* placed in him by a man has this man at his mercy. This is why *fidēs* becomes almost synonymous with *diciō* and *potestās*. In their primitive form these relations involved a certain reciprocity, placing one's *fidēs* in somebody secured in return his guarantee and his support. But this very fact underlines the inequality of the conditions. It is authority which is exercised at the same time as protection for somebody who submits to it, an exchange for, and to the extent of, his submission (Benveniste 1973, 97–98).

In this same vein, the strong tie between the two Latin terms *fides* and *credere*, which is so significant in its Christian context, becomes easily comprehensible: according to Benveniste, *credo* literally means "to give **kred*'," that is, to place magical powers in a person from whom one expects protection, and thus "to believe" in him. And because the old root-word **kred*' disappeared in Latin, the word *fides*, which expressed a very similar concept, took its place as a substantive corresponding to *credo*.

In reconstructing this notion of personal loyalty, Benveniste barely mentions the so-to-speak political aspect of this institution, in turn highlighted by Salvatore Calderone, which did not involve individuals as much ***Deditio in Fidem*** as it did the city and the people. At times of war, the enemy city could be conquered and destroyed by force (*kata kratos*) and its inhabitants killed or enslaved. But, on the other hand, what could also happen was that the weaker city could take recourse to the institution of the *deditio in fidem*, meaning that they could unconditionally surrender themselves to the hands of the enemy, making the victor hold to a more benevolent conduct (Calderone, 38–41). In this instance, the city could be saved and its inhabitants granted a personal freedom, while not being completely free. They comprised a special group, called the *dediticii*, who "gave themselves over" as what we would nowadays call stateless people. We should perhaps keep this particular group of nonslaves who were not completely free in mind when thinking of the status of the members of the messianic community according to Paul. This institution of giving oneself over was called *pistis* by the Greeks (*dounai eis pistin, peithesthai*) and *fides* by the Romans (*in fidem populi Romani venire* or *se tradere*, "to deliver oneself into the *fidēs* of the Roman people"). Let me first point out two important observations on this subject. Once again, we witness the direct connection and almost synonymous quality between faith and oath that we noted from the start. In all likelihood, this synonymy finds its raison d'être in this very context. The city and the people who were mutually linked together through the *dedito in fidem* exchanged solemn oaths to sanction this bond, yet on the other hand, as the etymological link between *fides* and *foedus* implies—well known to the Romans—this relation grants for numerous analogies to be made with a pact or treaty of alliance between people, even though modern scholars prefer to speak of "pseudotreaties" in the context of the *deditio in fidem*, in their desire to highlight the disparity between respective conditions.

In the Greco-Roman world, faith thus possesses a complex character, being both juridico-political and religious, and originating in the most ancient sphere of prelaw. But the tie to the juridical sphere never disappears, neither in Rome, where jurists elaborated on the notion of *bona fides*, a notion essential to the history of modern law, nor in Greece, where *pistis* and *pistos* referred to the credit and trust derived from contractual bonds in general.

If we want to comprehend the meaning that underlies the opposition between *pistis* and *nomos* in the Pauline text, we should keep in mind this rooting of faith in the sphere of the law—or rather, in prelaw, that is, where law, politics, and religion become tightly interwoven. In Paul, *pistis* retains something of the *deditio*, the unconditional self abandon to the power of another, which obliges the receiver as well.

Similar considerations could be made for the Hebrew *emunah*.
As you know, in the Bible Yahweh makes a *berit*, a pact or
a covenant with Israel, by virtue of which, as we read in   *Berit*
Deuteronomy 26:17–19:

> Thou hast avouched the Lord this day to be thy God, and to walk in his
> ways, and to keep to his statutes, and his commandments, and his judg-
> ments, and to hearken unto his voice . . . and you will be his special peo-
> ple, as he hath promised you, and that thou shouldest observe all his
> precepts. And on these conditions that he bestow thee high above all
> nations which he hath made, in praise, and in name, and in honor; and
> that thou mayest be an holy people to Yahweh, your God, as he hath
> spoken.

Now as much as it may embarrass those theologians who prefer to
speak of a theological intention being actualized in juridical terms,
this *berit* cannot be distinguished from a juridical pact like the one
between Jacob and Laban (Gen. 31:44 ff.). In both cases, *berit* designates a kind of sworn covenant whereby two parties are bound
together in reciprocal trust. Thus the *berit* seems to belong to the
same sphere of prelaw at the origin of what Benveniste recon-
structs as the relation of personal loyalty. The "blood of the
covenant" (Exod. 24:8, reiterated in Matt. 26:28) that Moses
sheds, half on the altar (which represents Yahweh) and half on the
people, is not so much a sacrifice as it is a sanctioning of the most
intimate union established between the two contracting parties of
the pact. This is why in Hebrew one speaks of "cutting a *berit*"
exactly in the way the Greek speaks of *horkia temnein* and the
Latin of *foedus ferire*. The problem of whether the *berit* between
Yahweh and Israel is a theological pact or a juridical pact loses significance once it is taken back to the sphere of personal loyalty and
prelaw. As we have seen, distinctions of this sort are untenable in
this sphere. (One definition of Judaism which is not that bad, is
that of an implacable reflection on the paradoxical situation that
emerges out of the desire to establish juridical relations with God.)

Thus the Hebrew word *emunah* signifies the very conduct that
should result from the *berit*, and in this way corresponds perfectly with the Greek *pistis*. In addition, according to the symmetrical

structure that defines the relation of loyalty, *emunah* is just as much the faith of men as it is the faith of Yahweh. This is seen in Deut. 7:9 where (according to the Greek of the Septuagint) *pistos* is God's attribute par excellence: "Know therefore that the Lord thy God is a faithful [*pistos* = *ne eman*] God, which keepeth covenant [*diathēkē* = *berit*] and his mercy [*ēleos* = *hesed*] with them that love him and keep his commandments to a thousand generations." Not only does the relation between faith and pact, *pistis* and the pact of personal loyalty between Yahweh and Israel, become evident in this passage, but Paul's other concept of *charis*, grace, which is opposed to laws and works of law, also finds its precursor in *hesed*, the goodness and favor that God reserves for his faithful (even if the Septuagint translates *hesed* with *ēleos* and reserves the word *charis* for *hen*).

I think that at this point it becomes clear why we can say that in Paul's setting *pistis* and *nomos* against each other, he does not merely oppose two heterogeneous elements. Rather, he brings to the fore two figures, two levels, or two elements that are present within the law—or within prelaw—in order to play them against each other, so to speak. What are these two levels? We saw that Paul calls the first *epaggelia*, "promise," or *diathēkē*, "pact," and the second *entolē*, "commandment" (or *nomos tōn entolōn*). In Genesis 15:18, the promise made by Yahweh to Abraham, which is so crucial to Paul's strategy, is defined simply as *diathēkē* and is Yahweh's originary pact with the descendants of Abraham. This pact precedes the pact of Mosaic law in every way (this is why in Ephesians 2:12 Paul refers to them as *diathēkai tēs epaggelias*, pacts of the promise). If we were to translate the Pauline antitheses into the language of modern law, we could say that Paul plays the constitution against positive law. Or even more precisely, we could say that he plays the level of constitutive power against the level of established law [*diritto costituito*]. In so doing, the Schmittian thesis on political theology ("the most meaningful concepts of the modern doctrine of the State are secularized theological concepts") receives further confirmation. The caesura between constitutive and constituted power, a divide that becomes so apparent in our times, finds its theological origins in the Pauline split between the level of faith and that of *nomos*, between personal loyalty and the positive obligation that derives from it. In this light, messianism appears as a struggle, within the law, whereby the element of the pact and constituent power leans toward setting itself against and emancipating itself from the element of the *entolē*, the norm in the strict sense. The messianic is therefore the historical process whereby the archaic link between law and religion (which finds its magical paradigm in *horkos*, oath) reaches a crises and the element of *pistis*, of faith in the pact, tends paradoxically to emancipate itself from any obligatory conduct and from positive law (from works fulfilled in carrying out the pact).

This is why we witness the theme of grace (*charis*) emerge so insistently alongside the theme of faith in Paul. Once again, as Benveniste demonstrated   Gratuitousness (Benveniste 1973, 160), *charis* essentially signifies a gratuitous service, freed from contractual obligations of counterservice and command. The significance of the opposition between law [*legge*] and grace (expressed in Romans 6:24) is readily misunderstood when not situated in its proper context, that of the rupture of the originary unity between *epaggelia* and *nomos*, law [*diritto*] and religion in the sphere of prelaw [*prediritto*].[1] It is not a matter of opposing two heterogeneous principles and excluding works in favor of faith, but of coming to terms with the aporia that emerges from this rupture. That which dissolves, along with the link between religion and law [*diritto*], is the link between service and counterservice, between execution and command. In this sense, what you have on the one side is a law that is "holy and just and good"—but which has become unobservable and incapable of producing salvation, namely the sphere of the law [*diritto*] in the strict sense—and on the other side, a faith, although originally deriving from the pact, that can make salvation operative "without law" [*senza legge*]. Having once been united in prelaw in a magical indifference, faith and law now fracture and give way to the space of gratuitousness [*gratuita*]. In the sphere of personal loyalty where faith finds its origin, faith obvi-

1. *Translator's note.* Unless indicated, all instances of the word "law" refer to the Italian "legge." In most of the European languages there are two different words for distinguishing the abstract and the concrete senses of the word *law*: in Italian *legge* and *diritto*, in Latin *lex* and *ius*, in German *Gesetzt* and *Recht* , in French *loi* and *droit*, and so on). The first of each pair refers to particular laws and so-called positive laws, i.e. laws that are actually legislated and enforced. The second of each pair is the basis in each case for the word for "rights" and relates to concepts of justice, fairness, rights, and obligation. In English, this distinction no longer is maintained.

ously implied fulfilling of acts of loyalty that sanctioned under oath. But now one element of the pact appears which constitutively exceeds any service that could seek to satisfy its exigency, thus introducing a dissymmetry and disconnect in the sphere of the law. The promise exceeds any claim that could supposedly ground itself in it, just as faith surpasses any obligation whatsoever of counterservice. Grace is that excess which, while it always divides the two elements of prelaw and prevents them from coinciding, does not even allow them to completely break apart. The *charis* issuing from this fracture between faith and obligation, between religion and law [*diritto*], cannot in turn be taken as a substantial and separate sphere, for it can only maintain itself through an antagonistic relation to faith and obligation. In other words, *charis* can only maintain itself as the insistence of a messianic exigency in the two, without which law [*diritto*] and religion would, in the long run, be condemned to atrophy.

Hence the complex relation between the spheres of grace and law in Paul, which never manage to reach a complete schism, but which, on the contrary, permit seeing in faith the fulfillment of the instance of the justice of the law (Rom. 8:4) and the law as a "pedagogue" leading to the messianic (Gal. 3:24), bearing the task of showing the impossibility of the execution of the law in a hyperbolic way (*kath'hyperbolēn*), making sin appear as such (Rom. 7:13). Nevertheless in Paul the relation between grace and sin, between gratuitousness and service is defined through a constitutive excess (*perisseia*): "But not as the offense, so is the gift of grace. For if through the offense of one, many be dead, much more the grace of God, and the gift by grace, which is by one man, Jesus Christ, has abounded to many. . . . Moreover the law entered, that the offense might abound. But where sin abounded, grace did much more abound [*hyperperisseusen*]" (Rom. 5:15–21). In one important passage, which perhaps has not been stressed enough, grace seems to even define a real "sovereignty" (*autarkeia*) of the messianic in relation to works of law: "God loves a cheerful giver. And God is able to abound all grace in you, so that always in everything having absolute sovereignty [*en panti pantole pasan autarkeian*], ye may abound with regard to every good work" (2

Cor. 9:7–8). What should be obvious is that *autarkeia* does not signify a sufficient disposition of goods (as some translations suggest), but the sovereign capacity to gratuitously carry out good works independently of the law. In Paul, there isn't any conflict between powers properly speaking; what you have is a disconnection between them, from which *charis* sovereignly emerges.

The juridical, or prejuridical, origin of the notion of faith and the situating of faith in the caesura between faith and obligation paves the way for a correct understanding of the ## The Two Covenants Pauline doctrine of the "new covenant" and of the two *diathēkai*. Mosaic law, the normative *diathēkē*, is preceded by the promise that was made to Abraham. This promise is hierarchically superior inasmuch as Mosaic law is powerless to render it inoperative— *katargein* (Gal. 3:17: "the law, which came four hundred and thirty years later, cannot annul the covenant which was previously ratified by God, and thus make the promise inoperative"). The Mosaic law of obligations and works, which is defined in 2 Corinthians 3:14 as "the old covenant" (*palai diathēkē*), is instead rendered inoperative by the Messiah. The *kainē diathēkē* (*kainē* means "new" in every sense, not just in the sense of *nea*, most recent), which Paul spoke of to the Corinthians (1 Cor. 11:25: "This cup is the new covenant in my blood"; and 2 Cor. 3:6: "Who also hath made us able ministers of the new covenant; not of the letter, but of the spirit"), represents the fulfillment of the prophesy in Jerome 31:31 ("Behold, the days come, says the Lord, that I will make a new covenant with the house of Israel, and with the house of Judah"), and goes back to the promise made to Abraham from which it draws its legitimacy.

In Galatians 4:22–26, Paul traces out an allegorical genealogy of two *diathēkai*:

It is written that Abraham had two sons, one by a slave woman, the other by a free woman. He who was born by the slave woman was born according to the flesh; but the son born by the free woman was through the promise. These things are an allegory: for these women are the two covenants; the one from mount Sinai, who bears children into bondage; this is Hagar. For this Hagar is mount Sinai in Arabia, and corresponds to the present Jerusalem, which is in bondage with her children. But the Jerusalem which is above is free, and she is our mother.

The two *diathēkai*, both of which go back to Abraham, represent two distinct genealogical lineages. Mosaic law comes from Hagar and corresponds to the servitude of commandments and obligations; the new covenant, which comes from Sarah, corresponds to the liberty of the law:

eppagelia—Abraham

Sarah
(*kainē diathēkē*)
the law of faith

Hagar
(*palaia diathēkē*)
the Mosaic law of the
commandments

katargein

The messianic instance, which takes place in historical time and renders Mosaic law inoperative, goes back genealogically before Mosaic law, toward the promise. The space that opens up between the two *diathēkai* is the space of grace. This is why the *kainē diathēkai* cannot be something like a written text containing new and diverse precepts (which is how it ends up). As stated in the extraordinary passage right before the affirmation of the new covenant, it is not a letter written in ink on tables of stone; rather, it is written with the breath of God on hearts of the flesh. In other words, it is not a text, but the very life of the messianic community, not a *writing*, but a *form of life*: *hē epistolē hemōn hymeis este*, "You are our letter" (2 Cor. 3:2)!

ℸ   This aporetic situating of grace in the fracturing of faith and law allows us to understand how, over the history of the Church, it gave way to those conflicts that emerge strongly for the first time in the Pelagian controversy, well documented by Augustine's *De natura e gratia.* According to Pelagius, grace was given to human nature once and for all through redemption. Human nature possesses it like an *inamissibile,* irrevocable, good that could never be lost, so that it always already exceeds the possibility and actuality of sin in the Christian. The Church would, however, advocate the *amissibile,* perishable, quality of grace as well as the necessity of further intervention so as to counter the loss of grace through sin. This amounts to reintroducing an openly juridical theme with regard to grace, a kind of compromise between *charis* and *nomos.* Through transgression and guilt, man constantly loses that grace which once figured as the only counterservice of loyalty to the pact. In a more general way, with the reintroduction of *nomos* into Christian theology, grace will end up occupying just as aporetic a place as does law in Judaism. A Kafkaesque universe of grace is specifically present in Christian dogma, just as a Kafkaesque universe of the law is present in Judaism.

꒯   At this point we should take a closer look at numerous analogies and divergences between Pauline *charis* and the system of *prestations totales,* or "total services,"   **Gift and Grace** described by Mauss in his book *The Gift: The Form and Reason for Exchange in Archaic Societies.* We should also question Mauss's strange silence concerning our culture's sphere of gratuitousness par excellence, the sphere of grace (in addition to using ethnographic material, Mauss also cites Greek and Roman texts and even Islamic texts). Mauss obviously conceives of the gift as preceding utilitarian services, but the determining—and simultaneously, the most aporetic—point of his doctrine is the absolute inextricability of gift and obligation. Not only is the obligation of the donor essential to potlatch, but the gift also furnishes the ground for the recipient's unconditional obligation to counterservice. In addition, as Mauss notes at the end of his book, the theory of total services requires that notions one is used to opposing (such as freedom/obligation; liberality/savings; generosity/interest; luxury/utility) become neutralized and hybridized. As is obvious in his concluding remarks, which are, in the end, social-democratic and progressivist, what is defined in *The Gift* is not a theory of gratuitousness, but a paradoxical bond between gratuitousness and obligation. (Even those who nowadays look to the gift as a fundamental social paradigm, substituting it with contract, do not have of anything other than this in mind.)

As we have seen, even in Paul, faith and grace are not simply disentangled from the sphere of the law; rather, they are placed within a complex web of relations with respect to the law. Nevertheless, in a different way than in Mauss, gratuitousness does not provide the grounds for obligatory service. Instead, it manifests itself as an irreducible excess with regard to all obligatory service. Grace does not provide the foundation for exchange and social obligations; it makes for their interruption. The messianic gesture does not found, it fulfills.

Georges Bataille sought to develop this constitutive excess of grace in his theory of the sovereignty of the unproductive expenditure (*dépense improductive*). (Odd that he fails to realize that the expression was already present in Paul!) In this endeavor, however, he transforms gratuitousness into a privileged category of acts (laughter, luxury, eroticism, etc.) that stands in opposition to utilitarian acts. It is obvious that for Paul grace cannot constitute a separate realm that is alongside that of obligation and law. Rather, grace entails nothing more than the ability to *use* the sphere of social determinations and services in its totality.

There are therefore no linguistic grounds for Buber's antithesis between Jewish *emunah* and Pauline *pistis*. As an expression of the condition that results from "cutting a pact," these terms are substantially equivalent with each other; no distinction can be made between one as "having confidence" and the other as "recognizing as true." In the additional postface to the newer German edition of *Two Types of Faith*, Flusser nevertheless discerns another meaning in Buber's distinction, understanding it as a split in faith within Christianity itself. In Christianity, according to Flusser, two types of faith cohabit each other but are so difficult to reconcile that they make for a "tragic problem, which the Christians have only just begun to recognize" (Buber, 241). The first faith is that *of* Jesus, the religion of the historical Jesus, the faith professed by him in words and actions, and the second faith is the faith *in* Jesus Christ, a faith that fully matured in the Christian community after the crucifixion and coincided with the construction of Christology and the recognition of Jesus as the only-begotten son of God, who was made man and died for the redemption of our sins.

Lessing was the first to clearly grasp this distinction in a fragment from 1780 entitled "The Religion of Christ":

Faith Divided

The religion of Christ and the Christian religion are two quite different things. The former, the religion of Christ, is that religion which as man he himself recognized and practiced. . . . The latter, the Christian religion, is that religion which accepts it as true that he was more than a man, and makes Christ himself, as such, the object of its worship. How these two religions, the religion of Christ and the Christian religion, can exist in Christ in one and the same person, is inconceivable. . . . The former, the religion of Christ, is contained in the evangelists quite differently from the Christian religion. The religion of Christ is therein contained in the clearest and most lucid language. On the other hand, the Christian religion is so uncertain and ambiguous, that there is scarcely a single passage which, in all the history of the world, has been interpreted in the same way by two men. (Lessing, 334–35)

The astuteness of Lessing's observation becomes all the more evident if, following Flusser's suggestion, we use this perspective to look, on the one hand, at the texts that comprise the New Testament, the Gospels and the Acts, and on the other, at the Letters of Paul, John, James, and so on. If only these latter texts had been preserved, our knowledge of the life of Jesus would have been far more fragmentary. (Paul hardly ever says anything concerning the historical Jesus.) And if only the first set had been preserved, we would have a very limited knowledge of Christian theology and of the Christological drama. This means that our knowledge of the faith of Jesus is limited to the Gospels, while the faith in Christ, something like Buber's *pistis*, is uniquely derived from the other texts.

In fusing Lessing's considerations with Buber's theory, Flusser grasps an antinomy that undoubtedly aids our understanding of the messianic problem and, even more so, the history of Christian theology. All of the pseudoproblems of Jesus' "messianic conscience" in fact came about in order to cover up the hiatus opened up between these two faiths. What did Jesus believe in? There is something grotesque in this question, especially if formulated in the following way: what could it mean for Jesus to believe in Jesus Christ? There is no answer to this question in the Gospels, and next to nothing is found in Mark 8:29–30, even if it is not interpolated, as certain people claim, and for good reason. "Jesus asks his disciples, 'But whom say you that I am?' And Peter answers,

'You are the Messiah [*su ei ho christos*].' And he charged them that they should tell no man of this." The same could be said for the Christological controversy that agitated the Church in the third century and culminated with Constantine's intervention in Nicea, which was inspired by the counsel of Eusebius of Caesarea, Constantine's *friseur* or personal hairdresser as Overbeck calls him. The mediation that is developed here, and which culminates in the Nicean formulation that many Catholics have repeated (*pisteuomen eis hena theon,* "We believe in one God, the almighty Father . . . and in one Lord, Jesus Christ, only-begotten son of the Father"), is a more or less successful attempt to reconcile Buber's two types of faith with Lessing's two religions.

But is this really the case in Paul? Could we also conceive of a split in faith in Paul in similar terms? I do not think so. Paul's faith starts with the resurrection, and he does not know Jesus in the flesh, only Jesus Messiah. This separation is already clear-cut in the greeting of the letter commented on at length. "Concerning his Son, who was made from the seed of David according to the flesh, he who was designated Son of God in power according to the spirit of holiness, by resurrection from the dead" (Rom. 1:3–4). And in 2 Corinthians 5:16 we read, "If we could have [or, if we had] known the Messiah in the flesh." Just as with the Jewish tradition wherein something like a "life of the Messiah" cannot exist (the Messiah—or, at least his name—was created before the creation of the world), the essential content of Pauline faith is not the life of Jesus but Jesus Messiah, crucified and risen. But what does faith in Jesus Messiah mean? How, in this instance, is the split between faith of Jesus and the faith in Jesus always and already overcome?

In answering these questions, we should start by using some linguistic data. In the Gospels the most common narrative formulas read: "Thus Jesus said to his disciples," "Jesus, ascending to Jerusalem," "Jesus entered into the temple." With the obvious exception of 1 Corinthians 11:23, these kind of diagetic sentences never occur in Paul; rather, he almost always uses his typical formula: *kyrios Iēsous christos,* "the Lord Jesus Messiah." In Acts 9:22, Luke shows the apostle in the

Belief In

synagogue affirming *hoti houtos estin ho christos,* "that that one [Jesus] is the Messiah." But this formula never occurs in the Pauline text, with the one unique exception of Romans 10:9, which we will turn to later. Instead, in his rendering of his faith, Paul uses the expression *pisteuein eis Iesoun christon,* "to believe *in* Jesus Messiah." This expression, which in the Latin translation became the canonical expression of faith, is an anomaly in Greek. *Pisteuō* is normally constructed with the dative, or with the accusative, or even with *hoti* plus a verb, in order to convey the content of faith. The Pauline formula becomes all the more significant as it never appears in the Synoptic Gospels, thus defining in a substantive way his conception of faith. It is as if, for Paul, there is no space between Jesus and Messiah for the copulative *is*; 1 Corinthians 2:2 is typical: "For I determined not to know anything among you except Jesus Messiah." He does not know that Jesus *is* the Messiah, he only knows *Jesus Messiah.* (This is how a misunderstanding could emerge later on that allowed for the syntagma *Iēsous christos* to be taken as proper name.)

From the standpoint of linguistics, this phrase is actually a nominal syntagma. The theory of the nominal

Nominal Sentence

sentence constitutes one of the most interesting chapters in linguistics. In Greek, as in Latin—as well as in Hebrew and Arabic—we often come across a proposition that is called a clause from a semantic standpoint, inasmuch as it expresses a complete assertion but does not contain a verbal predicate. There are two well-known examples in Pindar: *skias onar anthrōpos,* "from a dream the shade the man" (Pythian ode 8.95). (In current translations we read, "man is the dream of a shadow," and *ariston hydōr,* which is "best the water" [Olympian ode 1.1], usually translated as "best is water" or "water is the best of things.") But the work of contemporary linguists, especially that of Meillet and Benveniste, has shown us that it is quite simply wrong to interpret a nominal sentence as having an implied or present (zero degree) copula. The nominal sentence and the sentence with an explicit copula do not only differ morphologically, but semantically as well. "The nominal sentence and the sentence with *esti* do not make assertions in the same way and do not belong on the same plane. The first is from discourse, the second, from narration. The one establishes an absolute; the other describes a situation" (Benveniste 1971, 142). We should think through the philosophical implications of Benveniste's distinction. In Indo-European languages, we usually distinguish between two fundamental meanings of the verb *to be*, the existential meaning (the position of an existence, such as "the world is") and the predicative meaning (the predication of a quality or essence, "the world is eternal"). The fundamental division in ontology, the ontology of existence and the ontology of essence, stems from this double meaning. (The relation between these two ontologies is the relation of a presupposition: that all that is said is on the *hupokeimenon* of existence; cf. Aristotle, *Categories* 2a35). Yet the nominal sentence escapes this distinction, presenting a third type irreducible to the two other types: it is this one that requires thought.

What then does it mean that in Paul faith is expressed in the nominal syntagma "Jesus Messiah" and not the verbal syntagma "Jesus is the Messiah"? Paul does not believe that Jesus possesses the quality of being the Messiah; he believes in "Jesus Messiah" and that is all. *Messiah* is not a predicate tacked onto the subject *Jesus*, but something that is inseparable from him, without, however, constituting a proper name. For Paul, this is faith; it is an experience of being beyond existence and essence, as much beyond subject as beyond predicate. But isn't this precisely what happens in love? Love does not allow for copulative predication, it never has a quality or an essence as its object. "I love beautiful-brunette-tender Mary," not "I love Mary because she is beautiful, brunette, tender," in the sense of her possessing such and such an attribute. The moment when I realize that my beloved has such-and-such a quality, or such-and-such a defect, then I have irrevocably stepped out of love, even if, as is often the case, I continue to believe that I love her, especially after having given good reason for continuing to do so. Love has no reason, and this is why, in Paul, it is tightly interwoven with faith. This is why, as we read in the hymn in 1 Corinthians 13:4–7, "Love is magnanimous; it acts kindly. Love does not envy; love does not boast; it does not become haughty. It does not behave improperly; it does not seek its own; it is not provoked; it does not keep a record of evil. It does not rejoice over injustice, but it rejoices with the truth. It covers all things, believes all things, hopes all things, endures all things."

But what then is the world of faith? Not a world of substance and qualities, not a world in which the grass is green, the sun is warm, and the snow is white. No, it is not a world of predicates, of existences and of essences, but a world of indivisible events, in which I do not judge, nor do I believe that the snow is white and the sun is warm, but I am transported and displaced in the snow's-being-white and in the sun's-being-warm. In the end, it is a world in which I do not believe that Jesus, such-and-such a man, is the Messiah, only-begotten son of God, begotten and not created, cosubstantial in the Father. I only believe in Jesus Messiah; I am carried away and enraptured in him, in such a way that "I do not live, but the Messiah lives in me" (Gal. 2:20).

For Paul, this experience is above all an experience of the word, and this should be our starting point. The two dense nominal syntagmas in ### The Word of Faith Romans 10:17 categorically affirm "The faith from hearing, the hearing through the word of the Messiah." From the perspective of faith, to hear a word does not entail asserting the truth of any semantic content, nor does it simply entail renouncing understanding, as is implicit in the Pauline critique of glossolalia in 1 Corinthians 14. What then is the right relation to the word of faith? How does faith speak and what does hearing its word entail?

Paul defines the experience of the word of faith (*to rēma tes pisteōs*) in an important passage. Let us read this passage (Rom. 10:6–10) carefully.

But the just of faith says this: Do not say in your heart, "Who will go up into Heaven?" that is, to bring down the Messiah; or, "Who will go down into the abyss?" that is, to bring the Messiah up from the dead.

But what does it say? "The word is near you, in your mouth and in your heart," this is the word of faith [*to rēma tēs pisteōs*] which we proclaim. Because if you confess [*homologein*, literally, "to say the same thing"] Lord Jesus with your mouth, and believe in your heart that God raised Him from the dead, you will be saved. For with the heart one believes unto righteousness, and with the mouth one confesses unto salvation.

Paul is both paraphrasing and emending Deuteronomy 30:11–14, concerning the law God gives to the Jews:

For this command which I am commanding you today is not too high above you, nor is it too far off. It is not in the heavens that you should say, Who shall go up into the heavens for us, and bring it to us, and cause us to hear it, that we may do it? And it is not beyond the sea that you should say, Who shall cross over for us to the region beyond the sea and take it for us, and cause us to hear it, that we may do it? For the word is very near to you, in your mouth and in your heart, and in your hands that you may do it.

Having just affirmed that the Messiah is the *telos* of the law, Paul, in a typical gesture of hermeneutic violence, transfers onto faith and the Messiah what in Deuteronomy referred to Mosaic law. He substitutes the sea for the abyss, the *sheol* in which the Messiah descended, and takes out "and in your hands that you may do it," which referred to works of law and was actually an addition to the Septuagint. The word nearby, which was a word of command, now becomes a "word of faith." This is what Paul attempts to define in adding on verses 9 and 10. "If you confess Lord Jesus with your mouth. . . . " The word *homologein*, which Jerome translates as *confiteri* and which from that point on became the technical term for the profession of faith, signifies saying the same thing, making one word agree with another (hence, contractual agreement), or making it agree with a given reality (for example, in the correspondence between *logoi* and *erga*, "words" and "works"). But in Paul, the correspondence is not between different words, or between words and deeds; rather, this correspondence is internal to the word itself, between mouth and heart. In this light, *eggys*, "near," is a particularly interesting word. Not only does it signify nearness in space, but, above all, temporal proximity (hence, for example, Rom 13:11). The correspondence between mouth and heart in the word of faith is that of a nearing and almost coinciding in time. On the other hand, *eggys* etymologically derives from a root that indicates the openness or emptiness of the hand, and thus the act of giving or putting something in the hand. In this fashion *eggyēs* signifies the token put in one's hand, and the Greek ear would undoubtedly hear the resonance between the two terms, especially since in Hebrews 7:22 *eggyos* is Jesus, "the guarantor of a better covenant." The nearness is also a token and a guarantee of efficacy. The experience of the word of faith thus does not entail the experience of a denotative character of a word, its referring to things, but an experience of the word's being near, held in the harmony between mouth and heart, and, by means of this *homologein*, the word becomes the deliverer of salvation. The fact that Paul, for the first and only time, constructs *pisteuein* with *hoti* does not contradict this self-referential quality of the word of faith. As he clarifies immediately after, it is a matter of a purely logical articulation of the salvational efficacy of the word via two moments. The belief in the heart is neither a holding true, nor the description of an interior state, but a justification; only the professing of the mouth accomplishes salvation. Neither a glossolalia deprived of meaning, nor mere denotative word, the word of faith enacts its meaning through its utterance. When thinking of the nearness of the mouth and heart, we have to venture something like a performative efficacy of the word of faith realized in its very pronouncement.

Ever since John L. Austin defined the category of the performative in *How to Do Things with Words*, it took on increasing popularity not only with linguists, but with philosophers and jurists as well. The **Performative** performative is a linguistic enunciation that does not describe a state of things, but immediately produces a real fact. The paradox (which analytic philosophy summarized in the formula *speech act*) is that the meaning of an enunciation (expressed in syntagmas such as "I swear," "I declare," or "I promise") coincides with a reality that is itself produced through its utterance (this is why the performative can never be either true or false). In commenting on Austin's theses, Benveniste took care to distinguish what he took to be the performative, in the true sense of the term, from other linguistic categories with which the philosopher had muddied it (such as the imperative "Open the door!" or the sign "Dog" on a fence). He recognized that the speech can only function in circumstances, which, while authorizing it as an act, guarantee its effectiveness. "Anyone can shout in the public square, 'I decree a general mobilization,' and as it cannot be an *act* because the requisite authority is lacking, such an utterance is no more than words; it reduces itself to futile clamor, childishness, or lunacy" (Benveniste 1971, 236).

In this manner, what the great linguist brought to light was the closely knit link between the sphere of the performative and the sphere of the law [*diritto*] (which was affirmed in the close etymological tie between *ius* and *iurare*). The law [*diritto*] could be defined as the realm in which all language tends to assume a performative value. To do things with words could even be considered as a residue in language of a magical-juridical state of human existence, in which words and deeds, linguistic expression and real efficacy, coincide.

But how does the performative enact its end? What allows a certain syntagma to acquire, by means of its mere pronouncement, the efficacy of the deed, disproving the ancient maxim that words and deeds are separated by an abyss? Linguists make no mention of it, as though they come up against one final magical stratum of language, almost as though they truly believed in it. What is obviously most important here is the self-referential quality in each speech act. Yet this self-referentiality is not exhausted in the fact that the performative, as Benveniste notes, takes itself as its own referent inasmuch as it refers to a reality that it itself produces. Rather, what should be highlighted is that the self-referentiality of the performative is always constituted through a suspension of the normal denotative function of language. The performative verb is actually constructed with a *dictum* that, taken on its own, is of a purely constative nature, without which it would remain empty and inefficient. (*I swear* and *I declare* only are of value if they are followed or preceded by a *dictum* that complements them.) It is this constative quality of the *dictum* that is suspended and put into question at the very moment that it becomes the object of a performative syntagma. This is how the constatives "Yesterday I was in Rome" or "The population is mobilized" stop being constatives if they are respectively preceded by the performative "I swear" or "I declare." The performative thus substitutes normal denotative relations between words and deeds with a self-referential relation that, in ousting the first, posits itself as decisive fact. What is essential here is not a relation of truth between words and things, but rather, the pure form of the relation between language and world, now generating linkages and real effects. Just as, in the state of exception, law suspends its own application in order to ground its enforcement in a normal case, so too in the performative does language suspend its own denotation only in order to establish links with things. The ancient formula of the twelve tables that expresses the performative power of law [*diritto*] (*uti lingua nuncupassit, ita ius esto,* "as the tongue has uttered, thus be the law") does not mean that what is said is factually true, only that the *dictum* is itself a *factum,* and as such, obliges those among whom it was uttered.

This means that the performative bears witness to a phase in human culture in which—contrary to what we are used to thinking—language does not merely refer to things on the basis of a constative or truth relation, but through a very particular kind of operation, in which the word swears on itself, it itself becomes the fundamental fact. One could even say that what is produced by breaking the originary magical-performative relation between word and things is precisely the denotative relation between language and word.

How then should we understand Pauline *homologein* with regard to this performative sphere whose prejuridical paradigm is oath? In the last years of his life, Michel Foucault was working on a book on confession. Traces remain in a 1981 seminar given at the Catholic University of Leuven. Foucault places confession in the sphere of what he calls "forms of truth-telling [*véridiction*]," which insists less (or not only) upon the assertional content of confession, than upon the act itself of uttering truth. This act constitutes something like a performative, since, through confession, the subject is bound to the truth itself and changes his relation to others in addition to himself.[1] In the seminar at Leuven, Foucault begins by opposing confession and oath, which, in the ancient world represented the archaic form of the trial and—before moving onto his analysis of confession in the modern trial—he looks at the practice of Christian *exomologēsis*, the penitential confession of sins, which was formalized over the twelfth and thirteenth centuries. But between these two forms of *veridiction* or truth-telling—between the sacramental performative and the penitential performative—lies another that Foucault does not touch upon. This very form is the confession of faith documented in the Pauline passage on which we have been commenting. Between the performative of the oath and of penance, the *performativum fidei* defines the originary messianic—that is, Christian—experience of the word.

What is the relation between the *performativum fidei* and the penitential and sacramental performative? As is the case with every linguistic act, so too with Paul does the word of faith rise forth to go beyond the denotative relation between language and the world, toward a different and more originary status of the word. In the same way, for Paul, *homologia* does not consist in a relation between words and things, but in language itself in the nearness between mouth and heart. Each revelation is always and above all a revelation of language itself, an experience of a pure event of the word that exceeds every signification and is, nevertheless, animated by two opposing tensions. The first, which Paul calls *nomos*, attempts to encapsulate the excess by articulating it in precepts and in semantic contents. The second, which coin-

Performativum fidei

---

1. *Translator's note.* Agamben is referring to unpublished lectures entitled "Mal faire, dire vrai," given in 1981 in Leuven. Additional traces of these lectures can be found in "The Hermeneutics of the Self," in Foucault 1999, and in Foucault 1993.

cides with *pistis*, is oriented, on the contrary, toward maintaining it open beyond any determinate signification. It follows that there are two ways to go beyond the denotative function of language toward the experience of its event. The first, according to the oath paradigm, attempts to use it as a means to ground contract and obligation. For the other, however, the experience of the pure word opens up the space for gratuitousness and use. The latter is an expression of the subject's freedom ("our freedom which we have in the Messiah"; Gal. 2:3); the former is the expression of his subjection to a codified system of norms and articles of faith. (Already at the beginning of the fourth century, one finds a shift in conciliar symbols from the act of *homologein* and the experience of the nearness of the word of faith to the assertive dogmatic content of the confession.) As the history of the Church clearly demonstrates—as does that of *societas humana* in its entirety—the dialectic between these two experiences of the word is essential. If, as it inevitably happens and seems to be happening again today, the second falls to the wayside leaving only the word of *nomos* in absolute force, and if the *performativum fidei* is completely covered by the *performativum sacramenti*, then the law itself stiffens and atrophies and relations between men lose all sense of grace and vitality. The juridicizing of all human relations in their entirety, the confusion between what we may believe, hope, and love, and what we are supposed to do and not supposed to do, what we are supposed to know and not know, not only signal the crisis of religion but also, and above all, the crisis of law. The messianic is the instance, in religion and equally in law, of an exigency of fulfillment which—in putting origin and end in a tension with each other—restores the two halves of prelaw in unison. At this same moment, it shows the impossibility of their ever coinciding. (This is why the actual opposition between secular States, founded uniquely on law, and fundamentalist States, founded uniquely on religion, is only a seeming opposition that hides a similar political decline.) But in this, it points, beyond prelaw, toward an experience of the word, which—without tying itself denotatively to things, or taking itself as a thing, without being infinitely suspended in its openness or fastening itself up in dogma—manifests itself as a pure and common potentiality of saying, open to a free and gratuitous use of time and the world.

(•) The interpretation of the "word of faith" in Romans 10:9–10 in terms of a potentiality that exists as potentiality is already found in Origen. In *De anima* (417a21 ff.), Aristotle distinguishes between two figures of potentiality. The first is the generic one, according to which one says of a child that he can become a grammarian, craftsman, or pilot. The second is the effective potential (or potential according to *exis*), which belongs to the one who already enacts them. In the first, the passage to the act implies an exhaustion and destruction of potential. In the second, however, we find a conservation (*sōtēria*) of potential in the act and something like a giving of potentiality to itself (*epidosis eis heautō*). In applying the Aristotelian distinction to the Pauline text, Origen sets up the opposition between the merely virtual nearness of God's word to every man and to the meaning that actually exists (*efficacia vel efficentia*) in the one who confesses the word of faith in his mouth. "In this way, as well, then one must believe that Christ, who is the Word of God, is indeed potentially near us, i.e., near every human being, just as language is to children; but it will be said that he is in me in actuality when I shall have confessed with my mouth that Jesus is Lord and believed in my heart that God raised him from the dead" (Origen 2002, 138–39).

The word of faith manifests itself as the effective experience of a pure power [*potenza*] of saying that, as such, does not coincide with any denotative proposition, or with the performative value of a speech act. Rather, it exists as an absolute nearness of the word. One therefore understands why, for Paul, messianic power finds its *telos* in weakness. The act itself of a pure potentiality of saying, a word that always remains close to itself, cannot be a signifying word that utters true opinions on the state of things, or a juridical performative that posits itself as fact. There is no such thing as a content of faith, and to profess the word of faith does not mean formulating true propositions on God and the world. To believe in Jesus Messiah does not mean believing something about him, *legein ti kata tinos*, and the attempt of the Councils to formulate the content of faith in *symbola* can only be taken as a sublime irony. "Messianic and weak" is therefore that potentiality of saying,

The Nearness of the Word

which, in dwelling near the word not only exceeds all that is said, but also exceeds the act of saying itself, the performative power of language. This is the remnant of potentiality that is not consumed in the act, but is conserved in it each time and dwells there. If this remnant of potentiality is thus weak, if it cannot be accumulated in any form of knowledge or dogma, and if it cannot impose itself as a law, it does not follow that it is passive or inert. To the contrary, it acts in its own weakness, rendering the word of law inoperative, in de-creating and dismantling the states of fact or of law, making them freely available for use. *Katargein* and *chrēsthai* are the act of a potentiality that fulfills itself in weakness. That this potentiality finds its *telos* in weakness means that it does not simply remain suspended in infinite deferral; rather, turning back toward itself, it fulfills and deactivates the very excess of signification over every signified, it extinguishes languages (1 Cor. 13:8). In this way, it bears witness to what, unexpressed and insignificant, remains in use forever near the word.

You may recall the image of the hunchback dwarf in Benjamin's first thesis on the philosophy of history—a dwarf is hiding beneath a chessboard and, through his movements, assures victory to the mechanical puppet dressed in the garb of a Turk. Benjamin borrows this image from Poe; however, in transposing this image onto the terrain of the philosophy of history, he adds that the dwarf is in fact theology, who "today, as we know is wizened and has to keep out of sight," and if historical materialism knew how to put theology to use, it would win this historical battle, thus defeating its fearful adversary.

Benjamin invites us to conceive the very text of the philosophy of history as a chessboard upon which a crucial theoretical battle unfolds, and which, we are to assume, is even lent a hand by a hidden theologian concealed between the lines of the text. Who is this hunchback theologian, so well hidden by the author in his theses that not a single person yet has identified him? Is it possible to find clues and traces in the text that would allow us to name what should never be seen?

In one of the comments on section N of his index cards (which contains notes on a theory of consciousness), Citation Benjamin writes, "this work should fully develop the art of citing without citation marks" (Benjamin 1974–89, 5: 572). As you know, citation serves a strategic function in Benjamin's work. Just as through citation a secret meeting takes place between past generations and ours, so too between the writing of the past and the present a similar kind of meeting transpires; citations function as go-betweens in this encounter. It is therefore not surprising that they must be discrete and know how to perform their work incognito. This work consists not so much in conserving, but in destroying something. In his essay on Kraus we read, "[Citation] summons the word by its name, wrenches it destructively from its context, but precisely thereby calls it back to its origin"; at the same time it "saves and punishes" (Benjamin 1999b, 454). In the essay "What is Epic Theatre?" Benjamin writes, "to quote involves the interruption of its context" (Benjamin 1968, 151). Brechtian epic theater, to which Benjamin refers in this text, proposes to ensure that gesture be citable. "An actor," he writes, "must be able to space his gestures the way a typesetter produces spaced type" (Benjamin 1968, 151).

The German word translated as "spacing" is *sperren*. It refers to the method in typography, not exclusive to German, of substituting italics with a script that places a space between each letter of that word that is highlighted. Benjamin himself uses this method each time he uses a typewriter. From a palaeographic standpoint, this convention is the opposite of how scribes used abbreviations for reoccurring words in manuscripts that did not need to be read in their entirety (or, as is the case with Ludwig Traube's *nomina sacra*, for words that should not be read). These spaced words are, in a certain way, hyperread: they are read twice, and, as Benjamin suggests, this double reading may be the palimpsest of citation.

If we now turn to the *Handexemplar* of the *Theses*, you will see that Benjamin uses this typographical convention in second thesis. In the fourth line from the end, we read, *Dann ist uns wie jedem Geschlecht, das vor uns war, eine s c h w a c h e messianische Kraft mitgegeben*, "Like every generation that preceded us, we have been endowed with a w e a k messianic power." Why is *weak* spaced this way? Which time of citability is at stake here? And why is messianic power, to which Benjamin confides the redemption of the past, weak?

According to my knowledge, only one text explicitly theorizes

Walter Benjamin, *Handexemplar* of the *Theses on the Philosophy of History*, second thesis.

on the weakness of messianic power. As you may have guessed, the text is 2 Corinthians 12:9–10, which we have commented on at length, wherein Paul, having asked the Messiah to free him from that thorn in his flesh, hears the answer, *hē gar dynamis en astheneia teleitai*, "power fulfills itself in weakness." "Therefore," the apostle adds, "I take pleasure in infirmities, in reproaches, in necessities, in persecutions, in distresses for the sake of the Messiah: for when I am weak, then I am strong [*dynatos*]." The fact that this is an actual citation without citation marks is confirmed by Luther's translation, which Benjamin most likely had before his eyes. What Jerome translates as *virtus in infirmitate perficitur*, Luther translates, like the majority of modern translators, as *denn mein Kraft ist in den schwachen Mechtig*. Both of the terms (*Kraft* and *schwache*, power and weakness) are present, and it is precisely this hyperlegibility, this secret presence of the Pauline text in the *Theses*, that is signaled discretely by this spacing.

You can imagine that I was moved (to quite a degree) when discovering this hidden (although not so hidden) Pauline citation in the text within the *Theses*. To my knowledge, Taubes was the only scholar to note the possible influence of Paul on Benjamin, but his hypothesis referred to a text from the 1920s, the *Theological-*

Political Fragment, which he connected to Romans 8:19–23. Taubes's intuition is certainly on the mark; nevertheless, in that particular instance it is not only impossible to speak of citations (except perhaps in the case of Benjamin's term *Vergängnis,* "caducity," which could correspond to the Lutheran translation of verse 21, *vergengliches Wesen*), but there are also substantial differences between the two texts. While, for Paul, creation is unwillingly subjected to caducity and destruction and for this reason groans and suffers while awaiting redemption, for Benjamin, who reverses this in an ingenious way, nature is messianic precisely because of its eternal and complete caducity, and the rhythm of this messianic caducity is happiness itself.

Once the Pauline citation in the second thesis is uncovered—(I should remind you that the *Theses on the Philosophy of History* are one of Benjamin's last works and are a kind Image of testamentary compendium of his messianic conception of history)—the way is open to identify the hunchback theologian who secretly guides the hands of the puppet of historical materialism. One of the most enigmatic concepts in Benjamin's later thought is that of *Bild,* image. It appears several times in the text of the *Theses,* most markedly in the fifth thesis, where we read: "The true image [*das wahre Bild*] of the past *flees* by. The past can be seized only as an image which flashes up at the instant when it can be recognized and is never seen again. . . . For every image of the past that is not recognized by the present as one of its own concerns threatens to disappear irretrievably" (Benjamin 1968, 255). Several fragments in which Benjamin seeks to define this true *terminus technicus* of his conception of history are left, yet none is as clear as MS 474: "It is not that what is past casts its light on what is present, or what is present its light on what is past; rather, image is that wherein what has been comes together in a flash with the now to form a constellation. For while the relation of the present to the past is purely temporal (continuous), the relation of what-has-been to the now is dialectical, in leaps and bounds" (Benjamin 1999a, 463).[1]

1. In German, Benjamin 1974–89, 1: 1242 ff.

Bild thus encompasses, for Benjamin, all things (meaning all objects, works of art, texts, records, or documents) wherein an instant of the past and an instant of the present are united in a constellation where the present is able to recognize the meaning of the past and the past therein finds its meaning and fulfillment. We already found a similar constellation in Paul between past and future in terms of what we called a "typological relation." Even in this instance, a moment from the past (Adam, the passage through the Red Sea, the manna, etc.) must be recognized as the *typos* of the messianic now, and furthermore, as we have seen, messianic *kairos* is the relation itself. But why then does Benjamin speak of *Bild*, or image, and not of type or figure (the term used by the Vulgate)? Well, in this case, we have one more textual confirmation that permits our referring to an actual citation without citation marks. Luther translates Romans 5:14 (*typos tou mellontos*, "the type of the coming man") as *welcher ist ein Bilde des der zukunfftig war*, "he who is an image of the one who was to come" (1 Cor. 10:6 is rendered as *Furbilde*, and in Heb. 9:24 *antitypos* is rendered as *Gegenbilde*). Benjamin also spaces out words in this text, but he only does so three words after *Bild* for a word that seems to have no need to be highlighted. The passage states: *das wahre Bild der Vergangenheit h u s c h t vorbei* ("the true image of the past f l e e s by"), which may also be an allusion to 1 Corinthians 7:31 (*paragei gar to schēma tou kosmou toutou*, "for passing away is the figure of this world"), from which Benjamin may have taken the idea that the image of the past runs the risk of disappearing completely if the present fails to recognize itself in it.

You will undoubtedly recall that in the Pauline letters, the concepts of *typos* and *anakephalaiōsis*, recapitulation, are tightly intertwined, together defining messianic time. The first is also present in Benjamin's text in a particularly significant place, right at the end of the last thesis (which, after the discovery of the *Handexemplar*, is not the eighteenth, but the nineteenth thesis). Let us turn to the passage concerned: "Die Jetztzeit, die als Modell der Messianichen in einer ungeheuren Abbreviatur die Geschichte der ganzen Menschheit zusammenfasst, fällt haarscharf mit d e r Figur zusammen, die Geschichte der Menschheit im Universum macht (Benjamin 1974-89, 703) [Actuality, which, as a model of messianic time, comprises the entire history of mankind in an enormous abridgement, coincides exactly with *t h a t* figure which the history of mankind has in the universe (my translation)]."

Concerning the term *Jetztzeit*: in one of the manuscripts of the theses—the only manuscript in the technical sense of the term, owned by Hannah Arendt—as soon as the word   *Jetztzeit* is written for the first time in the fourteenth thesis, it appears in quotation marks. (Benjamin was writing by hand, so it was impossible for him to space the letters out, *sperren*.) This gave his first Italian translator, Renato Solmi, reason to translate the word as "now-time" [*tempo-ora*], which, although it is an arbitrary choice (since the German word simply means actuality), nevertheless embodies something of Benjamin's intention. After all we have said in this seminar about *ho nyn kairos* as a technical designation of messianic time in Paul, we must not overlook the literal correlation between the two terms ("the of-now-time"). All the more so, since recently in German the term harbors purely negative and anti-messianic connotations. Thus, from Schopenhauer ("This one here—our time—calls itself by a name that it bestowed upon itself, a name that is as characteristic as it is euphemistic: *Jetzt-Zeit*. Yes, precisely *Jetztzeit*, meaning, only the now is thought and the time that comes and judges is not even glanced at"; Schopenhauer, 213–14), to Heidegger ("What we call now-time [*Jetzt-Zeit*] is everyday time as it appears in the clock that counts the 'nows'. . . . When [these *Jetzt-Zeit*] are covered up, the ecstatic and horizonal constitution of temporality is *levelled off*"; Heidegger 1962, 474). Benjamin dispels this negative connotation and endows the term with the same qualities as those pertaining to the *ho nyn kairos* in Paul's paradigm of messianic time.

Let us go back to the problem of recapitulation. The last sentence of the thesis—messianic time as an enormous abridgment of the entire history—seems to clearly reiterate Ephesians 1:10 ("all things are recapitulated in the Messiah"). But even in this instance, if we look at Luther's translation, we immediately can tell that this reiteration is actually a citation without quotation marks: *alle ding zusamen verfasset würde in Christo*. Each time, the verb (*zusam-*

menfassen) corresponds to Pauline *anakephalaiōsasthai*.

This should be enough to prove a textual correspondence, and not mere conceptual correspondence, between the theses and the letters. In this light, the entire vocabulary of the theses appears to be truly stamped Pauline. It will not come as a surprise then that the term *redemption* (*Erlösung*)—an absolutely critical concept in Benjamin's notion of historical knowledge—is the term that Luther uses to convey Pauline *apolytrōsis*, just as crucial to the Letters. Whether this Pauline notion is Hellenistic in its origin (from the divine deliverance of the slaves, according to Deissmann), or strictly juridical, or the two together (which is most likely), in any case this orientation toward the past characteristic of Benjamin's messianism finds its canonic moment in Paul.

But there is another clue, an external clue, which allows us to infer that Scholem himself knew of this closeness between Benjamin's thought and Paul's. Scholem's attitude toward Paul, an author he knew well and once characterized as "the most outstanding example known to us of a revolutionary Jewish mystic" (Scholem 1965, 14), is certainly not lacking in ambiguity. Yet the discovery of a Pauline inspiration in aspects of his friend's messianic thought must have bothered him, although he certainly never would have raised the issue himself. Nevertheless, in one of his books—just as cautiously as when, in a book on Sabbatai Sevi, he establishes a relation between Paul and Nathan of Gaza—he seems to actually suggest, albeit in a cryptic fashion, that Benjamin may have identified with Paul. This occurs in his interpretation of *Agesilaus Santander*, the enigmatic fragment written by Benjamin in Ibiza in August 1933. Scholem's interpretation is based on the hypothesis that the name Agesilaus Santander, in which Benjamin seems to refer to himself, is actually an anagram for *der Angelus Satanas* (the angel Satan). If, as I believe to be the case, you keep in mind this *aggelos satana* who appears as a "thorn in the flesh" in 2 Corinthians 12:7, it is not so surprising that Scholem points to this very passage in Paul as Benjamin's possible source. The allusion is a fleeting one and never occurs again, yet if you take into account the fact that both Benjamin's text and the

Pauline passage are markedly autobiographic, this would imply that by mentioning his friend's evocation of his secret relation to the angel, Scholem is implying an identification with Paul on the part of Benjamin.

Whatever the case may be, there is no reason to doubt that these two fundamental messianic texts of our tradition, separated by almost two thousand years, both written in a situation of radical crisis, form a constellation whose time of legibility has finally come today, for reasons that invite further reflection. *Das Jetzt der Lesbarkeit*, "the now of legibility" (or of "knowability," *Erkennbarkeit*) defines a genuinely Benjaminian hermeneutic principle, the absolute opposite of the current principle according to which each work may become the object of infinite interpretation at any given moment (doubly infinite, in the sense that interpretations are never exhaustive and function independently of any historical-temporal situation). Benjamin's principle instead proposes that every work, every text, contains a historical index which indicates both its belonging to a determinate epoch, as well as its only coming forth to full legibility at a determinate historical moment. As Benjamin wrote in a note, in which he confided his most extreme messianic formulation and which will aptly conclude our seminar,

Each now is the now of a particular knowability (*Jedes Jetzt ist das Jetzt einer bestimmten Erkennbarkeit*). In it, truth is charged to the bursting point with time. (This point of explosion, and nothing else, is the death of the *intentio*, which thus coincides with the birth of authentic historical time, the time of truth.) It is not that what is past casts its light on what is present, or what is present its light on what is past; rather, image is that wherein what has been comes together in a flash with the now to form a constellation. In other words: image is dialectics at a standstill. For while the relation of the present to the past is purely temporal, the relation of what has been to the now is dialectical: not temporal in nature but imagistic [*bildlich*]. Only dialectical images are genuinely historical—that is, not archaic—images. The image that is read—which is to say, the image in the now of its recognizability—bears to the highest degree the imprint of the perilous critical moment on which all reading is founded. (Benjamin 1999a, 463)

Appendix: Interlinear Translation of Pauline Texts

From the Letter to the Romans:

1: 1–7

1 Παῦλος δοῦλος Χριστοῦ   Ἰησοῦ, κλητὸς
Paul   slave   of [the] Messiah   Jesus   called

ἀπόστολος, ἀφωρισμένος εἰς εὐαγγέλιον   θεοῦ,   2 ὁ
emissary   separated   unto [the] announcement   of God,   which

προεπηγγείλατο   διὰ   τῶν προφητῶν αὐτοῦ ἐν γραφαῖς ἁγίαις
[he] promised beforehand through the   prophets   of him   in   holy writings

3 περὶ   τοῦ υἱοῦ αὐτοῦ τοῦ   γενομένου ἐκ σπέρματος
concerning the   son   of him   the [one] having come   from [the] seed

Δαυὶδ κατὰ   σάρκα,   4 τοῦ ὁρισθέντος υἱοῦ θεοῦ ἐν
of David according to [the] flesh,   marked out as   son   of God in

δυνάμει κατὰ   πνεῦμα ἁγιωσύνης ἐξ ἀναστάσεως
power   according to [the] spirit of holiness   by [the] resurrection

νεκρῶν,   Ἰησοῦ Χριστοῦ τοῦ κυρίου ἡμῶν,   5 δι'
of [the] dead, of Jesus Messiah   the Lord   of us,   through

οὗ   ἐλάβομεν χάριν καὶ ἀποστολὴν εἰς ὑπακοὴν
whom we received grace   and [the] mandate   unto obedience

πίστεως ἐν   πᾶσιν τοῖς ἔθνεσιν ὑπὲρ τοῦ ὀνόματος
of [the] faith among all   the   people   for   the   name

αὐτοῦ,   6 ἐν   οἷς ἐστε καὶ ὑμεῖς κλητοὶ Ἰησοῦ Χριστοῦ,
of him,   among whom are   also   you   called   by Jesus Messiah,

7 πᾶσιν τοῖς οὖσιν ἐν Ῥώμῃ ἀγαπητοῖς θεοῦ, κλητοῖς
  to all   those being in Rome   beloved   of God, called

ἁγίοις· χάρις ὑμῖν καὶ εἰρήνη ἀπὸ θεοῦ πατρὸς ἡμῶν
saints; grace to you and peace   from God [the] father of us

καὶ κυρίου Ἰησοῦ Χριστοῦ.
and [the] Lord Jesus   Messiah.

1:14–17

14 Ἕλλησίν τε καὶ βαρβάροις, σοφοῖς τε καὶ
  To [the] Greeks - and to [the] barbarians, to [the] wise - and

ἀνοήτοις ὀφειλέτης εἰμί· 15 οὕτως τὸ κατ' ἐμὲ πρόθυμον
to [the] unwise [a] debtor   I am;   thus the part of me desire

καὶ ὑμῖν τοῖς ἐν Ῥώμῃ εὐαγγελίσασθαι. 16 οὐ γὰρ
also to you those in Rome to announce the good news.   For not

ἐπαισχύνομαι τὸ εὐαγγέλιον· δύναμις γὰρ θεοῦ ἐστιν
am I ashamed of the announcement; for [the] power   of God is

εἰς σωτηρίαν παντὶ τῷ πιστεύοντι, Ἰουδαίῳ τε πρῶτον
unto salvation for every -   believer,   to [the] Jew - first

καὶ Ἕλληνι. 17 δικαιοσύνη γὰρ θεοῦ ἐν αὐτῷ
and to [the] Greek.   For [the] justice   of God in him

ἀποκαλύπτεται ἐκ πίστεως εἰς πίστιν, καθὼς γέγραπται·
is revealed   from faith   to faith,   as   [it] is written:

ὁ δὲ δίκαιος ἐκ πίστεως ζήσεται.
the -   just   by faith   will live.

2:9–16

9 θλῖψις καὶ στενοχωρία ἐπὶ πᾶσαν ψυχὴν ἀνθρώπου
Tribulation and distress   to every   soul   of man

τοῦ κατεργαζομένου τὸ κακόν, Ἰουδαίου τε πρῶτον καὶ
who puts to work   - evil,   to [the] Jew - first   and

Ἕλληνος· 10 δόξα δὲ καὶ τιμὴ καὶ εἰρήνη παντὶ τῷ
to [the] Greek: glory - and honor and peace   to each one

ἐργαζομένῳ τὸ ἀγαθόν, Ἰουδαίῳ τε πρῶτον καὶ Ἕλληνι.
working   the good,   to [the] Jew - first   and to [the] Greek.

11 οὐ γὰρ ἐστιν προσωπολημψία παρὰ τῷ θεῷ.
For not is [there] [a] preference of faces according to -   God.

12 Ὅσοι γὰρ ἀνόμως ἥμαρτον, ἀνόμως καὶ ἀπολοῦνται·
For as many as without law sinned,   lawless   also will perish;

καὶ ὅσοι ἐν νόμῳ ἥμαρτον, διὰ νόμου κριθήσονται·
and as many as in [the] law sinned, through [the] law will be judged:

13 οὐ γὰρ οἱ ἀκροαταὶ νόμου δίκαιοι παρὰ [τῷ] θεῷ,
For not [are] the hearers of [the] law just in - God,

ἀλλ' οἱ ποιηταὶ νόμου δικαιωθήσονται. 14 ὅταν γὰρ
but the makers of [the] law will be justified. For whenever

ἔθνη τὰ μὴ νόμον ἔχοντα φύσει τὰ τοῦ νόμου
peoples who not law have by nature the [things] of the law

ποιῶσιν, οὗτοι νόμον μὴ ἔχοντες ἑαυτοῖς εἰσιν
make, these [the] law [although] not having to themselves are

νόμος· 15 οἵτινες ἐνδείκνυνται τὸ ἔργον τοῦ νόμου
law: whoever demonstrates [that] the work of the law

γραπτὸν ἐν ταῖς καρδίαις αὐτῶν, συμμαρτυρούσης αὐτῶν
is written in the hearts of them, bears witness of them

τῆς συνειδήσεως καὶ μεταξὺ ἀλλήλων τῶν λογισμῶν
the conscience and amongst one another the thoughts

κατηγορούντων ἢ καὶ ἀπολογουμένων, 16 ἐν ᾗ ἡμέρᾳ
accusing or also excusing, on the day [when]

κρίνει ὁ θεὸς τὰ κρυπτὰ τῶν ἀνθρώπων κατὰ τὸ
judges - God the hidden things of men according to the

εὐαγγέλιόν μου διὰ Χριστοῦ Ἰησοῦ.
announcement of me through [the] Messiah Jesus.

2:25–29
25 περιτομὴ μὲν γὰρ ὠφελεῖ ἐὰν νόμον πράσσῃς· ἐὰν δὲ
Circumcision on the one hand benefits if [the] law you practice; but if

παραβάτης νόμου ᾖς, ἡ περιτομή σου ἀκροβυστία
a transgressor of [the] law you are, the circumcision of you foreskin

γέγονεν. 26 ἐὰν οὖν ἡ ἀκροβυστία τὰ δικαιώματα
has become. If therefore the foreskin the prescriptions

τοῦ νόμου φυλάσσῃ, οὐχ ἡ ἀκροβυστία αὐτοῦ εἰς
of the law observes, not [will] the foreskin of him as

περιτομὴν λογισθήσεται; 27 καὶ κρινεῖ ἡ ἐκ φύσεως
circumcision be regarded? And will judge the by nature

ἀκροβυστία τὸν νόμον τελοῦσα σὲ τὸν διὰ
foreskin the law fulfilling you who through

γράμματος καὶ περιτομῆς παραβάτην νόμου. 28 οὐ γὰρ
the letter and circumcision [a] transgressor of [the] law. For not

ὁ ἐν τῷ φανερῷ Ἰουδαῖός ἐστιν, οὐδὲ ἡ ἐν τῷ φανερῷ
the in the visible   Jew   is,   nor   the in   the visible

ἐν σαρκὶ περιτομή· 29 ἀλλ' ὁ   ἐν   τῷ κρυπτῷ Ἰουδαῖος,
in [the] flesh [is] circumcision; but the [one] in - secret [is a] Jew,

καὶ περιτομὴ καρδίας ἐν πνεύματι οὐ γράμματι,
and circumcision [is] of [the] heart in [the] spirit not in [the] letter,

οὗ ὁ ἔπαινος οὐκ ἐξ ἀνθρώπων ἀλλ' ἐκ τοῦ θεοῦ.
of whom the praise [is] not from men   but from - God.

3:9–12

9 Τί οὖν; προεχόμεθα; οὐ πάντως· προῃτιασάμεθα γὰρ
What then? Are we superior? Not at all!   For we earlier accused

Ἰουδαίους τε καὶ Ἕλληνας πάντας ὑφ' ἁμαρτίαν εἶναι,
Jews   - and Greeks   all   under sin   to be,

10 καθὼς γέγραπται ὅτι οὐκ ἔστιν δίκαιος οὐδὲ εἷς,
as   it is written: that not is [there] [a] just [one], not even one,

11 οὐκ ἔστιν ὁ συνίων, οὐκ ἔστιν ὁ ἐκζητῶν τὸν θεόν.
Not is [there] one knowing, not is [there] one seeking - God.

12 πάντες ἐξέκλιναν, ἅμα ἠχρεώθησαν·   οὐκ ἔστιν
All   strayed,   and they became incapable of using; there is not

ὁ ποιῶν χρηστότητα, [οὐκ ἔστιν] ἕως ἑνός.
one making good use,   there is not   so much as one.

3:19–24

19 οἴδαμεν δὲ ὅτι ὅσα   ὁ νόμος λέγει τοῖς
We know   -   that as much as the law says   to those [who are]

ἐν τῷ νόμῳ λαλεῖ, ἵνα πᾶν στόμα φραγῇ καὶ ὑπόδικος
in the law [it] speaks, so that each mouth is closed and culpable

γένηται πᾶς ὁ κόσμος τῷ θεῷ· 20 διότι ἐξ ἔργων
becomes all the world before God;   thus from [the] works

νόμου οὐ δικαιωθήσεται πᾶσα σὰρξ ἐνώπιον αὐτοῦ·
of [the] law not will be justified all flesh before   him;

διὰ γὰρ νόμου ἐπίγνωσις   ἁμαρτίας.
for through the law [is] [the] aposteriori knowledge of sin.

21 Νυνὶ δὲ χωρὶς νόμου δικαιοσύνη θεοῦ πεφανέρωται,
But now without [the] law [the] justice of God has been manifested,

μαρτυρουμένη ὑπὸ τοῦ νόμου καὶ τῶν προφητῶν,
attested   by   the law   and the prophets,

22 δικαιοσύνη δὲ θεοῦ διὰ πίστεως ['Ιησοῦ] Χριστοῦ
the justice - of God through [the] faith of Jesus Messiah

εἰς πάντας τοὺς πιστεύοντας· οὐ γάρ ἐστιν διαστολή·
for all the believers; for [there] is not [a] difference;

23 πάντες γὰρ ἥμαρτον καὶ ὑστεροῦνται τῆς δόξης τοῦ
for all have sinned and come short of the glory of

θεοῦ, 24 δικαιούμενοι δωρεὰν τῇ αὐτοῦ χάριτι διὰ τῆς
God, being justified freely by the of him grace through the

ἀπολυτρώσεως τῆς ἐν Χριστῷ 'Ιησοῦ·
redemption which [is] in [the] Messiah Jesus.

3:27–31
27 Ποῦ οὖν ἡ καύχησις; ἐξεκλείσθη. διὰ ποίου
Where then [is] the boasting? It was excluded! By what

νόμου; τῶν ἔργων; οὐχί, ἀλλὰ διὰ νόμου πίστεως.
law? Of works? No, but by [the] law of faith.

28 λογιζόμεθα γὰρ δικαιοῦσθαι πίστει ἄνθρωπον χωρὶς
For we think to be justified by faith man without

ἔργων νόμου. 29 ἢ 'Ιουδαίων ὁ θεὸς μόνον; οὐχὶ καὶ
[the] works of [the] law. Or of Jews [is he] the God solely? Not also

ἐθνῶν; ναὶ καὶ ἐθνῶν, 30 εἴπερ εἷς ὁ θεὸς ὅς
of [the] peoples? Yes also of [the] peoples, since one [is] the God who

δικαιώσει περιτομὴν ἐκ πίστεως καὶ ἀκροβυστίαν διὰ τῆς
will justify circumcision by faith and [the] foreskin through -

πίστεως. 31 νόμον οὖν καταργοῦμεν διὰ τῆς πίστεως;
faith. [Is the] law therefore made inoperative through - faith?

μὴ γένοιτο, ἀλλὰ νόμον ἱστάνομεν.
Let it not be! Nay [the] law we uphold firmly.

4:2–3
2 εἰ γὰρ 'Αβραὰμ ἐξ ἔργων ἐδικαιώθη, ἔχει καύχημα·
For if Abraham from [the] works was justified, he has [cause for] boasting;

ἀλλ' οὐ πρὸς θεόν. 3 τί γὰρ ἡ γραφὴ λέγει;
but not before God. For what [does] the writing say?

ἐπίστευσεν δὲ 'Αβραὰμ τῷ θεῷ, καὶ ἐλογίσθη αὐτῷ
Believed - Abraham in God, and it was counted unto him

εἰς δικαιοσύνην.
in justice.

4:10–22

10 πῶς οὖν ἐλογίσθη; ἐν περιτομῇ ὄντι ἢ ἐν
How then was it reckoned? In circumcision being or in

ἀκροβυστίᾳ, οὐκ ἐν περιτομῇ ἀλλ' ἐν ἀκροβυστίᾳ·
the foreskin, not in [the] circumcision but in [the] foreskin!

11 καὶ σημεῖον ἔλαβεν περιτομῆς σφραγῖδα τῆς
And [the] sign he received of circumcision seal of the

δικαιοσύνης τῆς πίστεως τῆς ἐν τῇ ἀκροβυστίᾳ,
justification of faith that in the foreskin,

εἰς τὸ εἶναι αὐτὸν πατέρα πάντων τῶν πιστευόντων
in order - to be him father of all the believers

δι' ἀκροβυστίας, εἰς τὸ λογισθῆναι αὐτοῖς [τὴν]
through [the] foreskin, for - to be reckoned to them -

δικαιοσύνην, 12 καὶ πατέρα περιτομῆς τοῖς οὐκ ἐκ
justice, and father of circumcision to those not of

περιτομῆς μόνον ἀλλὰ καὶ τοῖς στοιχοῦσιν τοῖς
circumcision only, but also for those who walk in the

ἴχνεσιν τῆς ἐν ἀκροβυστίᾳ πίστεως τοῦ πατρὸς
steps of the in foreskin faith of the father

ἡμῶν Ἀβραάμ. 13 Οὐ γὰρ διὰ νόμου ἡ ἐπαγγελία
of us Abraham. For not through [the] law [was] the promise

τῷ Ἀβραὰμ ἢ τῷ σπέρματι αὐτοῦ, τὸ κληρονόμον
to Abraham or to the seed of him that heir

αὐτὸν εἶναι κόσμου, ἀλλὰ διὰ δικαιοσύνης πίστεως.
he be of [the] world, but through [the] justice of faith.

14 εἰ γὰρ οἱ ἐκ νόμου κληρονόμοι, κεκένωται
For if those from [the] law [be] heirs, has been emptied

ἡ πίστις καὶ κατήργηται ἡ ἐπαγγελία· 15 ὁ γὰρ νόμος
- faith and has made inoperative the promise; for the law

ὀργὴν κατεργάζεται· οὗ δὲ οὐκ ἔστιν νόμος, οὐδὲ
wrath puts to work; but of which [there] is not law, neither

παράβασις. 16 Διὰ τοῦτο ἐκ πίστεως, ἵνα
[is there] transgression. Wherefore [it is] of faith, in order that [it be]

κατὰ χάριν, εἰς τὸ εἶναι βεβαίαν τὴν ἐπαγγελίαν
by grace - - to be valid the promise

παντὶ τῷ σπέρματι, οὐ τῷ ἐκ τοῦ νόμου μόνον
for all the seed, not to the [one] from the law alone

ἀλλὰ καὶ τῷ   ἐκ πίστεως Ἀβραάμ, ὅς ἐστιν πατὴρ
but   also   to the one from [the] faith of Abraham, who is   father

πάντων ἡμῶν, 17 καθὼς γέγραπται ὅτι πατέρα
of all   of us,   as   it is written   that father

πολλῶν ἐθνῶν τέθεικά σε, κατέναντι οὗ
of many peoples I have placed you, before [him] whom

ἐπίστευσεν θεοῦ τοῦ ζῳοποιοῦντος τοὺς νεκροὺς
he believed God who makes alive   the   dead

καὶ καλοῦντος τὰ μὴ ὄντα ὡς ὄντα· 18 ὃς παρ'
and calls   things not being as being;   who against

ἐλπίδα ἐπ' ἐλπίδι ἐπίστευσεν, εἰς τὸ γενέσθαι
hope   in hope   believed,   that to become

αὐτὸν πατέρα πολλῶν ἐθνῶν κατὰ   τὸ
him   father   of many peoples according to what

εἰρημένον· οὕτως ἔσται τὸ σπέρμα σου, 19 καὶ
has been said; thus   will be the seed   of you,   and,

μὴ ἀσθενήσας τῇ πίστει κατενόησεν τὸ ἑαυτοῦ
not being weak in faith, he considered the of himself

σῶμα νενεκρωμένον, ἑκατονταέτης που ὑπάρχων,
body dead,   one hundred years roughly being,

καὶ τὴν νέκρωσιν τῆς μήτρας Σάρρας· 20 εἰς δὲ τὴν
and the deadness of the womb of Sarah;   for - the

ἐπαγγελίαν τοῦ θεοῦ οὐ διεκρίθη τῇ ἀπιστίᾳ, ἀλλ'
promise   of God [was] not doubted in lack of faith, but

ἐνεδυναμώθη τῇ πίστει, δοὺς δόξαν τῷ θεῷ 21 καὶ
was potentialized with faith, giving glory to God   and

πληροφορηθεὶς   ὅτι ὃ ἐπήγγελται δυνατός ἐστιν
having been carried into fullness that what he has promised able   he is

καὶ ποιῆσαι. 22 διὸ [καὶ] ἐλογίσθη αὐτῷ εἰς
also to make.   Therefore also it was imputed to him for

δικαιοσύνην.
justice.

5:12−14
12 Διὰ τοῦτο ὥσπερ δι' ἑνὸς ἀνθρώπου ἡ ἁμαρτία
   Through this just as by one man   - sin

εἰς τὸν κόσμον εἰσῆλθεν, καὶ διὰ   τῆς ἁμαρτίας
into the world   entered,   and because of - sin

ὁ θάνατος, καὶ οὕτως εἰς πάντας ἀνθρώπους ὁ
- death, and thus to all men -

θάνατος διῆλθεν, ἐφ' ᾧ πάντες ἥμαρτον· 13 ἄχρι γὰρ
death passed, because all sinned; for until

νόμου ἁμαρτία ἦν ἐν κόσμῳ, ἁμαρτία δὲ οὐκ
law sin was in [the] world, but sin not

ἐλλογεῖται μὴ ὄντος νόμου· 14 ἀλλὰ
imputed [since there] not being law; but

ἐβασίλευσεν ὁ θάνατος ἀπὸ Ἀδὰμ μέχρι Μωϋσέως
reigned - death from Adam until Moses

καὶ ἐπὶ τοὺς μὴ ἁμαρτήσαντας ἐπὶ τῷ ὁμοιώματι τῆς
even on those not sinning in the likeness as the

παραβάσεως Ἀδάμ, ὅς ἐστιν τύπος τοῦ μέλλοντος.
transgression of Adam, who is [a] figure of the coming one.

5:19–21

19 ὥσπερ γὰρ διὰ τῆς παρακοῆς τοῦ ἑνὸς ἀνθρώπου
For just as through the disobedience of one man

ἁμαρτωλοὶ κατεστάθησαν οἱ πολλοί, οὕτως καὶ διὰ
sinners [they] were made [as] - many, thus also through

τῆς ὑπακοῆς τοῦ ἑνὸς δίκαιοι κατασταθήσονται
the obedience of [only] one just shall be made

οἱ πολλοί. 20 νόμος δὲ παρεισῆλθεν ἵνα πλεονάσῃ
the many. [The] law then came forth that might abound

τὸ παράπτωμα· οὗ δὲ ἐπλεόνασεν ἡ ἁμαρτία,
the offence; but where abounded - sin,

ὑπερεπερίσσευσεν ἡ χάρις, 21 ἵνα ὥσπερ
much more did abound - grace, so that just as

ἐβασίλευσεν ἡ ἁμαρτία ἐν τῷ θανάτῳ, οὕτως καὶ
reigned - sin unto - death, even so

ἡ χάρις βασιλεύσῃ διὰ δικαιοσύνης εἰς ζωὴν
- grace might reign through justice unto life

αἰώνιον διὰ Ἰησοῦ Χριστοῦ τοῦ κυρίου ἡμῶν.
eternal through Jesus Messiah the Lord of us.

7:7–24

7 Τί οὖν ἐροῦμεν; ὁ νόμος ἁμαρτία; μὴ γένοιτο·
What therefore shall we say? The law [is] sin? May it not be!

ἀλλὰ τὴν ἁμαρτίαν οὐκ ἔγνων εἰ μὴ διὰ νόμου·
Nay - sin not did I know unless through [the] law;

τήν τε γὰρ ἐπιθυμίαν οὐκ ᾔδειν εἰ μὴ ὁ νόμος
for the desire not did I know unless the law

ἔλεγεν· οὐκ ἐπιθυμήσεις· 8 ἀφορμὴν δὲ λαβοῦσα
said: not shall you desire! But [once] [a] drive having taken

ἡ ἁμαρτία διὰ τῆς ἐντολῆς κατειργάσατο ἐν ἐμοὶ
- sin by way of the commandment made operative in me

πᾶσαν ἐπιθυμίαν· χωρὶς γὰρ νόμου ἁμαρτία νεκρά.
every desire; for without law sin [is] dead.

9 ἐγὼ δὲ ἔζων χωρὶς νόμου ποτέ· ἐλθούσης δὲ
I - was alive without law once; but having come

τῆς ἐντολῆς ἡ ἁμαρτία ἀνέζησεν, 10 ἐγὼ δὲ ἀπέθανον,
the commandment - sin revived, I then died,

καὶ εὑρέθη μοι ἡ ἐντολὴ ἡ εἰς ζωήν,
and [it] was discovered [that] for me the commandment the one for life,

αὕτη εἰς θάνατον· 11 ἡ γὰρ ἁμαρτία ἀφορμὴν
this [one] [was] unto death - for sin [a] drive

λαβοῦσα διὰ τῆς ἐντολῆς ἐξηπάτησέν με καὶ
taking occasion through the commandment deceived me and

δι' αὐτῆς ἀπέκτεινεν. 12 ὥστε ὁ μὲν νόμος
by means of it killed [me]. Wherefore the - law

ἅγιος, καὶ ἡ ἐντολὴ ἁγία καὶ δικαία καὶ ἀγαθή.
is holy, and the commandment holy and just and good.

13 Τὸ οὖν ἀγαθὸν ἐμοὶ ἐγένετο θάνατος; μὴ γένοιτο·
- Therefore good to me has become death? Let it not be!

ἀλλὰ ἡ ἁμαρτία, ἵνα φανῇ ἁμαρτία, διὰ τοῦ
But - sin, that it [might] appear [as] sin, through the

ἀγαθοῦ μοι κατεργαζομένη θάνατον, ἵνα γένηται
good to me making operative death, so that might become

καθ' ὑπερβολὴν ἁμαρτωλὸς ἡ ἁμαρτία διὰ τῆς
exceedingly sinful - sin through the

ἐντολῆς. 14 οἴδαμεν γὰρ ὅτι ὁ νόμος πνευματικός
commandment. For we know that the law spiritual

ἐστιν· ἐγὼ δὲ σάρκινός εἰμι, πεπραμένος ὑπὸ τὴν
is: but I carnal am, sold under -

ἁμαρτίαν. 15 ὃ γὰρ   κατεργάζομαι οὐ γινώσκω·
sin.   For that which I put to work   not do I know:

οὐ γὰρ ὃ   θέλω τοῦτο πράσσω, ἀλλ' ὃ   μισῶ
for not   what I want that   I do,   but   what I hate

τοῦτο ποιῶ. 16 εἰ δὲ ὃ   οὐ θέλω τοῦτο ποιῶ,
that   I make.   If   then what not I want this   I make,

σύμφημι τῷ   νόμῳ ὅτι καλός. 17 νυνὶ δὲ οὐκέτι ἐγὼ
I consent   unto the law   that [it is] good.   Now   then no more I

κατεργάζομαι αὐτὸ ἀλλὰ ἡ ἐνοικοῦσα ἐν ἐμοὶ ἁμαρτία.
put to work   it,   but   the dwelling   in me   sin.

18 οἶδα γὰρ ὅτι   οὐκ οἰκεῖ ἐν ἐμοί, τοῦτ' ἔστιν ἐν τῇ
For I know   that [it] not   dwells   in me,   that   is,   in the

σαρκί μου, ἀγαθόν· τὸ γὰρ θέλειν παράκειταί μοι,
flesh   of me, [the] good; for the   wanting is near   to me,

τὸ δὲ κατεργάζεσθαι τὸ καλὸν οὔ· 19 οὐ γὰρ ὃ
but the putting to work   the good   [is] not;   for not   what

θέλω ποιῶ ἀγαθόν, ἀλλὰ ὃ   οὐ θέλω κακὸν τοῦτο
I want I make good,   but   what not I want, evil   this

πράσσω. 20 εἰ δὲ ὃ   οὐ θέλω ἐγὼ τοῦτο ποιῶ,
I do.   But if   what not I want I   this   do,

οὐκέτι ἐγὼ κατεργάζομαι αὐτὸ ἀλλὰ ἡ οἰκοῦσα ἐν
no longer I   put to work   it   but   the dwelling   in

ἐμοὶ ἁμαρτία. 21 εὑρίσκω ἄρα τὸν νόμον τῷ θέλοντι
me   sin.   Therefore I find   the law   - wanting

ἐμοὶ ποιεῖν τὸ καλόν, ὅτι ἐμοὶ τὸ κακὸν παράκειται·
in me to make   the good,   when in me the evil   is near;

22 συνήδομαι γὰρ τῷ   νόμῳ τοῦ θεοῦ κατὰ   τὸν ἔσω
for I delight   in the law   of   God   according to the   inner

ἄνθρωπον, 23 βλέπω δὲ ἕτερον νόμον ἐν τοῖς μέλεσίν
man,   but I see   another   law   in the   members

μου ἀντιστρατευόμενον τῷ νόμῳ τοῦ νοός μου καὶ
of me fighting against   the law   of the mind of me and

αἰχμαλωτίζοντά με ἐν τῷ νόμῳ τῆς ἁμαρτίας τῷ
taking prisoner   me in   the law   of   sin   that

ὄντι ἐν τοῖς μέλεσίν μου. 24 Ταλαίπωρος ἐγὼ
which is in   the   members   of me.   [A] wretched   I [am]

ἄνθρωπος· τίς με ῥύσεται ἐκ τοῦ σώματος τοῦ
man! Who me shall deliver from the body -

θανάτου τούτου;
of death this?

8:19–25

19 ἡ γὰρ ἀποκαραδοκία   τῆς κτίσεως τὴν ἀποκάλυψιν
For the expectation of fulfillment of the creation   the   revelation

τῶν υἱῶν τοῦ θεοῦ ἀπεκδέχεται.   20 τῇ γὰρ ματαιότητι
of the sons of   God   is open to receive.   For to   vanity

ἡ κτίσις ὑπετάγη, οὐχ ἑκοῦσα, ἀλλὰ διὰ   τὸν
- creation was subjected, not willingly,   but   because of him who

ὑποτάξαντα, ἐφ' ἐλπίδι   21 διότι καὶ αὐτὴ ἡ κτίσις
was subjecting [it] with [the] hope   that   also itself - creation

ἐλευθερωθήσεται ἀπὸ τῆς δουλείας τῆς φθορᾶς εἰς
will be freed   from the   slavery   of   corruption for

τὴν ἐλευθερίαν τῆς   δόξης τῶν τέκνων τοῦ θεοῦ.
the freedom   of [the] glory of the sons of   God.

22 οἴδαμεν γὰρ ὅτι πᾶσα ἡ κτίσις συστενάζει καὶ
For we know   that all   the creation bewails together and

συνωδίνει   ἄχρι τοῦ νῦν·   23 οὐ μόνον δέ, ἀλλὰ
suffers the labour pains until   -   now;   but not only [this], but

καὶ αὐτοὶ τὴν ἀπαρχὴν τοῦ πνεύματος ἔχοντες [ἡμεῖς]
also us   the   initial source of the spirit   having,   we

καὶ αὐτοὶ ἐν   ἑαυτοῖς στενάζομεν υἱοθεσίαν
also ourselves within ourselves   bewail,   adoption

ἀπεκδεχόμενοι, τὴν ἀπολύτρωσιν τοῦ σώματος ἡμῶν.
open to receive,   the   redemption   of the body   of us.

24 τῇ γὰρ ἐλπίδι ἐσώθημεν· ἐλπὶς δὲ βλεπομένη οὐκ
For in   hope   we were saved; but hope   being seen   not

ἔστιν ἐλπίς· ὁ γὰρ βλέπει τίς,   τί καὶ ἐλπίζει;
is   hope: for what sees someone, what then should [he] hope?

25 εἰ δὲ ὃ   οὐ βλέπομεν ἐλπίζομεν, δι' ὑπομονῆς
But if   what not we see   we hope [for], through patience

ἀπεκδεχόμεθα.
we are open to receive.

9:3—9

3 ηὐχόμην γὰρ ἀνάθεμα εἶναι αὐτὸς ἐγὼ ἀπὸ τοῦ
For I could wish [a] curse were myself I from the

Χριστοῦ ὑπὲρ τῶν ἀδελφῶν μου τῶν συγγενῶν μου
Messiah for the sake of the brothers of me the kinsmen of me

κατὰ σάρκα, 4 οἵτινές εἰσιν Ἰσραηλῖται, ὧν
according to [the] flesh, who are Israelites, to whom [pertains]

ἡ υἱοθεσία καὶ ἡ δόξα καὶ αἱ διαθῆκαι καὶ ἡ
the adoption as sons and the glory and the covenants and the

νομοθεσία καὶ ἡ λατρεία καὶ αἱ ἐπαγγελίαι, 5 ὧν
giving of the law and the worship and the promises, of whom

οἱ πατέρες, καὶ ἐξ ὧν ὁ Χριστὸς τὸ κατὰ σάρκα
are the fathers, and of whom [is] the Messiah that according to [the] flesh

ὁ ὢν ἐπὶ πάντων θεὸς εὐλογητὸς εἰς τοὺς αἰῶνας,
the being above all God blessed throughout the ages,

ἀμήν. 6 Οὐχ οἷον δὲ ὅτι ἐκπέπτωκεν ὁ λόγος τοῦ
amen. Not as such [is] - what has fallen from the word of

θεοῦ. οὐ γὰρ πάντες οἱ ἐξ Ἰσραήλ, οὗτοι Ἰσραήλ·
God. For not all those from Israel, these [are] Israel;

7 οὐδ' ὅτι εἰσὶν σπέρμα Ἀβραάμ, πάντες τέκνα, ἀλλ'·
nor because are seed of Abraham, all [are] children, but,

ἐν Ἰσαὰκ κληθήσεταί σοι σπέρμα. 8 τοῦτ' ἔστιν, οὐ
in Isaac shall be called for you seed. That is, not

τὰ τέκνα τῆς σαρκὸς ταῦτα τέκνα τοῦ θεοῦ,
they the children of the flesh [are] these [the] children of God,

ἀλλὰ τὰ τέκνα τῆς ἐπαγγελίας λογίζεται εἰς σπέρμα.
but the children of the promise are counted as seed.

9 ἐπαγγελίας γὰρ ὁ λόγος οὗτος, κατὰ τὸν καιρὸν
For of promise [is] the word this, at the time

τοῦτον ἐλεύσομαι καὶ ἔσται τῇ Σάρρᾳ υἱός.
this I will come and [there] will be to Sarah [a] son.

9:24—28

24 οὓς καὶ ἐκάλεσεν ἡμᾶς οὐ μόνον ἐξ Ἰουδαίων
Those whom also he called us not only of [the] Jews

ἀλλὰ καὶ ἐξ ἐθνῶν; 25 ὡς καὶ ἐν τῷ Ὡσηὲ λέγει,
but also of [the] Gentiles? As also in - Osee he says:

καλέσω τὸν οὐ λαόν μου λαόν μου καὶ τὴν οὐκ
I will call the not people of me people of me, and the not

ἠγαπημένην ἠγαπημένην· 26 καὶ ἔσται ἐν τῷ τόπῳ οὗ
beloved beloved: and [it] shall be in the place where

ἐρρέθη [αὐτοῖς]· οὐ λαός μου ὑμεῖς, ἐκεῖ κληθήσονται
it was said to them: Not [the] people of me [are] you, there they will be called

υἱοὶ θεοῦ ζῶντος. 27 Ἡσαΐας δὲ κράζει ὑπὲρ τοῦ
children of God living. Esaias then cries on behalf of

Ἰσραήλ, ἐὰν ᾖ ὁ ἀριθμὸς τῶν υἱῶν Ἰσραὴλ ὡς
Israel: If also be the number of the sons of Israel as

ἡ ἄμμος τῆς θαλάσσης, τὸ ὑπόλειμμα σωθήσεται·
the sand of the sea, a remnant shall be saved:

28 λόγον γὰρ συντελῶν καὶ συντέμνων ποιήσει κύριος
for [the] word fulfilling and contracted will make [the] Lord

ἐπὶ τῆς γῆς.
upon the earth.

10:2–12

2 μαρτυρῶ γὰρ αὐτοῖς ὅτι ζῆλον θεοῦ ἔχουσιν, ἀλλ'
For I bear witness to them that zeal of God they have, but

οὐ κατ' ἐπίγνωσιν· 3 ἀγνοοῦντες γὰρ τὴν τοῦ θεοῦ
not according to knowledge: for not knowing the of God

δικαιοσύνην, καὶ τὴν ἰδίαν ζητοῦντες
justice, and their own [justice] seeking

στῆσαι, τῇ δικαιοσύνῃ τοῦ θεοῦ οὐχ
to uphold firmly, unto the justice of God not

ὑπετάγησαν· 4 τέλος γὰρ νόμου Χριστὸς εἰς
did they submit. For [the] end of law [is] [the] Messiah for

δικαιοσύνην παντὶ τῷ πιστεύοντι. 5 Μωϋσῆς γὰρ
justice to every one that believes. For Moses

γράφει ὅτι τὴν δικαιοσύνην τὴν ἐκ νόμου ὁ
writes that - justice the one from [the] law: The

ποιήσας ἄνθρωπος ζήσεται ἐν αὐτῇ. 6 ἡ δὲ
having made man shall live by them. But the

ἐκ πίστεως δικαιοσύνη οὕτως λέγει· μὴ εἴπῃς ἐν
from faith justice thus speaks: Do not say in

τῇ καρδίᾳ σου· τίς ἀναβήσεται εἰς τὸν οὐρανόν; τοῦτ'
the heart of you: Who shall ascend into - heaven? This

ἔστιν Χριστὸν καταγαγεῖν·   7 ἤ· τίς καταβήσεται
is   [the] Messiah to bring down;   or: Who shall lead down

εἰς τὴν ἄβυσσον; τοῦτ' ἔστιν Χριστὸν ἐκ νεκρῶν
into the abyss?   That   is [for] [the] Messiah from [the] dead

ἀναγαγεῖν.   8 ἀλλὰ τί λέγει;   Ἐγγύς σου τὸ ῥῆμά
to bring up.   But   what does [it] say? Near   to you the word*

ἔστιν, ἐν τῷ στόματί σου καὶ ἐν τῇ καρδίᾳ σου· τοῦτ'
is,   in the mouth   of you and in the heart   of you: that

ἔστιν τὸ ῥῆμα τῆς πίστεως ὃ κηρύσσομεν.   9 ὅτι ἐὰν
is   the word of faith   that we announce.   That if

ὁμολογήσῃς ἐν τῷ στόματί σου κύριον Ἰησοῦν, καὶ
you shall confess in the mouth   of you Lord   Jesus,   and

πιστεύσῃς ἐν τῇ καρδίᾳ σου ὅτι ὁ θεὸς αὐτὸν
you shall believe in the heart   of you that - God him

ἤγειρεν ἐκ νεκρῶν, σωθήσῃ·   10 καρδίᾳ γὰρ
raised   from [the] dead, you shall be saved: for with [the] heart

πιστεύεται εἰς δικαιοσύνην, στόματι   δὲ ὁμολογεῖται
it is believed unto justice,   with the mouth then it is confessed

εἰς σωτηρίαν.   11 λέγει γὰρ ἡ γραφή· πᾶς ὁ πιστεύων
unto salvation.   For says   the writing,   all who believe

ἐπ' αὐτῷ οὐ καταισχυνθήσεται.   12 οὐ γὰρ ἐστιν
in him   not shall be ashamed.   For not   is [there]

διαστολὴ Ἰουδαίου τε καὶ Ἕλληνος, ὁ γὰρ αὐτὸς
a difference of Jew   - and Greek,   for the same

κύριος πάντων, πλουτῶν εἰς πάντας τοὺς
Lord   over all, [is] rich   to all   those

ἐπικαλουμένους αὐτόν·
calling upon   him.

11:1–16

1 Λέγω οὖν, μὴ ἀπώσατο ὁ θεὸς τὸν λαὸν αὐτοῦ;
Therefore I say, did not cast away - God   the people of him?

μὴ γένοιτο· καὶ γὰρ ἐγὼ Ἰσραηλίτης εἰμί, ἐκ
Let it not be!   For even I   [an] Israelite   am,   from

σπέρματος Ἀβραάμ, φυλῆς Βενιαμίν.   2 οὐκ ἀπώσατο
the seed   of Abraham, of [the] tribe of Benjamin.   Not thrust off

ὁ θεὸς τὸν λαὸν αὐτοῦ ὃν προέγνω. ἢ οὐκ οἴδατε
 - God   the people of him whom he foreknew. Or not do you know

*Translator's note: Agamben translates *lexis* as *parola*, which means both
word and utterance, the substance of speech and speech itself, like the logos.

ἐν Ἠλίᾳ τί λέγει ἡ γραφή, ὡς ἐντυγχάνει τῷ θεῷ κατὰ
in Elias what says the writing, as [an] encounter with God according to

τοῦ Ἰσραήλ; 3 κύριε, τοὺς προφήτας σου ἀπέκτειναν,
- Israel? Lord, the prophets of you they killed,

τὰ θυσιαστήριά σου κατέσκαψαν, κἀγὼ ὑπελείφθην
the altars of you they razed, and I was left

μόνος καὶ ζητοῦσιν τὴν ψυχήν μου. 4 ἀλλὰ
alone, and they seek the life of me. But

τί λέγει αὐτῷ ὁ χρηματισμός; κατέλιπον ἐμαυτῷ
what says to him the oracle? I reserved for myself

ἑπτακισχιλίους ἄνδρας, οἵτινες οὐκ ἔκαμψαν γόνυ
seven thousand men, who [did] not bend [a] knee

τῇ Βάαλ. 5 οὕτως οὖν καὶ ἐν τῷ νῦν καιρῷ λεῖμμα
to Baal. Thus then also in the of now time [a] remnant

κατ' ἐκλογὴν χάριτος γέγονεν· 6 εἰ δὲ χάριτι,
according to [the] election of grace has become; but if by grace, [and]

οὐκέτι ἐξ ἔργων, ἐπεὶ ἡ χάρις οὐκέτι γίνεται χάρις.
no more from works, then - grace no more becomes grace.

7 Τί οὖν; ὁ ἐπιζητεῖ Ἰσραήλ, τοῦτο οὐκ ἐπέτυχεν,
What then? What seeks Israel, this [it did] not obtain,

ἡ δὲ ἐκλογὴ ἐπέτυχεν· οἱ δὲ λοιποὶ ἐπωρώθησαν,
- but election [it] obtained: but those remnants were hardened,

8 καθάπερ γέγραπται· ἔδωκεν αὐτοῖς ὁ θεὸς
thus it has been written: Gave to them - God

πνεῦμα κατανύξεως, ὀφθαλμοὺς τοῦ μὴ βλέπειν
[a] spirit of torpor, eyes for not seeing

καὶ ὦτα τοῦ μὴ ἀκούειν, ἕως τῆς σήμερον
and ears for not hearing, unto - this

ἡμέρας. 9 καὶ Δαυὶδ λέγει· γενηθήτω ἡ τράπεζα
day. And David says: Let be made a table

αὐτων εἰς παγίδα καὶ εἰς θήραν καὶ εἰς σκάνδαλον
theirs for [a] snare and for [a] trap and for [a] stumbling block

καὶ εἰς ἀνταπόδομα αὐτοῖς, 10 σκοτισθήτωσαν
and for [a] recompense unto them, were darkened

οἱ ὀφθαλμοὶ αὐτῶν τοῦ μὴ βλέπειν, καὶ τὸν νῶτον
the eyes of them so as not to see, and the backs

αὐτῶν διὰ παντὸς σύγκαμψον. 11 Λέγω οὖν,
of them through all bent downward. Therefore I say,

μὴ ἔπταισαν ἵνα πέσωσιν; μὴ γένοιτο·
have they stumbled that they should fall? Let it not be!

ἀλλὰ τῷ αὐτῶν παραπτώματι ἡ σωτηρία τοῖς
Rather by their false steps the salvation [is come] to the

ἔθνεσιν, εἰς τὸ παραζηλῶσαι αὐτούς. 12 εἰ δὲ τὸ
peoples, for - making jealous them. But if the

παράπτωμα αὐτῶν πλοῦτος κόσμου καὶ τὸ ἥττημα
false steps of them [is] [the] wealth of [the] world and the diminishing

αὐτῶν πλοῦτος ἐθνῶν, πόσῳ μᾶλλον τὸ πλήρωμα
of them [the] wealth of peoples, by how much more the fullness

αὐτῶν. 13 Ὑμῖν δὲ λέγω τοῖς ἔθνεσιν. ἐφ' ὅσον μὲν
of them. But to you I say to the peoples.* Inasmuch as

οὖν εἰμι ἐγὼ ἐθνῶν ἀπόστολος, τὴν διακονίαν μου
- am I of Gentiles emissary, the ministry of me

δοξάζω, 14 εἴ πως παραζηλώσω μου τὴν σάρκα
I honor, if somehow I make jealous of me the flesh

καὶ σώσω τινὰς ἐξ αὐτῶν. 15 εἰ γὰρ ἡ ἀποβολὴ
and I will save some of them. For if the casting away

αὐτῶν καταλλαγὴ κόσμου, τίς ἡ πρόσλημψις
of them [be] reconciliation of [the] world, what [will be] the reintegration

εἰ μὴ ζωὴ ἐκ νεκρῶν; 16 εἰ δὲ ἡ ἀπαρχὴ ἁγία, καὶ
if not life from the dead? But if the initial source [is] holy, so [is]

τὸ φύραμα· καὶ εἰ ἡ ῥίζα ἁγία, καὶ οἱ κλάδοι.
the dough; and if the root [is] holy, so [are] the branches.

11:25-26

25 Οὐ γὰρ θέλω ὑμᾶς ἀγνοεῖν, ἀδελφοί, τὸ
For not do I want you not to know, brothers, the

μυστήριον τοῦτο, ἵνα μὴ ἦτε ἑαυτοῖς
mystery this, in order that not you be for yourselves

φρόνιμοι, ὅτι πώρωσις ἀπὸ μέρους τῷ Ἰσραὴλ
wise, that hardness in part to Israel

γέγονεν ἄχρι οὗ τὸ πλήρωμα τῶν ἐθνῶν εἰσέλθῃ,
has happened until - the fullness of the peoples enters,

26 καὶ οὕτως πᾶς Ἰσραὴλ σωθήσεται, καθὼς
and thus all Israel shall be saved, thus

Translator's note: Agamben translates the Greek "ethnos" as "gentili" or "pagani," which I have translated as either "people" or "Gentile" depending on the context.

γέγραπται· ἥξει ἐκ Σιὼν ὁ ῥυόμενος, ἀποστρέψει
it has been written: will come from Zion   the saviour,   he will expel

ἀσεβείας ἀπὸ Ἰακώβ.
impiety   from Jacob.

13:8—10

8 Μηδενὶ μηδὲν ὀφείλετε, εἰ μὴ τὸ ἀλλήλους ἀγαπᾶν·
To no one anything be owed,   except   one another   to love;

ὁ γὰρ ἀγαπῶν τὸν ἕτερον νόμον πεπλήρωκεν.
for the one loving   the   other   law   has fulfilled.

9 τὸ γὰρ οὐ μοιχεύσεις, οὐ φονεύσεις, οὐ κλέψεις,
- For: Not shall you adulter, not shall you kill, not shall you steal,

οὐκ ἐπιθυμήσεις, καὶ εἴ τις ἑτέρα ἐντολή,   ἐν
not shall you desire, and if some other   commandment, in

τῷ λόγῳ τούτῳ ἀνακεφαλαιοῦται, [ἐν τῷ]· ἀγαπήσεις
the word this   is recapitulated,   in   it: Love

τὸν πλησίον σου ὡς σεαυτόν. 10 ἡ ἀγάπη τῷ
the neighbor of you as yourself.   The love   to the

πλησίον κακὸν οὐκ ἐργάζεται· πλήρωμα οὖν   νόμου
neighbor evil   not works: fulfilling   therefore of [the] law

ἡ ἀγάπη.
- [is] love.

From the First Letter to the Corinthians

1:22—29

22 ἐπειδὴ καὶ Ἰουδαῖοι σημεῖα αἰτοῦσιν καὶ
Since   both Jews   signs   ask for   and

Ἕλληνες σοφίαν ζητοῦσιν, 23 ἡμεῖς δὲ κηρύσσομεν
Greeks   wisdom   seek,   but we   announce

Χριστὸν ἐσταυρωμένον, Ἰουδαίοις μὲν   σκάνδαλον,
the Messiah crucified,   unto Jews   on one hand [a] stumbling block

ἔθνεσιν δὲ   μωρίαν, 24 αὐτοῖς δὲ   τοῖς κλητοῖς,
to Gentiles on the other foolishness,   for themselves instead those called,

Ἰουδαίοις τε καὶ Ἕλλησιν, Χριστὸν θεοῦ δύναμιν
Jews   and even Greeks,   [the] Messiah of God power

καὶ θεοῦ σοφίαν. 25 ὅτι   τὸ μωρὸν τοῦ θεοῦ
and of God wisdom.   Because the foolishness of   God

σοφώτερον τῶν ἀνθρώπων ἐστίν, καὶ τὸ ἀσθενὲς
wiser   than men   is,   and the weakness

τοῦ θεοῦ ἰσχυρότερον τῶν ἀνθρώπων. 26 Βλέπετε
of God [is] stronger than men.   For you see

γὰρ τὴν κλῆσιν ὑμῶν, ἀδελφοί, ὅτι οὐ πολλοὶ σοφοὶ
the calling of you, brothers, that not many [are the] wise

κατὰ   σάρκα, οὐ πολλοὶ δυνατοί,   οὐ πολλοὶ εὐγενεῖς·
according to flesh, not many [the] powerful, not many [the] wellborn;

27 ἀλλὰ τὰ μωρὰ   τοῦ κόσμου ἐξελέξατο ὁ θεὸς
but the foolish things of [the] world were chosen [by] - God

ἵνα   καταισχύνῃ τοὺς σοφούς, καὶ τὰ ἀσθενῆ τοῦ
in order to shame   the wise,   and the weak things of

κόσμου ἐξελέξατο ὁ θεὸς ἵνα   καταισχύνῃ τὰ
the world were chosen [by] - God in order to shame   the

ἰσχυρά, 28 καὶ τὰ ἀγενῆ τοῦ κόσμου καὶ τὰ
mighty,   and the base of [the] world and the

ἐξουθενημένα ἐξελέξατο ὁ θεός, τὰ μὴ ὄντα, ἵνα
contemptible were chosen [by] - God, the things not being, in order

τὰ ὄντα   καταργήσῃ, 29 ὅπως   μὴ καυχήσηται πᾶσα
the things being to abolish,   in order [that] not may boast   all

σὰρξ ἐνώπιον τοῦ θεοῦ.
flesh before   - God.

2:1–5
1 Κἀγὼ ἐλθὼν πρὸς ὑμᾶς, ἀδελφοί, ἦλθον οὐ καθ'
And I coming toward you, brothers, came not according to

ὑπεροχὴν λόγου ἢ σοφίας καταγγέλλων ὑμῖν τὸ
superiority of word or of wisdom announcing   to you the

μαρτύριον τοῦ θεοῦ. 2 οὐ γὰρ ἔκρινά τι   εἰδέναι
testimony of God.   For not I judged anything to know

ἐν   ὑμῖν εἰ μὴ Ἰησοῦν Χριστὸν καὶ τοῦτον
among you except Jesus Messiah and this one

ἐσταυρωμένον. 3 κἀγὼ ἐν ἀσθενείᾳ καὶ ἐν φόβῳ
crucified.   And I in weakness and in fear

καὶ ἐν τρόμῳ πολλῷ ἐγενόμην πρὸς ὑμᾶς, 4 καὶ ὁ
and in trembling much was   toward you,   and the

λόγος μου καὶ τὸ κήρυγμά μου   οὐκ ἐν πειθοῖς
word of me and the announcement of me [was] not in persuasive

σοφίας λόγοις, ἀλλ' ἐν ἀποδείξει πνεύματος καὶ
of wisdom words,   but   with demonstration of spirit   and

δυνάμεως, 5 ἵνα   ἡ πίστις ὑμῶν μὴ ᾖ ἐν σοφίᾳ
potentiality,   in order that the faith   of you not be in [the] wisdom

ἀνθρώπων ἀλλ' ἐν δυνάμει θεοῦ.
of men   but in [the] power of God.

7:17–24

17 Εἰ μὴ ἑκάστῳ ὡς μεμέρικεν ὁ κύριος, ἕκαστον
Unless to each as portioned out the Lord, each

ὡς κέκληκεν ὁ θεός, οὕτως περιπατείτω. καὶ
as called - God, so walk. And

οὕτως ἐν ταῖς ἐκκλησίαις πάσαις διατάσσομαι.
thus among the communities all I order.

18 περιτετμημένος τις ἐκλήθη; μὴ ἐπισπάσθω·
[Of the] circumcised who was called? Let him not be uncircumcised!

ἐν ἀκροβυστίᾳ κέκληταί τις; μὴ περιτεμνέσθω.
With the foreskin [was] called someone? Let him not be circumcised!

19 ἡ περιτομὴ οὐδέν ἐστιν, καὶ ἡ ἀκροβυστία οὐδέν
- Circumcision nothing is, and the foreskin nothing

ἐστιν, ἀλλὰ τήρησις ἐντολῶν θεοῦ. 20 ἕκαστος ἐν
is, but [the] guarding of commandments of God. Each in

τῇ κλήσει ᾗ ἐκλήθη, ἐν ταύτῃ μενέτω. 21 δοῦλος
the calling in which he was called, in this let him remain. A slave

ἐκλήθης; μή σοι μελέτω· ἀλλ' εἰ καὶ δύνασαι
you were called? Let it not to you be a concern! But if also you are able

ἐλεύθερος γενέσθαι, μᾶλλον χρῆσαι. 22 ὁ γὰρ ἐν
free to become, rather make use [of it]. For the one in

κυρίῳ κληθεὶς δοῦλος ἀπελεύθερος κυρίου ἐστίν·
the Lord being called slave freed of [the] Lord is;

ὁμοίως ὁ ἐλεύθερος κληθεὶς δοῦλός ἐστιν Χριστοῦ.
in like manner, the free one being called slave is of [the] Messiah.

23 τιμῆς ἠγοράσθητε· μὴ γίνεσθε δοῦλοι
With a price you were bought; do not become slaves

ἀνθρώπων. 24 ἕκαστος ἐν ᾧ ἐκλήθη, ἀδελφοί,
of men. Each in which he was called, brothers,

ἐν τούτῳ μενέτω παρὰ θεῷ.
in this let him remain before God.

7:29–32

29 τοῦτο δέ φημι, ἀδελφοί, ὁ καιρὸς
But this   I say,   brethren   time

συνεσταλμένος ἐστίν· τὸ λοιπὸν ἵνα   καὶ οἱ
contracted   is;   the rest   in order that also   the

ἔχοντες γυναῖκας ὡς μὴ ἔχοντες ὦσιν, 30 καὶ οἱ
ones having wives   as not having   may be,   and the

κλαίοντες ὡς μὴ κλαίοντες, καὶ οἱ χαίροντες ὡς
ones weeping as not weeping,   and the ones rejoicing as

μὴ χαίροντες, καὶ οἱ ἀγοράζοντες ὡς μὴ
not rejoicing,   and the ones buying   as not

κατέχοντες, 31 καὶ οἱ χρώμενοι τὸν κόσμον ὡς
possessing,   and the ones using   the world   as

μὴ καταχρώμενοι· παράγει γὰρ τὸ σχῆμα τοῦ
not using it up: for passes away   the figure   of

κόσμου τούτου. 32 Θέλω δὲ ὑμᾶς ἀμερίμνους
world   this.   I want now you   without care

εἶναι.
to be.

9:19–22

19 Ἐλεύθερος γὰρ ὢν ἐκ πάντων πᾶσιν ἐμαυτὸν
For free   being from all   to all   myself

ἐδούλωσα, ἵνα τοὺς πλείονας κερδήσω· 20 καὶ
I remained a slave, that the more   I may gain   and

ἐγενόμην τοῖς Ἰουδαίοις ὡς Ἰουδαῖος, ἵνα
become   to the Jews   as Jew,   so that

Ἰουδαίους κερδήσω· τοῖς ὑπὸ νόμον   ὡς ὑπὸ
Jews   I may win over; with those under [the] law [who are] as under

νόμον, μὴ ὢν αὐτὸς ὑπὸ νόμον, ἵνα τοὺς   ὑπὸ
the law, not being myself under [the] law, so that those [who are] under

νόμον κερδήσω· 21 τοῖς ἀνόμοις ὡς ἄνομος, μὴ
the law I may gain;   with [the] lawless   as without law, not

ὢν ἄνομος θεοῦ ἀλλ' ἔννομος Χριστοῦ, ἵνα
being without law of God but   in [the] law of [the] Messiah, so that

κερδάνω τοὺς ἀνόμους· 22 ἐγενόμην τοῖς
I win over   the lawless;   I became   with the

ἀσθενέσιν ἀσθενής, ἵνα   τοὺς ἀσθενεῖς κερδήσω·
weak   weak,   in order that the   weak   I may win over;

τοῖς πᾶσιν γέγονα   πάντα, ἵνα   πάντως τινὰς σώσω.
with all   I have become all,   in order that assuredly someone I may save.

10:1–6

1 Οὐ θέλω γὰρ ὑμᾶς ἀγνοεῖν,   ἀδελφοί, ὅτι οἱ
For I do not want you to be ignorant, brothers, that the

πατέρες ἡμῶν πάντες ὑπὸ τὴν νεφέλην ἦσαν καὶ
fathers of us all   under the cloud   were and

πάντες διὰ   τῆς θαλάσσης διῆλθον, 2 καὶ πάντες
all   through the sea   passed,   and all

εἰς τὸν Μωϋσῆν ἐβαπτίσαντο ἐν τῇ νεφέλῃ καὶ
unto -   Moses   were immersed in the cloud   and

ἐν τῇ θαλάσσῃ 3 καὶ πάντες τὸ αὐτὸ πνευματικὸν
in the sea   and all   the same spiritual

βρῶμα ἔφαγον, 4 καὶ πάντες τὸ αὐτὸ πνευματικὸν
food   ate,   and all   the same spiritual

ἔπιον πόμα· ἔπινον γὰρ ἐκ πνευματικῆς
drink drank: for they drank from [a] spiritual

ἀκολουθούσης   πέτρας, ἡ πέτρα δὲ ἦν ὁ Χριστός.
that accompanied [them] rock,   the rock really was the Messiah.

5 Ἀλλ' οὐκ ἐν τοῖς πλείοσιν αὐτῶν εὐδόκησεν ὁ
But   not in the most   of them was pleased   -

θεός· κατεστρώθησαν γὰρ ἐν τῇ ἐρήμῳ. 6 ταῦτα
God; for they were prostrated in the desert.   These things

δὲ τύποι ἡμῶν ἐγενήθησαν, εἰς τὸ μὴ εἶναι ἡμᾶς
- [as] figures of us were generated, for the not to be us

ἐπιθυμητὰς κακῶν,   καθὼς κἀκεῖνοι ἐπιθύμησαν.
desirous   of evil things, like   those who also desired [them].

10:11

11 ταῦτα δὲ τυπικῶς συνέβαινεν ἐκείνοις, ἐγράφη
But these things as figure   that happened to them,   were written

δὲ πρὸς νουθεσίαν ἡμῶν, εἰς οὓς τὰ τέλη τῶν
for admonition of us, in whom the ends of the

αἰώνων κατήντηκεν.
times   came face to face.

13:1–13

1 Ἐὰν ταῖς γλώσσαις τῶν ἀνθρώπων λαλῶ καὶ
If also with the tongues of men I speak and

τῶν ἀγγέλων, ἀγάπην δὲ μὴ ἔχω, γέγονα χαλκὸς
of angels, but love not I have, I have become brass

ἠχῶν ἢ κύμβαλον ἀλαλάζον. 2 καὶ ἐὰν ἔχω
resounding or [a] cymbal clanging. And if also I have

προφητείαν καὶ εἰδῶ τὰ μυστήρια πάντα καὶ
prophecy and I know the mysteries all and

πᾶσαν τὴν γνῶσιν, κἂν ἔχω πᾶσαν τὴν πίστιν
all - science and if also I have all the faith

ὥστε ὄρη μεθιστάναι, ἀγάπην δὲ μὴ ἔχω, οὐθέν
so that mountains move, but love not I have, nothing

εἰμι. 3 κἂν ψωμίσω πάντα τὰ ὑπάρχοντά μου, καὶ
am I. And if I distribute all the belongings of me and

ἐὰν παραδῶ τὸ σῶμά μου ἵνα καυθήσωμαι,
if I give up the body of me in order that I may burn,

ἀγάπην δὲ μὴ ἔχω, οὐδὲν ὠφελοῦμαι. 4 Ἡ ἀγάπη
but love not I have, nothing will I be of use. - Love

μακροθυμεῖ, χρηστεύεται ἡ ἀγάπη, οὐ ζηλοῖ, ἡ
is magnaminous, knows how to use love, not jealous [is], -

ἀγάπη οὐ περπερεύεται, οὐ φυσιοῦται, 5 οὐκ
love [does] not boast, [is] not inflated, [does] not

ἀσχημονεῖ, οὐ ζητεῖ τὰ ἑαυτῆς, οὐ παροξύνεται,
act unseemly, [does] not seek things of itself, [is] not provoked

οὐ λογίζεται τὸ κακόν, 6 οὐ χαίρει ἐπὶ
does not contemplate - evil, [does] not rejoice in

τῇ ἀδικίᾳ, συγχαίρει δὲ τῇ ἀληθείᾳ· 7 πάντα στέγει,
- injustice but rejoices in [the] truth; all it covers,

πάντα πιστεύει, πάντα ἐλπίζει, πάντα ὑπομένει.
all it believes, all it hopes, all it endures.

8 Ἡ ἀγάπη οὐδέποτε πίπτει· εἴτε δὲ προφητεῖαι,
- Love never falls off, whether prophecies

καταργηθήσονται· εἴτε γλῶσσαι, παύσονται· εἴτε
will be abolished, whether tongues will be stopped, whether

γνῶσις, καταργηθήσεται. 9 ἐκ μέρους γὰρ
knowledge will be rendered inoperative. For in part

γινώσκομεν καὶ ἐκ μέρους προφητεύομεν· 10 ὅταν
we know   and in part   we prophesize;   but whenever

δὲ ἔλθῃ τὸ τέλειον, τὸ ἐκ μέρους καταργηθήσεται.
comes the perfection, the from [a] part   will be rendered inoperative.

11 ὅτε ἤμην νήπιος, ἐλάλουν ὡς νήπιος, ἐφρόνουν
When I was [a] child, I spoke   as [a] child, I thought

ὡς νήπιος, ἐλογιζόμην ὡς νήπιος· ὅτε γέγονα
as [a] child, I reasoned   as [a] child;   when I became

ἀνήρ, κατήργηκα   τὰ τοῦ νηπίου.   12 βλέπομεν
a man,   I rendered inoperative the things of the child.   For we look

γὰρ ἄρτι δι'   ἐσόπτρου ἐν αἰνίγματι, τότε δὲ
now through [a] mirror   in [an] enigma,   but then

πρόσωπον πρὸς πρόσωπον· ἄρτι γινώσκω
face   to face,   now I know

ἐκ μέρους, τότε δὲ ἐπιγνώσομαι καθὼς καὶ
in part,   but then I will know   as   also

ἐπεγνώσθην. 13 νυνὶ δὲ μένει πίστις, ἐλπίς, ἀγάπη,
I was known.   But now remains faith,   hope,   love,

τὰ τρία ταῦτα· μείζων δὲ τούτων ἡ ἀγάπη.
these three things: but greater than them [is] - love

15:7–9
7 ἔπειτα ὤφθη   Ἰακώβῳ, εἶτα τοῖς ἀποστόλοις
Then   he appeared to James,   thus   to the apostles

πᾶσιν· 8 ἔσχατον δὲ πάντων ὡσπερεὶ τῷ
all;   but last then of all   just as if   to a

ἐκτρώματι ὤφθη   κἀμοί. 9 Ἐγὼ γάρ εἰμι ὁ ἐλάχιστος
miscarriage he appeared also to me.   For I   am   the least

τῶν ἀποστόλων, ὃς οὐκ εἰμὶ ἱκανὸς καλεῖσθαι
of the apostles,   who not am   worthy to be called

ἀπόστολος, διότι ἐδίωξα   τὴν ἐκκλησίαν
apostle,   because I persecuted the   community

τοῦ θεοῦ·
of God.

15:20–28
20 Νυνὶ δὲ Χριστὸς ἐγήγερται ἐκ νεκρῶν, ἀπαρχὴ
But now   [the] Messiah has been awoken from [the] dead, initial source

τῶν κεκοιμημένων. 21 ἐπειδὴ γὰρ δι' ἀνθρώπου
of those having slept. For since through [a] man

θάνατος, καὶ δι' ἀνθρώπου ἀνάστασις νεκρῶν.
death [came], also through [a] man resurrection from death.

22 ὥσπερ γὰρ ἐν τῷ Ἀδὰμ πάντες ἀποθνήσκουσιν,
For just as in - Adam all die

οὕτως καὶ ἐν τῷ Χριστῷ πάντες ζωοποιηθήσονται.
so also in the Messiah all will be made alive.

23 Ἕκαστος δὲ ἐν τῷ ἰδίῳ τάγματι· ἀπαρχὴ
But each in his own order: [the] first fruit [is]

Χριστός, ἔπειτα οἱ τοῦ Χριστοῦ ἐν τῇ παρουσίᾳ
the Messiah, then those of [the] Messiah in the coming

αὐτοῦ, 24 εἶτα τὸ τέλος, ὅταν παραδιδοῖ τὴν
of him, then the end, when he gives the

βασιλείαν τῷ θεῷ καὶ πατρί, ὅταν καταργήσῃ
kingdom to God and Father, when he renders inoperative

πᾶσαν ἀρχὴν καὶ πᾶσαν ἐξουσίαν καὶ δύναμιν.
all rule and all authority and power.

25 δεῖ γὰρ αὐτὸν βασιλεύειν ἄχρι οὗ θῇ
For it is necessary [that] he rule until - he puts

πάντας τοὺς ἐχθροὺς ὑπὸ τοὺς πόδας αὐτοῦ.
all the enemies under the feet of him.

26 ἔσχατος ἐχθρὸς καταργεῖται ὁ θάνατος·
The last enemy rendered inoperative [is] - death;

27 πάντα γὰρ ὑπέταξεν ὑπὸ τοὺς πόδας αὐτοῦ.
for all he subjects under the feet of him.

ὅταν δὲ εἴπῃ ὅτι πάντα ὑποτέτακται, δῆλον ὅτι
But when he says that all have been subjected, [it is] clear that

ἐκτὸς τοῦ ὑποτάξαντος αὐτῷ τὰ πάντα.
it excepts the one subjecting to him - all things.

28 ὅταν δὲ ὑποταγῇ αὐτῷ τὰ πάντα, τότε καὶ
But when he will subject to him - all things, then also

αὐτὸς ὁ υἱὸς ὑποταγήσεται τῷ ὑποτάξαντι
himself the son will be subjected to the one subjecting

αὐτῷ τὰ πάντα, ἵνα ᾖ ὁ θεὸς πάντα ἐν πᾶσιν.
to him - all things, in order that be - God all in all.

From the Second Letter to the Corinthians

3:1–3
1 Ἀρχόμεθα πάλιν ἑαυτοὺς συνιστάνειν; ἢ μὴ
  Do we begin   again   ourselves   to commend?   Oh [do] not

χρήζομεν ὥς τινες συστατικῶν ἐπιστολῶν πρὸς
we need   as   some   of recommendation   letters   to

ὑμᾶς ἢ ἐξ ὑμῶν; 2 ἡ ἐπιστολὴ ἡμῶν ὑμεῖς ἐστε,
you   or from you?   The letter   of us   you   are,

ἐγγεγραμμένη ἐν ταῖς καρδίαις ἡμῶν, γινωσκομένη
written   on   the   hearts   of us,   being known

καὶ ἀναγινωσκομένη ὑπὸ πάντων ἀνθρώπων,
and   being read   by   all   men,

3 φανερούμενοι ὅτι ἐστὲ ἐπιστολὴ Χριστοῦ
  manifesting   that   you are [the] letter   of [the] Messiah

διακονηθεῖσα ὑφ' ἡμῶν, ἐγγεγραμμένη οὐ μέλανι
served   by   us,   written   not with ink

ἀλλὰ πνεύματι θεοῦ ζῶντος, οὐκ ἐν πλαξὶν
but   with [the] spirit of God living,   not   on tablets

λιθίναις ἀλλ' ἐν πλαξὶν καρδίαις σαρκίναις.
of stone   but   on tablets   [of the] heart fleshy.

3:12–18
12 Ἔχοντες οὖν τοιαύτην ἐλπίδα πολλῇ
   Therefore   having this sort of   hope   great

παρρησία χρώμεθα, 13 καὶ οὐ καθάπερ Μωϋσῆς
freedom in speaking we use,   and   not just as   Moses

ἐτίθει κάλυμμα ἐπὶ τὸ πρόσωπον αὐτοῦ, πρὸς
placed   [a] veil   on   the face   of him,   for

τὸ μὴ ἀτενίσαι τοὺς υἱοὺς Ἰσραὴλ εἰς τὸ τέλος
not to stare   the   sons   of Israel   to   the end

τοῦ καταργουμένου. 14 ἀλλὰ ἐπωρώθη
of   that which has been made inoperative.   But   were hardened

τὰ νοήματα αὐτῶν. ἄχρι γὰρ τῆς σήμερον ἡμέρας
the thoughts   of them.   For as far as   this   very   day

τὸ αὐτὸ κάλυμμα ἐπὶ τῇ ἀναγνώσει τῆς παλαιᾶς
the same   veil   upon -   reading   the   old

διαθήκης μένει, μὴ ἀνακαλυπτόμενον ὅτι ἐν
covenant remains, not uncovered since in

Χριστῷ καταργεῖται· 15 ἀλλ' ἕως σήμερον
[the] Messiah it is rendered inoperative, but unto today

ἡνίκα ἂν ἀναγινώσκηται Μωϋσῆς κάλυμμα ἐπὶ τὴν
when is read Moses [the] veil on the

καρδίαν αὐτῶν κεῖται· 16 ἡνίκα δὲ ἐὰν ἐπιστρέψῃ
heart of them lays. But when so ever [he] turns

πρὸς κύριον, περιαιρεῖται τὸ κάλυμμα.
toward [the] Lord, is removed the veil.

17 ὁ δὲ κύριος τὸ πνεῦμά ἐστιν· οὗ δὲ τὸ πνεῦμα
The Lord the spirit is; where - the spirit

κυρίου, ἐλευθερία. 18 ἡμεῖς δὲ πάντες
of [the] Lord [is], freedom [is]. But we all

ἀνακεκαλυμμένῳ προσώπῳ τὴν δόξαν κυρίου
uncovered of face the glory of [the] Lord

κατοπτριζόμενοι τὴν αὐτὴν εἰκόνα
we are reflecting as in a mirror the same image

μεταμορφούμεθα ἀπὸ δόξης εἰς δόξαν, καθάπερ
our being transformed from glory to glory, just as

ἀπὸ κυρίου πνεύματος.
from Lord's spirit.

5:16-17

16 Ὥστε ἡμεῖς ἀπὸ τοῦ νῦν οὐδένα οἴδαμεν κατὰ
So that we from - now no one we know according to

σάρκα· εἰ καὶ ἐγνώκαμεν κατὰ σάρκα Χριστόν,
[the] flesh; and if we knew according to [the] flesh [the] Messiah,

ἀλλὰ νῦν οὐκέτι γινώσκομεν. 17 ὥστε εἴ τις ἐν
but now no longer we know [him so]. So that if someone [is] in

Χριστῷ, καινὴ κτίσις· τὰ ἀρχαῖα παρῆλθεν, ἰδοὺ
[the] Messiah, [a] new creation, the old things have passed away, behold

γέγονεν καινά.
they have become new.

12:1-10

1 Καυχᾶσθαι δεῖ, οὐ συμφέρον μέν, ἐλεύσομαι
To boast is necessary not helpful though, I will come

δὲ εἰς ὀπτασίας καὶ ἀποκαλύψεις κυρίου. 2 οἶδα
- unto visions and revelations of [the] Lord. I know

ἄνθρωπον ἐν Χριστῷ πρὸ ἐτῶν δεκατεσσάρων,
a man in [the] Messiah ago years fourteen,

— εἴτε ἐν σώματι οὐκ οἶδα, εἴτε ἐκτὸς τοῦ σώματος
— whether in [the] body not I know, or out of the body

οὐκ οἶδα, ὁ θεὸς οἶδεν, — ἁρπαγέντα τὸν τοιοῦτον
not I know, God knows, — being seized by force this one

ἕως τρίτου οὐρανοῦ. 3 καὶ οἶδα τὸν τοιοῦτον
until third heaven. And I know [that] this

ἄνθρωπον — εἴτε ἐν σώματι εἴτε χωρὶς τοῦ
man — whether in [the] body or outside of the

σώματος [οὐκ οἶδα], ὁ θεὸς οἶδεν — 4 ὅτι ἡρπάγη
body not I know, - God knows, — that he was seized by force

εἰς τὸν παράδεισον καὶ ἤκουσεν ἄρρητα ῥήματα,
into - paradise and he heard ineffable words,

ἃ οὐκ ἐξὸν ἀνθρώπῳ λαλῆσαι. 5 ὑπὲρ
which not are allowed by man to be spoken. Concerning

τοῦ τοιούτου καυχήσομαι, ὑπὲρ δὲ ἐμαυτοῦ
- this one I will boast, but concerning myself

οὐ καυχήσομαι εἰ μὴ ἐν ταῖς ἀσθενείαις.
not will I boast unless - in - weaknesses.

6 ἐὰν γὰρ θελήσω καυχήσασθαι, οὐκ ἔσομαι ἄφρων,
For if I wish to boast, not will I be mindless,

ἀλήθειαν γὰρ ἐρῶ· φείδομαι δὲ, μή τις εἰς
for truth I will speak; but I withhold, lest someone concerning

ἐμὲ λογίσηται ὑπὲρ ὃ βλέπει με ἢ ἀκούει
me reckon beyond that which he sees me [being] or hears

ἐξ ἐμοῦ 7 καὶ τῇ ὑπερβολῇ τῶν ἀποκαλύψεων. διὸ
from me and by the excesses of the revelations. Therefore

ἵνα μὴ ὑπεραίρωμαι, ἐδόθη μοι σκόλοψ τῇ σαρκί,
in order that not I be elevated, was given to me [a] thorn in the flesh,

ἄγγελος σατανᾶ, ἵνα με κολαφίζῃ, ἵνα μὴ
an angel of Satan, so that me he might disturb, so that not

ὑπεραίρωμαι. 8 ὑπὲρ τούτου τρὶς τὸν κύριον
I should not be elevated. For this thrice the Lord

παρεκάλεσα ἵνα ἀποστῇ ἀπ' ἐμοῦ. 9 καὶ εἴρηκέν
I beseeched   that it leave   from me.   And he said

μοι· ἀρκεῖ σοι ἡ χάρις μου· ἡ γὰρ δύναμις ἐν
to me: Enough to you the grace   of me, -   for   power   in

ἀσθενείᾳ τελεῖται. Ἥδιστα οὖν   μᾶλλον
weakness   is realized.   Most sweet therefore rather

καυχήσομαι ἐν ταῖς ἀσθενείαις, ἵνα
will I boast   in -   weaknesses,   so that

ἐπισκηνώσῃ ἐπ' ἐμὲ ἡ δύναμις τοῦ Χριστοῦ.
should set up tent over me   the power   of   [the] Messiah.

10 διὸ   εὐδοκῶ ἐν ἀσθενείαις, ἐν ὕβρεσιν, ἐν
Therefore I am pleased in   weaknesses.   in injuries,   in

ἀνάγκαις, ἐν διωγμοῖς καὶ στενοχωρίαις, ὑπὲρ
necessities,   in persecutions and constraints   for

Χριστοῦ· ὅταν γὰρ ἀσθενῶ, τότε δυνατός εἰμι.
[the] Messiah; for whenever I am weak, then   powerful   am I.

From the Letter to the Galatians

1:11–17

11 γνωρίζω γὰρ ὑμῖν, ἀδελφοί, τὸ εὐαγγέλιον τὸ
For I make known to you, brothers,   the announcement -

εὐαγγελισθὲν ὑπ' ἐμοῦ ὅτι οὐκ ἔστιν κατὰ
announced   by me   that not is   according to

ἄνθρωπον· 12 οὐδὲ γὰρ ἐγὼ παρὰ ἀνθρώπου
man;   for neither I   from   man

παρέλαβον αὐτὸ οὔτε ἐδιδάχθην, ἀλλὰ δι'
received   it,   nor   was I taught,   but   through

ἀποκαλύψεως Ἰησοῦ Χριστοῦ. 13 Ἠκούσατε
the revelation   of Jesus Messiah.   For you heard

γὰρ τὴν ἐμὴν ἀναστροφήν ποτε ἐν τῷ Ἰουδαϊσμῷ,
- of my   upheaval   one time in -   Judaism,

ὅτι καθ' ὑπερβολὴν ἐδίωκον τὴν ἐκκλησίαν τοῦ
that according to excesses I persecuted the community   of

θεοῦ καὶ ἐπόρθουν αὐτήν, 14 καὶ προέκοπτον
God and ravaged   it,   and I was advancing

ἐν τῷ Ἰουδαϊσμῷ ὑπὲρ πολλοὺς συνηλικιώτας
in -   Judaism   beyond many   contemporaries

ἐν τῷ γένει μου, περισσοτέρως ζηλωτὴς ὑπάρχων
in the kin   of me, more fully   zealous   being

τῶν πατρικῶν μου παραδόσεων.   15 Ὅτε δὲ
than the fathers   of me of [the] traditions.   But when

εὐδόκησεν ὁ ἀφορίσας με ἐκ κοιλίας
was pleased   who separated   me from [the] womb

μητρός   μου καὶ καλέσας διὰ   τῆς χάριτος
of [the] mother of me and   called [me] through the   grace

αὐτοῦ   16 ἀποκαλύψαι τὸν υἱὸν αὐτοῦ ἐν ἐμοί, ἵνα
of him   to reveal   the son of him in me,   so that

εὐαγγελίζωμαι   αὐτὸν ἐν   τοῖς ἔθνεσιν, εὐθέως
I announce the good news, him   among the   peoples   right away

οὐ προσανεθέμην σαρκὶ καὶ αἵματι,   17 οὐδὲ ἀνῆλθον
not I conferred   with flesh and blood,   nor   did I go up

εἰς Ἱεροσόλυμα πρὸς τοὺς πρὸ ἐμοῦ ἀποστόλους,
to Jerusalem   with those before me   emissaries,

ἀλλὰ ἀπῆλθον εἰς Ἀραβίαν, καὶ πάλιν ὑπέστρεψα
but   I went away to   Arabia   and again   I returned

εἰς Δαμασκόν.
to Damascus.

2:1–14
1 Ἔπειτα διὰ δεκατεσσάρων ἐτῶν πάλιν ἀνέβην
Then   after fourteen   years again   I went up

εἰς Ἱεροσόλυμα μετὰ Βαρναβᾶ, συμπαραλαβὼν
to Jerusalem   with Barnabas,   bringing along

καὶ Τίτον·   2 ἀνέβην δὲ κατὰ   ἀποκάλυψιν· καὶ
also Titus;   and I went up according to [a] revelation;   and

ἀνεθέμην αὐτοῖς τὸ εὐαγγέλιον ὃ   κηρύσσω ἐν
presented   to them   the announcement which I declare   among

τοῖς ἔθνεσιν, κατ' ἰδίαν δὲ τοῖς δοκοῦσιν, μή πως
the peoples,   but in private   to the esteemed,   lest somehow

εἰς κενὸν τρέχω ἢ ἔδραμον.   3 ἀλλ' οὐδὲ Τίτος ὁ
for naught I run   or had run.   But not even Titus   who [was]

σὺν ἐμοί, Ἕλλην ὤν, ἠναγκάσθη περιτμηθῆναι·
with me,   Greek   being, was forced   to be circumcised;

4 διὰ δὲ   τοὺς παρεισάκτους ψευδαδέλφους,
but on account of the   intruding   false brothers,

οἵτινες παρεισῆλθον κατασκοπῆσαι τὴν ἐλευθερίαν
who   entered   to spy out   the   freedom

ἡμῶν ἣν ἔχομεν ἐν Χριστῷ Ἰησοῦ, ἵνα ἡμᾶς
of us   that we have   in [the] Messiah Jesus,   so that of us

καταδουλώσουσιν· 5 οἷς οὐδὲ πρὸς ὥραν
they enslave;   to whom not even for   [a] moment

εἴξαμεν τῇ ὑποταγῇ, ἵνα ἡ ἀλήθεια τοῦ εὐαγγελίου
did we give in to   subjection,   so that the truth   of the announcement

διαμείνῃ πρὸς ὑμᾶς. 6 ἀπὸ δὲ τῶν δοκούντων
remain   with   you.   But from those esteemed

εἶναί τι,   — ὁποῖοί ποτε ἦσαν οὐδέν μοι διαφέρει·
to be something— whatever then   they were nothing to me it matters:

πρόσωπον [ὁ] θεὸς ἀνθρώπου οὐ λαμβάνει   — ἐμοὶ
the face   - God   of man   not takes into account — for to me

γὰρ οἱ δοκοῦντες οὐδὲν προσανέθεντο, 7 ἀλλὰ
for   those reputable nothing conferred,   but

τοὐναντίον ἰδόντες ὅτι πεπίστευμαι τὸ εὐαγγέλιον
the opposite having seen that I believe in   the announcement

τῆς ἀκροβυστίας καθὼς Πέτρος τῆς περιτομῆς,
of the foreskin   just as   Peter   of the circumcision,

8 ὁ γὰρ ἐνεργήσας Πέτρῳ εἰς ἀποστολὴν τῆς
for he having activated in Peter   for the mission   of the

περιτομῆς ἐνήργησεν καὶ ἐμοὶ εἰς τὰ ἔθνη, 9 καὶ
circumcision he activated   also in me for the Gentiles,   and

γνόντες τὴν χάριν τὴν δοθεῖσάν μοι, Ἰάκωβος
having known the grace given   to me, James

καὶ Κηφᾶς καὶ Ἰωάννης, οἱ δοκοῦντες στῦλοι
and Cephas and John,   who esteemed   pillars

εἶναι, δεξιὰς ἔδωκαν ἐμοὶ καὶ Βαρναβᾷ κοινωνίας,
to be, [the] right hands they gave to me and Barnabas of communion,

ἵνα ἡμεῖς εἰς τὰ ἔθνη, αὐτοὶ δὲ εἰς τὴν περιτομήν·
so that we   for the Gentiles, but they instead for the circumcision;

10 μόνον τῶν πτωχῶν ἵνα μνημονεύωμεν, ὃ καὶ
only   the   poor   that we remember,   which also

ἐσπούδασα αὐτὸ τοῦτο ποιῆσαι. 11 Ὅτε δὲ ἦλθεν
I concentrated [this] same thing to make.   But when came

Κηφᾶς εἰς Ἀντιόχειαν, κατὰ πρόσωπον αὐτῷ
Cephas to   Antioch,   in   face   to him

ἀντέστην, ὅτι κατεγνωσμένος ἦν. 12 πρὸ τοῦ
I opposed,   because about to be blamed   he was.   For before the

γὰρ ἐλθεῖν τινας ἀπὸ Ἰακώβου μετὰ τῶν ἐθνῶν
coming   some   from James   with   the   Gentiles

συνήσθιεν· ὅτε δὲ ἦλθον, ὑπέστελλεν καὶ
he ate with;   but when they came, he withdrew   and

ἀφώριζεν ἑαυτόν, φοβούμενος τοὺς ἐκ περιτομῆς·
separated   himself,   fearing   those   of   circumcision;

13 καὶ συνυπεκρίθησαν αὐτῷ [καὶ] οἱ λοιποὶ
and   pretended   with him also   the other

Ἰουδαῖοι, ὥστε καὶ Βαρναβᾶς συναπήχθη αὐτῶν
Jews,   so that also   Barnabas   was split off   from them

τῇ ὑποκρίσει. 14 ἀλλ' ὅτε εἶδον ὅτι οὐκ
by the hypocrisy.   But   when I saw   that   not

ὀρθοποδοῦσιν πρὸς τὴν ἀλήθειαν τοῦ εὐαγγελίου,
did they go rightly   according to the   truth   of the announcement,

εἶπον τῷ Κηφᾷ ἔμπροσθεν πάντων· εἰ σὺ Ἰουδαῖος
I said   to   Cephas in front of   all: if   you   Jew

ὑπάρχων ἐθνικῶς καὶ οὐκ Ἰουδαϊκῶς ζῇς, πῶς
being,   Gentiles   and   not   like Jew   live,   how

τὰ ἔθνη ἀναγκάζεις ἰουδαΐζειν;
the Gentiles will you compel to live as Jews?

3:10−14

10 ὅσοι γὰρ ἐξ ἔργων νόμου εἰσὶν ὑπὸ κατάραν
For as many as from works   of law   are,   under curse

εἰσίν· γέγραπται γὰρ ὅτι ἐπικατάρατος πᾶς ὃς
are;   for it has been written that: Cursed [be]   each who

οὐκ ἐμμένει πᾶσιν τοῖς γεγραμμένοις ἐν τῷ βιβλίῳ
not dwells   in all   the   things written   in the book

τοῦ νόμου τοῦ ποιῆσαι αὐτά. 11 ὅτι δὲ ἐν νόμῳ
of the law   to make   them.   But -   by law

οὐδεὶς δικαιοῦται παρὰ τῷ θεῷ δῆλον, ὅτι ὁ
no one   is justified   with -   God [is] manifest, because the

δίκαιος ἐκ πίστεως ζήσεται· 12 ὁ δὲ νόμος οὐκ
just one   by faith   shall live;   but the law   not

ἔστιν ἐκ πίστεως, ἀλλ' ὁ ποιήσας αὐτὰ   ζήσεται
is   of faith,   but: He having made these things will live

ἐν αὐτοῖς.   13 Χριστὸς   ἡμᾶς ἐξηγόρασεν ἐκ
in them.   [The] Messiah us   ransomed   from

τῆς κατάρας τοῦ νόμου γενόμενος ὑπὲρ ἡμῶν
the curse   of the law   having become for   us

κατάρα, ὅτι γέγραπται· ἐπικατάρατος πᾶς
a curse, as   it has been written: Cursed   [be] each

ὁ κρεμάμενος ἐπὶ ξύλου, 14 ἵνα   εἰς τὰ ἔθνη ἡ
- hanging   from [the] wood, so that to   the peoples the

εὐλογία τοῦ Ἀβραὰμ γένηται ἐν Ἰησοῦ Χριστῷ,
blessing of Abraham   may come in Jesus   Messiah,

ἵνα   τὴν ἐπαγγελίαν τοῦ πνεύματος λάβωμεν διὰ
so that the promise   of the spirit   we may receive through

τῆς πίστεως.
-    faith.

4:21–26
21 Λέγετέ μοι, οἱ ὑπὸ νόμον θέλοντες εἶναι, τὸν
Tell   to me, ones under law   wanting   to be,   the

νόμον οὐκ ἀκούετε; 22 γέγραπται γὰρ ὅτι Ἀβραὰμ
law   not do you hear?   For it has been written that Abraham

δύο υἱοὺς ἔσχεν, ἕνα ἐκ τῆς παιδίσκης καὶ ἕνα
two sons   had,   one from the maidservant   and one

ἐκ τῆς ἐλευθέρας. 23 ἀλλ' ὁ [μὲν] ἐκ τῆς παιδίσκης
from the free woman.   But the one   from the   maidservant

κατὰ   σάρκα γεγέννηται, ὁ δὲ ἐκ τῆς ἐλευθέρας
according to flesh   was born,   the other from the   free woman

διὰ   τῆς ἐπαγγελίας. 24 ἅτινά   ἐστιν ἀλληγορούμενα·
through the promise.   These things are   being allegorized

αὗται γὰρ εἰσιν δύο διαθῆκαι, μία μὲν ἀπὸ ὄρους
for these   are   two covenants, one -   from Mount

Σινᾶ, εἰς δουλείαν γεννῶσα, ἥτις ἐστὶν Ἁγάρ.
Sinai, to   slavery   generating, which is   Hagar.

25 τὸ δὲ Ἁγὰρ Σινᾶ ὄρος ἐστὶν ἐν τῇ Ἀραβίᾳ,
-   But Hagar Sinai Mount is   in -   Arabia;

συστοιχεῖ δὲ τῇ νῦν Ἰερουσαλήμ, δουλεύει γὰρ
and corresponds to now Jerusalem,   for enslaved

μετὰ τῶν τέκνων αὐτῆς. 26 ἡ δὲ ἄνω Ἰερουσαλὴμ
with the children of her. - But above Jerusalem

ἐλευθέρα ἐστίν, ἥτις ἐστὶν μήτηρ ἡμῶν·
free is, who is mother of us.

From the Letter to the Ephesians

1:9—10

9 γνωρίσας ἡμῖν τὸ μυστήριον τοῦ θελήματος
having made known to us the mystery of the will

αὐτοῦ, κατὰ τὴν εὐδοκίαν αὐτοῦ, ἣν προέθετο
of him, according to the good thoughts of him, which he decided beforehand

ἐν αὐτῷ 10 εἰς οἰκονομίαν τοῦ πληρώματος
in him for [the] economy of the fullness

τῶν καιρῶν, ἀνακεφαλαιώσασθαι τὰ πάντα ἐν τῷ
of the times, recapitulating - all things in the

Χριστῷ, τὰ ἐπὶ τοῖς οὐρανοῖς καὶ τὰ ἐπὶ τῆς γῆς·
Messiah, things in the heavens and things on - earth

ἐν αὐτῷ . . .
in him . . .

From the Letter to the Phillipians

2:5—11

5 τοῦτο φρονεῖτε ἐν ὑμῖν ὃ καὶ ἐν Χριστῷ Ἰησοῦ,
This you think in you that [was] also in [the] Messiah Jesus,

6 ὃς ἐν μορφῇ θεοῦ ὑπάρχων οὐχ ἁρπαγμὸν
who in [the] form of God existing, not theft [was it]

ἡγήσατο τὸ εἶναι ἴσα θεῷ, 7 ἀλλὰ ἑαυτὸν
[to be] reputed to be equal to God, but himself

ἐκένωσεν μορφὴν δούλου λαβών, ἐν ὁμοιώματι
emptied [the] form of [a] slave having taken, in likeness

ἀνθρώπων γενόμενος· καὶ σχήματι εὑρεθεὶς
of man having become; and [in] figure discovered

ὡς ἄνθρωπος 8 ἐταπείνωσεν ἑαυτὸν γενόμενος
as a man he lowered himself having become

ὑπήκοος μέχρι θανάτου, θανάτου δὲ σταυροῦ.
subjected until death, death - of [the] cross.

9 διὸ καὶ ὁ θεὸς αὐτὸν ὑπερύψωσεν καὶ ἐχαρίσατο
Therefore even - God him highly exalted and granted

αὐτῷ τὸ ὄνομα τὸ ὑπὲρ πᾶν ὄνομα, 10 ἵνα ἐν τῷ
to him the name - above every name, so that in the

ὀνόματι Ἰησοῦ πᾶν γόνυ κάμψῃ ἐπουρανίων καὶ
name of Jesus every knee may bend of [things] of heaven and

ἐπιγείων καὶ καταχθονίων, 11 καὶ πᾶσα γλῶσσα
of earth and below, and each tongue

ἐξομολογήσηται ὅτι ΚΥΡΙΟΣ ΙΗΣΟΥΣ ΧΡΙΣΤΟΣ εἰς
will confess that [the] Lord [is] Jesus Messiah in

δόξαν θεοῦ πατρός.
glory of God [the] Father.

3:3–14

3 ἡμεῖς γάρ ἐσμεν ἡ περιτομή, οἱ πνεύματι θεοῦ
For we are the circumcision, the ones in spirit of God

λατρεύοντες καὶ καυχώμενοι ἐν Χριστῷ Ἰησοῦ
serving and boasting in [the] Messiah Jesus

καὶ οὐκ ἐν σαρκὶ πεποιθότες, 4 καίπερ ἐγὼ ἔχων
and not in [the] flesh convinced, though I having

πεποίθησιν καὶ ἐν σαρκί. Εἴ τις δοκεῖ ἄλλος
conviction also in flesh. If someone thinks another

πεποιθέναι ἐν σαρκί, ἐγὼ μᾶλλον· 5 περιτομῇ
to be convinced in flesh, I more: circumcision

ὀκταήμερος, ἐκ γένους Ἰσραήλ, φυλῆς Βενιαμίν,
[on the] eighth day, from [the] kin of Israel, tribe of Benjamin

Ἑβραῖος ἐξ Ἑβραίων, κατὰ νόμον Φαρισαῖος,
Hebrew of Hebrews, according to [the] law [a] Pharisee,

6 κατὰ ζῆλος διώκων τὴν ἐκκλησίαν, κατὰ
according to zeal persecuting the community, according to

δικαιοσύνην τὴν ἐν νόμῳ γενόμενος ἄμεμπτος.
justice, that in [the] law having become blameless.

7 ἀλλὰ ἅτινα ἦν μοι κέρδη, ταῦτα ἥγημαι διὰ
But whatever was to me [as] gain, these [I] thought through

τὸν Χριστὸν ζημίαν. 8 ἀλλὰ μενοῦν γε καὶ ἡγοῦμαι
the Messiah [as] loss. But certainly - also I think through

πάντα ζημίαν εἶναι διὰ τὸ ὑπερέχον τῆς γνώσεως
all things loss to be on account of the superiority of the knowledge

Χριστοῦ Ἰησοῦ τοῦ κυρίου μου, δι' ὃν τὰ πάντα
of [the] Messiah Jesus the Lord of me, through whom all things

ἐζημιώθην, καὶ ἡγοῦμαι   σκύβαλα ἵνα   Χριστὸν
I esteemed lost, and   I think through excrement   in order that [the] Messiah

κερδήσω 9 καὶ εὑρεθῶ ἐν αὐτῷ, μὴ ἔχων ἐμὴν
I may earn   and be found in him,   not having my

δικαιοσύνην τὴν ἐκ νόμου, ἀλλὰ τὴν διὰ πίστεως
justice, [be]   that from law,   but   the one through faith

Χριστοῦ,   τὴν ἐκ θεοῦ δικαιοσύνην ἐπὶ τῇ πίστει,
of [the] Messiah, the from God justice   upon the faith,

10 τοῦ γνῶναι αὐτὸν καὶ τὴν δύναμιν τῆς
for knowing him   and the power   of the

ἀναστάσεως αὐτοῦ καὶ κοινωνίαν
resurrection   of him and communion [of the]

παθημάτων αὐτοῦ, συμμορφιζόμενος τῷ θανάτῳ
sufferings   of him,   sharing form with   the death

αὐτοῦ, 11 εἴ πως   καταντήσω εἰς τὴν ἐξανάστασιν
of him,   if somehow I will end up at   the resurrection

τὴν ἐκ νεκρῶν. 12 Οὐχ ὅτι ἤδη ἔλαβον ἢ ἤδη
-   of [the] dead.   Not that already I seized or already

τετελείωμαι, διώκω δὲ εἰ καὶ καταλάβω, ἐφ' ᾧ καὶ
have completed, but I seek since   also I seize hold   for which also

κατελήμφθην ὑπὸ Χριστοῦ Ἰησοῦ. 13 ἀδελφοί,
I was seized hold of by [the] Messiah Jesus.   Brothers,

ἐγὼ ἐμαυτὸν οὔπω λογίζομαι κατειληφέναι· ἐν δέ,
I myself   not   reckon   to have been seized; but one thing:

τὰ μὲν   ὀπίσω ἐπιλανθανόμενος
things on one hand [that are] behind   being forgotten,

τοῖς δὲ   ἔμπροσθεν ἐπεκτεινόμενος,
towards the things that on the other hand are before me,   I extend,

14 κατὰ σκοπὸν διώκω εἰς τὸ βραβεῖον
toward [the] goal I pursue to   the prize

τῆς ἄνω   κλήσεως τοῦ θεοῦ ἐν Χριστῷ Ἰησοῦ.
of the from above calling   of   God in [the] Messiah Jesus.

From the First Letter to the Thessalonians

1:3–5

3 μνημονεύοντες ὑμῶν τοῦ ἔργου τῆς πίστεως
Remembering   of you the work   of   faith

καὶ τοῦ κόπου τῆς ἀγάπης καὶ τῆς ὑπομονῆς
and of the toil of love and the patience

τῆς ἐλπίδος τοῦ κυρίου ἡμῶν Ἰησοῦ Χριστοῦ
of hope of the Lord of us Jesus Messiah

ἔμπροσθεν τοῦ θεοῦ καὶ πατρὸς ἡμῶν, 4 εἰδότες,
before - God and [the] Father of us. Knowing,

ἀδελφοὶ ἠγαπημένοι ὑπὸ [τοῦ] θεοῦ, τὴν ἐκλογὴν
brothers beloved by - God, the election

ὑμῶν, 5 ὅτι τὸ εὐαγγέλιον ἡμῶν οὐκ ἐγενήθη
of you, that the announcement of us not generated

εἰς ὑμᾶς ἐν λόγῳ μόνον, ἀλλὰ καὶ ἐν δυνάμει
in you in word only, but also in power

καὶ ἐν πνεύματι ἁγίῳ καὶ πληροφορίᾳ πολλῇ,
and in spirit holy and transported in fullness,

καθὼς οἴδατε οἷοι ἐγενήθημεν ἐν ὑμῖν δι' ὑμᾶς.
just as you know what sort we became among you for you.

4:13–17
13 Οὐ θέλομεν δὲ ὑμᾶς ἀγνοεῖν, ἀδελφοί, περὶ τῶν
But we do not want you to be ignorant, brothers, concerning those

κοιμωμένων, ἵνα μὴ λυπῆσθε καθὼς καὶ οἱ λοιποὶ
who fell asleep, so that not you become saddened just as also the others

οἱ μὴ ἔχοντες ἐλπίδα. 14 εἰ γὰρ πιστεύομεν ὅτι
ones not having hope. For if we believe that

Ἰησοῦς ἀπέθανεν καὶ ἀνέστη, οὕτως καὶ ὁ θεὸς
Jesus died and rose, thus also - God

τοὺς κοιμηθέντας διὰ τοῦ Ἰησοῦ ἄξει σὺν αὐτῷ.
those asleep through - Jesus will lead with him.

15 Τοῦτο γὰρ ὑμῖν λέγομεν ἐν λόγῳ κυρίου,
For this to you we speak in [the] word of [the] Lord,

ὅτι ἡμεῖς οἱ ζῶντες οἱ περιλειπόμενοι εἰς τὴν
that we the living who are remaining in the

παρουσίαν τοῦ κυρίου οὐ μὴ φθάσωμεν τοὺς
coming of the Lord not do we come to be those

κοιμηθέντας· 16 ὅτι αὐτὸς ὁ κύριος ἐν κελεύσματι,
asleep; since himself the Lord in [a] word of command,

ἐν φωνῇ ἀρχαγγέλου καὶ ἐν σάλπιγγι θεοῦ,
in [the] voice of [an] archangel and in [a] trumpet of God,

καταβήσεται ἀπ' οὐρανοῦ, καὶ οἱ νεκροὶ ἐν
shall come down from heaven, and the dead in

Χριστῷ ἀναστήσονται πρῶτον, 17 ἔπειτα ἡμεῖς
[the] Messiah shall rise up first, thereupon we

οἱ ζῶντες οἱ περιλειπόμενοι ἅμα σὺν αὐτοῖς
the living who remain along with them

ἁρπαγησόμεθα ἐν νεφέλαις εἰς ἀπάντησιν τοῦ
will be snatched up in [the] clouds for encountering the

κυρίου εἰς ἀέρα· καὶ οὕτως πάντοτε σὺν κυρίῳ
Lord in [the] air; and thus always with [the] Lord

ἐσόμεθα.
we will be.

5:1–3
1 Περὶ δὲ τῶν χρόνων καὶ τῶν καιρῶν, ἀδελφοί,
But concerning the times and the moments, brothers,

οὐ χρείαν ἔχετε ὑμῖν γράφεσθαι· 2 αὐτοὶ γὰρ
not need do you have in you to be written; for yourselves

ἀκριβῶς οἴδατε ὅτι ἡμέρα κυρίου ὡς κλέπτης
exactly you know that [the] day of [the] Lord as thief

ἐν νυκτὶ οὕτως ἔρχεται. 3 ὅταν λέγωσιν· εἰρήνη
in [the] night thus it comes. Whenever they will say: Peace

καὶ ἀσφάλεια, τότε αἰφνίδιος αὐτοῖς ἐφίσταται
and security, then suddenly for them comes

ὄλεθρος ὥσπερ ἡ ὠδὶν τῇ ἐν γαστρὶ ἐχούσῃ, καὶ
destruction just as the labour to her in womb having, and

οὐ μὴ ἐκφύγωσιν.
not - will they escape.

From the Second Letter to the Thessalonians

2:3–11
3 μή τις ὑμᾶς ἐξαπατήσῃ κατὰ μηδένα τρόπον·
Not someone you will deceive in any way!

ὅτι ἐὰν μὴ ἔλθῃ ἡ ἀποστασία πρῶτον
For [it will not be] unless comes the apostasy first

καὶ ἀποκαλυφθῇ ὁ ἄνθρωπος τῆς ἀνομίας, ὁ υἱὸς
and was revealed the man of lawlessness, the son

τῆς ἀπωλείας, 4 ὁ   ἀντικείμενος καὶ ὑπεραιρόμενος
- of destruction,   the one opposing   and   exalting

ἐπὶ πάντα   λεγόμενον θεὸν ἢ σέβασμα,
above all those things called   God   or object of worship,

ὥστε αὐτὸν εἰς τὸν ναὸν τοῦ θεοῦ καθίσαι,
so as   for him in   the   temple of   God   to sit,

ἀποδεικνύντα ἑαυτὸν ὅτι ἔστιν θεός. 5 Οὐ
demonstrating   himself   that he is   God.   Not

μνημονεύετε ὅτι ἔτι ὢν πρὸς ὑμᾶς ταῦτα   ἔλεγον
do you remember that still being with   you   these things I said

ὑμῖν; 6 καὶ νῦν τὸ   κατέχον οἴδατε,   εἰς τὸ
to you?   And now the one withholding all of you know, for   -

ἀποκαλυφθῆναι αὐτὸν ἐν τῷ αὐτοῦ καιρῷ.
being revealed   himself in   -   his   moment.

7 τὸ γὰρ μυστήριον ἤδη ἐνεργεῖται τῆς ἀνομίας·
For the   mystery   already works   of   lawlessness;

μόνον ὁ   κατέχων ἄρτι ἕως ἐκ μέσου γένηται.
only   the one restraining now   until from the middle he becomes [removed].

8 καὶ τότε ἀποκαλυφθήσεται ὁ ἄνομος, ὃν ὁ κύριος
And then   will be revealed   the lawless,   whom the Lord

['Ιησοῦς] ἀνελεῖ τῷ   πνεύματι τοῦ στόματος
Jesus   will abolish with the breath   of the mouth

αὐτοῦ καὶ καταργήσει   τῇ   ἐπιφανείᾳ τῆς
of him   and   will render inoperative with the appearance   of the

παρουσίας αὐτοῦ, 9 οὗ   ἐστιν ἡ παρουσία
coming   of him,   of which [the impious] is   the presence

κατ'   ἐνέργειαν τοῦ σατανᾶ ἐν πάσῃ δυνάμει καὶ
according to [the] working of   Satan   in every   power   and [in]

σημείοις καὶ τέρασιν ψεύδους 10 καὶ ἐν πάσῃ
signs   and prodigies   of falsehood   and   with every

ἀπάτῃ ἀδικίας τοῖς ἀπολλυμένοις, ἀνθ' ὧν τὴν
trick   of injustice to those being destroyed,   because of the

ἀγάπην τῆς ἀληθείας οὐκ ἐδέξαντο εἰς τὸ
love   of   truth   not   did they accept for   -

σωθῆναι αὐτούς. 11 καὶ διὰ τοῦτο πέμπει αὐτοῖς
being saved   them.   And for   this   sends   to them

ὁ θεὸς ἐνέργειαν πλάνης   εἰς τὸ πιστεῦσαι αὐτοὺς
God   power   of miscarriage to   the believing   them

τῷ ψεύδει . . .
in   falsehood . . .

From the Letter to Philemon

1 : 15—16
15 τάχα γὰρ διὰ   τοῦτο ἐχωρίσθη   πρὸς
For perhaps   because of this   he was separated [from you] for

ὥραν, ἵνα αἰώνιον αὐτὸν ἀπέχῃς,   16 οὐκέτι ὡς δοῦλον
[a] time, until eternally   him   you may have,   no longer as   slave

ἀλλὰ ὑπὲρ δοῦλον, ἀδελφὸν ἀγαπητόν, μάλιστα ἐμοί,
but   super- slave,   [a] brother beloved,   certainly   to me,

πόσῳ δὲ   μᾶλλον σοὶ καὶ ἐν σαρκὶ καὶ ἐν κυρίῳ.
but by how much more   to you it be in   flesh   than in   [the] Lord.

References

Translator's note. The bibliography contains works cited in the text in addition to those significant works referenced by Agamben. In the case of works not originally published in English, translations were consulted and occasionally modified. Page references refer to works as they are listed here.

Adorno, Theodor W. 1974. *Minima Moralia: Reflections from Damaged Life.* Trans. E. F. N. Jephcott. London: Verso. Originally published as *Minima Moralia: Reflexionen aus dem beschädigten Leben* (Berlin: Suhrkamp, 1951).

Augustine. 1997. *On Christian Doctrine.* Trans. R. P. H. Green. New York: Oxford University Press.

Aristeas. 1951. *Letter of Aristeas.* Ed. and trans. Moses Hadas. New York: Harper.

Badiou, Alain. 1997. *Saint Paul: The Foundation of Universalism.* Translated by Ray Brassier. Stanford, Calif.: Stanford University Press, 2003. Originally published as *Saint Paul: La Fondation de l'universalisme* (Paris: Presses Universitaires de France).

Barth, Karl. 1954. *Der Römerbrief.* 9th ed. Zollikon-Zurich: Evangelischer Verlag.

Bartolo of Sassoferrato. 1555. *Tractatus minoricarum.* In *Opera.* Lugduni: Blasius.

Benjamin, Walter. 1966. *Briefe.* Ed. Gershom Scholem and Theodor W. Adorno. Frankfurt am Main: Suhrkamp. Translated by Manfred R.

Jacobson and Evelyn M. Jacobson as *The Correspondence of Walter Benjamin, 1910–1940* (Chicago: University of Chicago Press, 1994).

———. 1974–89. "Über den Begriff der Geschichte." In *Gesammelte Schriften*, vol. 1, pt. 2, ed. Rolf Tiedemann and Herbert Schweppenhäuser. Translated by Harry Zohn as "Theses on the Philosophy of History," in *Illuminations*, ed. and intro. Hannah Arendt (New York: Schocken Books, 1968).

———. 1999a. *The Arcades Project*. Ed. and intro. Hannah Arendt. Trans. Howard Eiland and Kevin McLaughlin. Cambridge, Mass.: Harvard University Press. German edition, *Gesammelte Schriften*, vol. 5, pt. 1, *Passagenwerk*, ed. Rolf Tiedemann (Frankfurt am Main: Suhrkamp, 1982).

———. 1999b. *Selected Writings*. Vol. 2, 1927–1934. Ed. Michael W. Jennings, Howard Eiland, and Gary Smith. Trans. Rodney Livingstone et al. Cambridge, Mass.: Harvard University Press. German edition, *Gesammelte Schriften*, vol. 2, pt. 1, ed. Rolf Tiedemann and Herbert Schweppenhäuser (Frankfurt am Main: Suhrkamp, 1974–89).

Benveniste, Émile. 1971. *Problems in General Linguistics*. Trans. Mary Elizabeth Meek. Coral Gables: University of Miami Press. Originally published as *Problèmes de linguistique générale* (Paris: Gallimard, 1966).

———. 1973. *Indo-European Language and Society*. Trans. Elizabeth Palmer. Coral Gables: University of Florida Press, 1973. Originally published as *Le Vocabulaire des institutions indo-européennes* (Paris: Éditions de Minuit, 1969).

Bernays, Jacob. 1996. *Jacob Bernays, un philologue juif.* Ed. John Glucker and André Lask. Villeneuve: Presses Universitaires du Septentrion.

Blanchot, Maurice. 1969. *The Infinite Conversation*. Translated by Susan Hanson. Minneapolis: University of Minnesota Press, 1993. Originally published as *L'Entretien infini* (Paris: Gallimard).

Buber, Martin. 1994. *Two Types of Faith*, with a paper by David Flusser. Translated by N. P. Goldhawk. Syracuse, N.Y.: Syracuse University Press, 1973. Originally published as *Zwei Glaubensweisen*. Afterword by David Flusser (Gerlingen: Schneider).

Bultmann, Rudolf. 1960. *Glauben und Versteben: Gesammelte Aufsätze*. Vol. 3. Tübingen: Mohr.

Calderone, Salvatore. 1964. *Pistis-Fides: Ricerche di storia e diritto internazionale nell'antichità*. Messina: Università degli Studi.

Canello, Ugo A., ed. 1883. *La vita e le opere del trovatore Arnaldo Daniello.* Halle: Niemeyer. Redited by René Lavaud as *Les Poésies d'Arnaut Daniel* (Toulouse: Privat, 1910; rpt. Geneva: Slatkine, 1973).

Carchia, Gianni. 2000. *L'amore del pensiero.* Macerata: Quodlibet.

Casanova, Paul. 1911. *Mohammed et la fin du monde.* Paris: Geuthner.

Chrysostom, John. 2002. *On the Incomprehensible Nature of God.* Trans. Paul W. Harkins. Fathers of the Church, vol. 72. Washington, D.C.: Catholic University of America Press. French edition, *Sur l'incompréhensibilité de Dieu,* vol. 1 of *Homélies,* vols. 1–5, ed. Anne-Marie Malingrey (Paris: Éditions du Cerf, 1970).

Cohen, Boaz. 1966. *Jewish and Roman Law: A Comparative Study.* New York: Jewish Theological Seminary of America.

Coppens, Joseph. 1968. *Le Messianisme royal, ses origins, son développement, son accomplissement.* Paris: Éditions du Cerf.

Davies, William David. 1958. *Paul and Rabbinic Judaism: Some Rabbinic Elements in Pauline Theology.* 2nd ed., with additional notes. London: S.P.C.K.

Deissmann, Gustav Adolf. 1923. *Licht vom Osten: Das Neue Testament und die neuentdeckten Texte der hellenistish-römischen Welt.* 4th ed. Tübingen: Mohr.

Derrida, Jacques. 1973. *Speech and Phenomena, and Other Essays on Husserl's Theory of Signs.* Trans. David B. Allison. Evanston, Ill.: Northwestern University Press. Originally published as *La Voix et le phénomène: Introduction au problème du signe dans la phénoménologie de Husserl* (Paris: Presses Universitaires de France, 1967).

———. 1982. *Margins of Philosophy.* Trans. Alan Bass. Chicago: University of Chicago Press. Originally published as *Marges de la philosophie* (Paris: Éditions de Minuit, 1972).

Dessau, Hermann. 1910. "Der Name des Apostels Paulus." *Hermes* 45.

Durling, Robert, and Ronald L. Martinez. 1990. *Time and the Crystal: Studies in Dante's "Rime Petrose."* Berkeley: University of California Press.

Foucault, Michel. 1993. "About the Beginning of the Hermeneutics of the Self: Two Lectures at Dartmouth." *Political Theory* 21, no. 2 (May): 198–227.

———. 1994. *Dits et écrits, 1954–1988.* Vol. 3, 1976–79. Ed. Daniel Defert and François Ewald. Paris: Gallimard.

———. 1999. *Religion and Culture.* Ed. Jeremy R. Carette. New York: Routledge.

———. 2001. *Fearless Speech.* Sel. and ed. Joseph Pearson. Los Angeles:

Semiotexte.

Fränkel, Eduard. 1916. "Zur Geschichte des Wortes 'fides.'" *Rheinisches Museum* 71.

Genesis Rabbah. 1985. *Genesis Rabbah: The Judaic Commentary to the Book of Genesis.* Ed. Jacob Neusner. Atlanta: Scholars Press.

Guillaume, Gustave. 1970. *Temps et verbe: Théorie des aspects, des modes, et des temps. Suivi de l'architectonique du temps dans les langues classiques.* Paris: Champion.

Harrer, Gustave Adolphus. 1940. "Saul Who Also Is Called Paul." *Harvard Theological Review* 33.

Hegel, Georg Wilhelm Friedrich. 1969. *Science of Logic.* Trans. A. V. Miller. Atlantic Highlands, N.J.: Humanities Press International. Originally published as *Wissenschaft der Logik,* ed. Eva Moldenhauer and Karl Markus Michel, vol. 5 of *Werke in zwanzig Bänden* (Frankfurt am Main: Suhrkamp, 1971).

Heidegger, Martin. 1962. *Being and Time.* Trans. John Macquarrie and Edward Robinson. New York: Harper and Row. Originally published as *Sein und Zeit* (Tübingen: Niemeyer, 1972).

————. 1995. *Einleitung in die Phänomenologie der Religion.* Ed. Matthias Jung. Vol. 60, pt. 1, of *Gesamtausgabe.* Frankfurt am Main: Klostermann.

Hengel, Martin. 1991. *The Pre-Christian Paul.* Trans. John Bowden Philadelphia: Trinity Press International. Originally published as "Der vorchristliche Paulus," in *Paulus und das antike Judentum,* ed. Martin Hengel and Ulrich Heckel (Tübingen: Mohr, 1992).

Huby, Joseph, ed. 1957. *Saint Paul, Épître aux Romains.* Notes by Stanislas Lyonnet. Paris: Beauchesne.

Jüngel, Eberhard. 1983. *God as the Mystery of the World.* Trans. Darrell L. Guder. Grand Rapids, Mich.: William B. Eerdmans Publishing. Originally published as *Gott als Geheimnis der Welt: Zur Begründung der Theologie des Gekreuzigten im Streit zwischen Theismus und Atheismus* (Tübingen: Mohr, 1978).

Justinian. 1998. *The Digest of Justinian.* Bilingual edition. Ed. and trans. Alan Watson. Philadelphia: University of Pennsylvania Press.

Kafka, Franz. 1966 [1953]. *Hochzeitsvorbereitung auf dem Lande und andere Prosa aus dem Nachlass.* Vol. 8 of *Gesammelte Werke.* Ed. Max Brod. Frankfurt am Main: Fischer.

Kant, Immanuel. 1996. *Religion and Rational Theology.* Trans. and ed. Allen W. Wood. New York: Cambridge University Press. Originally published as *Das Ende aller Dinge,* in *Akademie-Textausgabe,* vol. 8,

Abhandlungen nach 1781 (Berlin: de Gruyter, 1968).

Kojève, Alexandre. 1952. "Les Romans de la sagesse." *Critique* 60.

Koyré, Alexandre. 1935. "Hegel à Jena." *Revue d'Histoire et de Philosophie Religieuse* 26.

Lambertini, Roberto. 1990. *Apologia e crescita dell'identità francescana (1255–1279)*. Rome: Istituto Storico del Medio Evo.

Lambertz, Moritz. 1906–8. "Die griechische Sklavennamen." *Jahresbericht über das Staatsgymnasium im VIII Bezirk Wiens* 57–58.

————. 1914. "Zur Ausbreitung der Supernomen oder Signum." *Glotta* 5.

Lessing, Gotthold Ephraim. 1991. *"Nathan the Wise," "Minna von Barnhelm," and Other Plays and Writings.* Ed. Peter Demetz. New York: Continuum. Published as *Theologiekritische Schriften 1 und 2*, ed. Helmut Göbel, vol. 7 of *Werke*, 8 vols., ed. Herbert G. Göpfert (Munich: Carl Hanser, 1976).

Lévi-Strauss, Claude. 1987. *Introduction to the Works of Marcel Mauss.* Trans. Felicity Baker. London: Routledge. Originally published as "Introduction à l'oeuvre de Marcel Mauss," *Sociologie et anthropologie* (Paris: Presses Universitaires de France, 1957).

Lote, Georges. 1949. *Histoire du vers français.* Vol. 1. Paris: Boivin et Companie.

Manganelli, Giorgio. 1996. *La notte*. Milan: Adelphi.

Marx, Karl, and Friedrich Engels. 1975–. *Collected Works.* London: Lawrence and Wishart. German edition, vols. 1–4 of *Werke*, 45 vols. (Berlin: Dietz, 1977).

Mauss, Marcel. 1990. *The Gift: The Form and Reason for Exchange in Archaic Societies.* Trans. W. D. Halls. London: Routledge. Originally published as "Essai sur le don," *Sociologie et Anthropologie* (1950).

Nietzsche, Friedrich Wilhelm. 1990. *The Anti-Christ.* Trans. and intro. H. L. Mencken. Tuscon: See Sharp Press. Published as *Der Antichrist*, vol. 2 of *Werke in Drei Bänden*, 3 vols., ed. Karl Schlechta (Munich: Carl Hanser, 1955).

Norden, Eduard. 1898. *Die antike Kunstprosa: vom VI. Jahrhundert v. Chr. bis in die Zeit der Renaissance.* 2 vols. Leipzig: Teubner.

Origen. 1989. *Commentary on the Gospel According to John, Books 1–10.* Trans. Ronald E. Heine. Washington, D.C.: Catholic University of America Press. Also edited by Theresia Heither as *Commentaire sur Saint Jean*, vol. 1 of 4 (Freiburg: Herder, 1996), and by Cécile Blanc as *Commentaire sur saint Jean, 1: Livres 1–5* (Paris: Editions du Cerf, 1996).

————. 2001. *Commentary on the Epistle to the Romans, Books 1–5.* Trans. Thomas P. Scheck. Washington, D.C.: Catholic University of America Press.

————. 2002. *Commentary on the Epistle to the Romans, Books 6–10.* Trans. Thomas P. Scheck. Washington, D.C.: Catholic University of America Press.

Philo of Alexandria. 1984. *Quaestiones et solutiones in Genesin.* Vol. 3. Ed. Charles Mercier. Paris: Éditions du Cerf.

Rancière, Jacques. 1999. *Dis-agreement: Politics and Philosophy.* Trans. Julie Rose. Minneapolis: University of Minnesota Press. Originally published as *La Mésentente: Politique et philosophie* (Paris: Galilée, 1995).

Rosenzweig, Franz. 1970. *The Star of Redemption.* Trans. William W. Hallo. Chicago: Holt, Rinehart, and Winston. Originally published as *Stern der Erlösung* (The Hague: Nijhoff, 1981).

Rüstow, Alexander. 1960. "*Entos ymon estin*: Zur Deutung von Lukas 17:20–21." *Zeitschrift für die neutestamentliche Wissenschaft* 51.

Schmitt, Carl. 1974. *Der Nomos der Erde im Völkerrecht des Jus Publicum Europaeum.* Berlin: Duncker and Humblot.

————. 1985. *Political Theology: Four Chapters on the Concept of Sovereignty.* Cambridge, Mass.: MIT Press. Originally published as *Politische Theologie: Vier Kapitel zur Lehre von der Souveränität* (Munich: Duncker and Humboldt, 1922).

Scholem, Gershom. 1965. *On the Kabbalah and Its Symbolism.* Trans. Ralph Manheim. New York: Schocken Books. German edition, *Zur Kabbalah und ihrer Symbolik* (Zurich: Rhein Verlag, 1980).

————. 1971. *The Messianic Idea in Judaism and Other Essays on Jewish Spirituality.* New York: Schocken Books. German edition, in *Judaica,* vol. 1 (Frankfurt am Main: Suhrkamp, 1963).

————. 1995. *Gershom Scholem Zwischen die Disziplinen.* Ed. Peter Schäfer and Gary Smith. Frankfurt am Main: Suhrkamp.

Schopenhauer, Arthur. 1963. *Sämtliche Werke.* Vol. 4. Ed. Hans Wolfgang Friedrich von Löhneysen. Frankfurt am Main: Cotta-Insel Verlag.

Shapiro, Marianne. 1980. *Hieroglyph of Time: The Petrarchan Sestina.* Minneapolis: University of Minnesota Press.

Strobel, August. 1961. *Untersuchungen zum eschatologischen Verzögerungsproblem, auf Grund der spätjüdisch-urchristlichen Geschichte von Habakuk 2. 2ff.* Leiden: Brill.

Taubes, Jacob. 2003. *The Political Theology of Paul.* Trans. Dana Hollander. Stanford, Calif.: Stanford University Press. Originally published as *Die politische Theologie des Paulus,* ed. Aleida Assmann and Jan Assmann (Munich: Fink, 1993).

Thomas, Yan. 1995. "*Fictio legis:* L'Empire de la fiction romaine et ses limites médiévales." *Droit* 21.

Ticonius. 1989. *The Book of Rules.* Bilingual edition. Ed. and trans. William S. Babcock. Atlanta: Scholars Press.

Tomson, Peter. 1990. *Paul and the Jewish Law.* Minneapolis: Fortress Press.

Vaihinger, Hans. 1965. *The Philosophy of "As If": A System of the Theoretical, Practical, and Religious Fictions of Mankind.* 2nd ed. London: Routledge and Kegan Paul. Originally published as *Die Philosophie der Als Ob: System der theoretischen, praktischen und religiösen Fiktionen der Menschheit auf Grund eines idealistischen Positivismus. Mit einem Anhang über Kant und Nietzsche* (Berlin: Reuther und Reithard, 1911).

Watson, Alan. 1996. *Jesus and the Law.* Athens: University of Georgia Press.

———. 1998. *Ancient Law and Modern Understanding.* Athens: University of Georgia Press.

Weber, Max. 2002. *The Protestant Ethic and the Spirit of Capitalism.* Ed., trans., and intro. Peter Baehr and Gordon C. Wells. New York: Penguin Books. Published as *Die protestantische Ethik: Eine Aufsatzsammlung,* 8th ed., ed. Johannes Winckelmann (Gütersloh: Gütersloher Verlaghaus, 1991).

Whorf, Benjamin Lee. 1956. *Language, Thought, and Reality: Selected Writings.* Ed. John B. Carroll. Cambridge, Mass.: MIT Press.

Wilamovitz-Möllendorf, Ulrich von. 1907. "Die griechische Literatur des Altertums." In *Die griechische und lateinische Literatur und Sprache,* 2nd ed., ed. Ulrich von Wilamovitz-Möllendorf et al. Berlin-Leipzig: Teubner.

Wilcke, Hans-Alwin. 1967. *Das Problem eines messianischen Zwischenreichs bei Paulus.* Zurich: Zwingli Verlag.

Wilhelm, James J. 1982. *Il Miglior Fabbro: The Cult of the Difficult in Daniel, Dante, and Pound.* Orono: National Poetry Foundation, University of Maine.

Wolbert, Werner. 1981. *Ethische Argumentation und Paränese in 1 Kor 7.* Düsseldorf: Patmos Verlag.

Index of Names

MERIDIAN

Crossing Aesthetics